Relationship Marketing

A Consumer Experience Approach

Steve Baron
Tony Conway
Gary Warnaby

SAGE

Los Angeles | London | New Delhi
Singapore | Washington DC

First published 2010

SAGE Publications Ltd
1 Oliver's Yard
55 City Road
London EC1Y 1SP

SAGE Publications Inc.
2455 Teller Road
Thousand Oaks, California 91320

SAGE Publications India Pvt Ltd
B 1/I 1 Mohan Cooperative Industrial Area
Mathura Road
New Delhi 110 044

SAGE Publications Asia-Pacific Pte Ltd
33 Pekin Street #02-01
Far East Square
Singapore 048763

Library of Congress Control Number: 2009938438

British Library Cataloguing in Publication data

A catalogue record for this book is available from the British Library

ISBN 978-1-4129-3121-2
ISBN 978-1-4129-3122-9 (pbk)

Typeset by C&M Digitals (P) Ltd, Chennai, India
Printed and bound in Great Britain by TJ International Ltd, Padstow, Cornwall
Printed on paper from sustainable resources

Contents

Relationship Marketing

Other titles in this series

Part I

Relationship Marketing: The State of the Art

Origins and History of Relationship Marketing

Background

As the world and society change over time, so do business and management processes and practices. As one of the established business and management disciplines, marketing has developed accordingly. Different perspectives on marketing have been adopted, most notably 'relationship marketing' in the 1980s and the 'service-dominant logic [S-D logic] of marketing' in the mid-2000s. In tandem, information and communication technology (ICT) has, through internet access and mobile telephony, become a customer, as well as supplier resource since the mid–late 1990s, and so the customer/consumer role in marketplaces has changed significantly. This book is entitled '*Relationship Marketing*: *A Consumer Experience Approach*' because we feel that it is an appropriate time to expand the ideas behind relationship marketing into an era where the customer/consumer perspective on relationships is being recognized as being increasingly important.

In Table 1.1, we summarize some of the key developments in marketing and ICT over time, followed by an explanation of the rationale adopted in this book.

The 1960s

In the 1960s, westernized economies were dominated by manufacturing industries, and effort was geared towards the marketing of tangible goods. This was the case in Kotler's first marketing textbook in 1967, where marketing was equated with marketing management (Bourassa et al. 2007). Even in the fourth edition of Kotler's *Marketing Management* text (1980) there were only five of 772 pages devoted to services, and of the nine discussion questions in the chapter on 'market segmentation and targeting', seven were on manufacturing organizations (automobile, printing equipment, motorboats, beverages, chemicals, hair products,

Table 1.1   Key developments in marketing and ICT

Time period	Economy type	ICT environment	Marketing priorities and distinctions	Relationship marketing
1960s	Manufacturing/ goods-based	Main-frame computing: land-line telephones	Marketing of goods; often concentration on fast-moving consumer goods	Not really articulated
1970s– 1990s	Shift to service-based economies	Advent of micro- and personal computers. Mobile/ cell-phones in 1990s. Era of digitalization. Data mining by organizations	Distinctions made between business-to-consumer (B2C) and business-to-business (B2B) Marketing, and between the marketing of goods and services	Relationships seen as important in B2B and services marketing (both characterized by interpersonal interactions), leading to the development of relationship marketing. Focus on customer retention
2000–	More service-based economies. Experience Economy?	Widespread use of internet (world wide web) and mobile technology by consumers. Social networking	Debate about goods-dominant and service-dominant logics of marketing. Increased importance of consumer-to-consumer (C2C) interactions	Increased recognition of customer experiences and the effect of customer and consumer communities

automotive), with the remaining two questions on demand forecasting at industry and company level.

Marketing practice was adopted by companies producing fast-moving-consumer-goods (fmcg) such as toothpaste, soap powders, chocolate and soup, and also by those selling higher-priced items (cars, washing machines). The companies were guided by marketing mix considerations (the 4Ps – product, price, place, promotion) in operationalizing their marketing plans. The focus was on tangible goods. As such, attracting more customers for the goods was an important goal, which brought with it the need to understand customers' needs and the development of a marketing orientation. Computers were generally owned by organizations and personal computers were a development for the future.

The 1970s–90s

During this period, the balance in many economies moved towards services, with more than half the countries' GDP and employment attributed to service industries. In the 1970s, relationships in marketing were given more overt prominence, especially in the areas of B2B (industrial) marketing and services marketing, because interactions between people played a central role in each of these marketing sub-disciplines. A greater focus on customer retention and loyalty became the goal, and relationship marketing (sometimes called 'customer relationship management') was born. The increasing access by businesses to customer databases, and use by consumers of ICT, meant that relationship marketing had the potential to be applied in the B2C marketplace – to develop one-to-one relationships with consumers.

During this period, Berry (1983) is credited with introducing the term 'relationship marketing', but the relationship marketing concept did not gain widespread access until the publication of the first relationship marketing book by Christopher et al. (1991). One of the most influential features of the book was the concept of a loyalty ladder, where strategies for organizations were to be geared towards moving customers up the rungs of a ladder from 'suspects' to 'prospects' to 'first time customers' to 'repeat customers' to 'supporters' to 'advocates'; the top three rungs being where relationship marketing took over from traditional (at the time) marketing. Also, in this period, relationship marketing was seen by some as a new marketing paradigm (Grönroos 1997). These aspects are discussed in more detail later in this chapter.

The year 2000 onwards

In the late 1990s and the early 2000s, there was an even greater swing to service-based economies, with upwards of 70 per cent of GDP of many countries attributed to services. By this time Kotler's *Marketing Management* textbook (12th edition, co-authored with Keller in 2006) had a 30-page chapter on 'designing and managing services', as well as a 34-page chapter on 'creating customer value, satisfaction and loyalty' which addresses customer relationship management and database marketing. There is also a final chapter on a new theme for this edition, 'managing a holistic marketing organization', in which relationship marketing is an explicit element.

Some authors even suggested that many countries are entering the era of the experience economy (Pine and Gilmore 1999): indeed, the European edition of Kotler's co-authored *Marketing Management* textbook contains nine pages on the experience economy (Kotler et al. 2009). Whether or not we are entering such an era, there is ample evidence that customer experiences are the key to many business and social relationships. For example, in the UK, the Department of Trade and Industry (DTI) published the findings of an extensive research project into innovation in experiential services (Voss and Zomerdijk 2007), and universities and health services are actively monitoring the student and patient experiences, respectively, and being judged on how they manage these experiences.

In parallel, there has been an upsurge in interest in consumer-to-consumer (C2C) interactions, partly because of the evidence of the effects of social networking. According to the *New York Times* (18 August 2008), for example, the Fox News Channel wanted more friends, and so decided to network on the Facebook social networking site. They aimed to use every feature that Facebook offered – discussion boards, wall for user comments, reviews, polls and photo submissions – as well as designing a video player for social networking, with facilities for users to create customized playlists and share clips with Facebook friends. This example also provides evidence of the notion of co-creation of value (between suppliers and customers), and the employment of consumer resources, that are key features of the S-D logic of marketing (see Chapter 4).

Rationale for this book

The developments outlined above – described in more detail in Vargo and Lusch (2004) and Harwood et al. (2008) – provided a rationale for this book; one that is in keeping with marketplaces in the early twenty-first century. We move toward *a consumer experience perspective of* relationship marketing. The current insights into relationship marketing are definitely not being abandoned. Indeed, Chapters 2 and 3 of Part I are devoted to a summary of the main elements of relationship marketing that have been researched, discussed and applied in practice since the 1980s. However, in Part II, new ideas are presented which examine interactions and relationships from a consumer/customer perspective, which resonate with the S-D logic marketing. Such an approach also offers opportunities for active student learning of consumer experiences.

Figure 1.1 is taken from Harwood et al. (2008) and represents the traditional focal firm perspective on networks of relationships. The firm is the centre of the network and the network consists of entities with which the firm has direct interactions and relationships. Such a view is implicit in the discussions in Chapters 2 and 3, but what happens if the customer or consumer replaces the focal firm at the centre of a network of direct interactions that they have during experiences? This is the angle being explored in Part II.

In the remainder of this chapter, we look at current definitions of relationship marketing (RM), consider whether RM is a new marketing paradigm, and trace in more detail the historical development of RM. Underpinning these discussions is a case study of Liverpool Football (Soccer) Club, where relationships from the focal firm and from a customer (Liverpool soccer fan) perspective are contrasted, so as to highlight the features of this book.

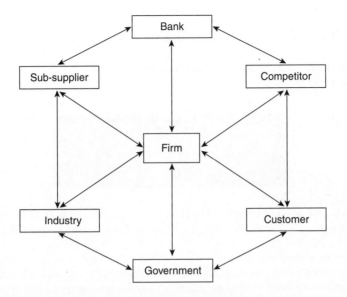

Figure 1.1   A firm-centred perspective on relationships

Source: Harwood, T., Garry, T. and Broderick, A. (2008) *Relationship Marketing*. Reproduced with the kind permission of The McGraw-Hill Companies. All rights reserved

Liverpool Football Club and relationship marketing

Liverpool Football Club is a football (soccer) club in the English Premier League. It has been a successful club for forty years or more at the time of writing, and has built up a loyal fan base not just in Liverpool (in northwest England) and the UK but also in other parts of Europe, and in Asia.

To begin the case study, we reproduce a press release that appeared on the 'How-Do' website that provides news and opinions for the media industry of northwest England (see Exhibit 1.1). Ostensibly, this is an announcement of a new TV channel devoted entirely to Liverpool Football Club (LFC from now on). However, it is worth asking why LFC should invest in over 20 new employees, and on this new initiative. The answer clearly lies in the desire to enhance LFC's relationships with its fans (supporters). As the chief executive says, 'we always welcome the opportunity to engage with our fantastic fan base', and he believes that the TV initiative 'will bring them closer to the club and the team they love'. Here, in a nutshell, are the desired outcomes of relationship marketing efforts of organizations with their customers – customers should be *loyal to*, and have a *close affinity* with the organization, and even *love* the organization and what it represents.

Exhibit 1.1 Press release, 12 July 2008

Liverpool confirms September launch date for LFC TV
Thursday, 12 July 2008

Following the announcement in April that LFC was to launch its own TV channel employing over 20 staff, the club yesterday confirmed the channel will launch in September.

The new station intends to broadcast at least six hours of original programming content a day, five days a week across the whole year. LFC TV has been trialling a three hour weekly programme over the spring.

The club also announced that it had signed an exclusive three year deal with broadcaster Setanta Sports to carry the new channel in the UK and Ireland as part of the Setanta Sports Pack, a nine channel satellite offering.

The channel will also be broadcast live on www.liverpoolfc.tv as part of e-Season Ticket, the official club website's premium content service.

Rick Parry, chief executive of LFC, said: 'The channel heralds a new era for Liverpool Football Club. We always welcome the opportunity to engage with our fantastic fan base and LFC TV will bring them closer to the club and the team they love, at what is a very exciting time both on and off the pitch.'

We will deal with definitions of relationship marketing later, but for now, we will look a little more closely at what else is implied by the press release.

The dedicated TV channel is seen by LFC as an initiative for increasing its interactions and relationships with its fans; providing them with news, interviews with players and match highlights on a continuous basis. But the interactions and relationships with the fans are not the only ones that take place in the provision of the service offered by the TV channel. For example, LFC has business-to-business (B2B) external relationships with the broadcaster Setanta Sports (replaced in 2009 by ESPN), and the LFC website designers and internal relationships have to be in place to ensure that loyal fans can purchase e-season tickets.

This one press release gives only an inkling of the potential relationships that have to be in place for an organization such as LFC to seek to encourage loyalty, close affinity and love from their fans. Exhibits 1.2, 1.3 and 1.4, taken from the home page of LFC's website, give a picture of the complexity of interactions and relationships that underpin the organization's marketing efforts.

Exhibit 1.2   Customized ring-tones for the mobile/cell phone

LFC REALTONES

 Have the Kop singing on your mobile. You'll Never Walk Alone and so many more are all available!

Items available in UK ONLY.

You must have a WAP enabled handset to download. Check compatibility before ordering. Click for *help* and our *Terms & Conditions.*

If you need further assistance please call on 0870 750 7886 to speak to a customer support representative.

Ring-tones (Exhibit 1.2) are a means of constantly reminding the user of LFC. To provide this service, LFC need also to engage in B2B relationships with mobile phone manufacturers and operators, and recording experts. (The Kop is the part of the stadium – behind one of the goals – where the most vociferous fans sit, and sing and chant. 'You'll Never Walk Alone' is the anthem of LFC.)

Exhibit 1.3   Replica kit at an early age!

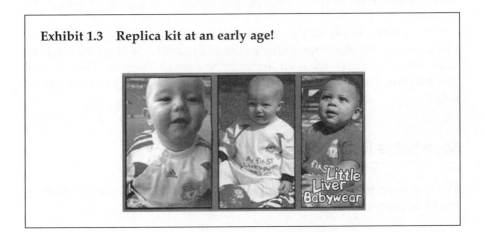

E-shopping (Exhibit 1.3) is available for fans across the world. The nurturing of fans from a very early age is integral to a football club's relationship marketing strategy (and worthy of ethical debate?). Again, such an offer involves LFC in other B2B relationships with kit manufacturers and designers, and child-modelling agencies.

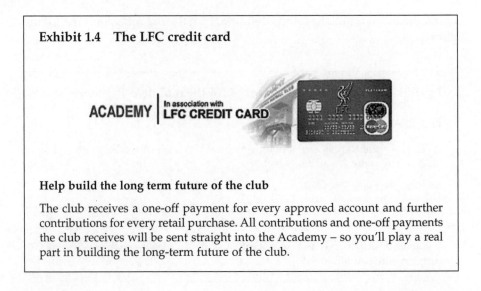

Exhibit 1.4   The LFC credit card

Help build the long term future of the club

The club receives a one-off payment for every approved account and further contributions for every retail purchase. All contributions and one-off payments the club receives will be sent straight into the Academy – so you'll play a real part in building the long-term future of the club.

The Academy, based in the Kirkby area of Liverpool, is the training facility for the youth teams. The LFC credit card (Exhibit 1.4), therefore, not only provides its owner with a physical reminder of the club, but also provides a means for fans to invest in the future playing talent. Once more, many interactions and relationships support the initiative. Deals have to be struck with MasterCard, and the card designers, and internal relationships are required between LFC's finance department and the staff running the Academy.

Although the labels of the network partners may be slightly different, LFC is essentially the 'firm' at the centre of Figure 1.1, and all the relationships talked of above are seen through the eyes of the firm. This, we call the traditional relationship marketing approach. This is expanded upon below.

So, what is Relationship Marketing?

The two statements below provide the essence of a traditional relationship marketing approach.

- Relationship Marketing (RM) draws attention to the importance of *retaining* as well as attracting customers, with emphasis being placed on the development of *long-term relationships* with customers.
- The primary goal of RM is to *build* and *maintain* a base of *committed* customers who are profitable for the organization.

So, from the perspective of LFC, an RM approach is being adopted to retain fans, not just through providing them with a team to support on match days, but also through other devices that enhance their commitment to the club; ring-tones and credit cards, for example. Even the attraction of new fans, through the replica kits for toddlers, is achieved via the existing committed fans, the parents.

An RM approach is often compared to transactional marketing, as follows (Jackson 1985):

- Transaction marketing – *attracting* customers using *offensive* strategies, e.g. encouragement of brand switching; recruiting dissatisfied customers of competitors.
- Relationship Marketing – *retaining* customers using *defensive* strategies, e.g. minimizing customer turnover, maximizing customer retention.

There is a recognition that, in the context of soccer fans, 'consumption becomes exclusively oriented toward their team, no matter its on-field performance' (Harris and Ogbonna 2008: 383). Therefore, brand switching is relatively rare, and so transaction marketing using offensive strategies is not really a feasible approach for an organization such as LFC.

As is emphasized above, the focus of RM is on customer retention and the nurturing of long-term customer relationships (loyal customers), as opposed to a focus on individual transactions.

RM has been difficult to define. By 1999, Harker (1999: 14) had identified 26 definitions of RM. The earlier definitions specify that RM is about:

- 'attracting, maintaining and enhancing customer relationships' (Grönroos 1994);
- 'turning new customers into regular purchasers ... to strong supporters ... to active, vocal advocates of the company' (Christopher et al. 1991);
- 'developing mutual trust and commitment' (Morgan and Hunt 1994).

Largely, they refer to dyadic relationships between an organization and its customers (for example, LFC and its fans). Later definitions emphasize more the interactions that take place and the relationship networks that underpin the activities. For example, RM is said to be:

- 'the ongoing process of engaging in cooperative and collaborative activities and programs with immediate and end user customers to create or enhance mutual economic value, at reduced cost' (Parvatiyar and Sheth 1999: 8);
- 'marketing based on interaction within networks of relationships' (Gummesson 2002: 587);
- 'the process of identifying and establishing, maintaining, enhancing, and when necessary terminating relationships with customers and other stakeholders, at a profit, so that the objectives of all parties involved are met, when this is done by mutual giving and fulfilment of promises' (Grönroos 2004: 101).

Thus, the interactions of LFC with their many partners and stakeholders, in addition to those with its fans, are integral to an RM *process*. Also the notion of mutuality (that is, that the relationships should benefit both or all parties, not just the provider organization) is explicitly recognized. In particular, RM benefits to customers are seen to be as important as those for the organization. This will be explored later.

Is RM a new marketing paradigm?

A paradigm is a fundamental set of assumptions that is shared by members of a particular scientific community (Kuhn 1970). A paradigm is in crisis when:

- *too many exceptions* result in loss of credibility, acceptance;
- it *ceases to inform research* in useful ways.

It has been proposed that RM could be a new marketing paradigm, as the traditional, transaction-based marketing paradigm, centred on the marketing mix (the 4Ps), is believed to be inadequate especially with respect to the service and experience economies (Pine and Gilmore 1999) of the late twentieth and early twenty-first centuries, and the increasing accessibility and use of information and communication technology. One of the first advocates of RM as a new paradigm was Grönroos who argued that 'the simplicity of the marketing mix paradigm, with its Four P model, has become a strait-jacket, fostering toolbox thinking rather than an awareness that marketing is a multi-faceted social process' (1997: 322). Ballantyne et al. agree that marketing activity should be understood as 'systemic, holistic, and, above all, as dynamically complex' (2003: 164). Sheth observed that 'relationship marketing emerged as a popular new paradigm in the 1980s due to shift in focus from customer acquisition to customer retention' (2002: 591).

There is general agreement that the marketing mix approach has reduced credibility and has ceased to inform research in the twenty-first century in useful ways. However, the S-D logic (Vargo and Lusch 2004, 2008) may be the new paradigm. It advocates a move away from a goods-dominant logic of marketing to a service-dominant logic of marketing; a logic that is underpinned by intangible resources (service), co-creation of value by producers and consumers, and *relationships*. Therefore, relationships and RM are deemed to be integral to a new logic of marketing. The S-D logic of marketing will be explained in detail, and discussed, in Chapter 5.

The historical development of RM

In order to provide a context for the material that follows in this book, we expand on Table 1.1 by concentrating more on the historical development of RM. O'Malley and Tynan (1998) provide a concise summary of how RM grew from obscurity to popularity in business-to-consumer (B2C) markets.

In the late 1970s and early 1980s, RM emerged as an alternative to mainstream marketing for B2B and service marketers. It was seen as an alternative paradigm where:

- markets are heterogeneous;
- buyers and sellers both active;
- interactions and relationships are important.

An example is holiday tour companies, which compete for holiday seekers of many types, and must engage in B2B relationships with hotels, airlines, tourism departments, etc., as well as with the consumers of their services. Here, a relationship focus was deemed more appropriate, especially with a view to the creation and maintenance of loyal customers.

In the late 1980s, it was proposed that RM may be of benefit in B2C markets. Technology advances made it conceivable as:

- customer databases offered potential to *personalize* interaction with customers;
- there were opportunities to identify *the most important customers*; thereby identifying lifetime value accruing from individual customers or customer types, and also making cross-selling more achievable.

However, the increased use of customer databases raised concerns about invasion of privacy.

In the early twenty-first century, we are all used to personalized messages from organizations ranging from utility companies to fitness centres, each of which is treating the individual customer as a 'valued friend', and it is often a shock to realize that these activities only became mainstream in the 1990s.

By the mid-1990s, there was a general acceptance, by academics, that RM was feasible, and indeed helpful, for organizations engaged in B2C marketing:

- there was academic weight/support for RM in consumer markets;
- there were the arguments for a paradigm shift from transaction to relationship marketing;
- there was an assumption that both consumers and organizations want relationships (B2C).

From the mid-1990s until the early 2000s, there was an explosion of work/ research on RM, especially in the B2C marketplace. A number of issues and questions were given great attention, for example:

- what motivates consumers and organizations to engage in RM?;
- the identification of feasible scenarios for relationship building;
- a keen interest in explaining the processes of relationship development.

These issues and questions will be addressed in Chapters 2, 3 and 4 of the book.

Interactions and relationships from a consumer perspective

Since the emergence of the S-D logic of marketing in 2004, there has been an increased focus on how consumers, through their experiences and interactions, co-create value with organizations. Interactions and relationships from the consumer perspective are less well understood than those from an organizational perspective. Part II of the book attempts to redress the balance by putting the consumer at the centre of a network of interactions and relationships.

This brings us back to the story of LFC. We use an account by a Liverpool fan, published in the fanzine 'Red All Over the Land' (http://raotl.co.uk/), of his personal experience in following his team, Liverpool, to the final of the European Champions League (aka European Cup) in Istanbul in 2005, to illustrate this different perspective on relationships.

A personal experience as a fan of LFC

The narrative in Exhibit 1.5 is quite long (but only half the length of the original published story in the fanzine), but should be read in full, as it gives a rich account of the interactions and relationships that contribute to this fan's experience with LFC. The description of the match itself (where Liverpool recovered from 3–0 down at half-time to eventually win the game) has been kept to a minimum as it is well documented elsewhere. This is deliberate as the intention is to delve into the complete consumer experience; something that extends well beyond the match itself.

As is the norm with personalized accounts, a certain amount of jargon and colloquialisms are used. Therefore, a short glossary of (perhaps) unfamiliar terms is provided after the account.

Exhibit 1.5   A consumer experience in the context of LFC

Growing up in Birkenhead, and becoming accustomed to winning the European cup as a 10 year old, meant the full significance of being European champions often passed you by. Birkenhead wasn't exactly a cosmopolitan, ethnically diverse place. Foreigners were rarely encountered and foreign travel was a luxury. We were largely unaware of the awe with which the Reds were coming to be regarded across the world. Nevertheless, each triumph delivered a fully turbo-charged electric buzz. Such was the magic of the European Cup …

There was something magically mystical about us reaching the Istanbul final in such unexpected circumstances. We were becoming an irresistible force and a pilgrimage to the banks of the Bosphorous of religious proportions ensued. Istanbul is a lively, exotic, passionate and crazy city. Without a lively, exotic, passionate and crazy travelling horde, Istanbul would have been disappointed with hosting the European Cup final. Fortunately, we delivered all of the above, in spades, and Istanbul enjoyed one of the greatest nights in its modern history. It staged the greatest European cup final in living memory and played host to the greatest fans in the world who were on a mission to fulfil their destiny and recreate their glorious past in the most special of competitions. The truth is that for the duration of our stay, there was a curious symbiosis between visiting scousers and the city of Istanbul. Anyone who didn't sense this, either wasn't there, or is completely incapable of any form of sensory perception …

BEFORE THE MATCH

My own visit to Istanbul began with check-in at Belfast International airport at 8am Tuesday 24th May for an Easyjet flight to Amsterdam. It was not an auspicious start, although it was a fortunate one. The check-in attendant was unhappy with my well worn passport. If you dug your nail round the bottom edge, which she delighted in doing, you could make it flake away slightly. She disappeared with the parting words, 'I don't know if you'll be able to travel.' Imagine the scene. There I was with luggage, match ticket, passport and Turkish airline tickets to Istanbul, on the eve of the most momentous night in Liverpool's history, certainly since Rome' 77 and here I was being informed that I might not be able to leave Belfast. It was 7.30 on a cold grey Belfast morning, but sweat began to trickle from my arm pit. I was left stranded in a state of purgatory at the check-in desk for about five minutes before she returned scowling with the message, that they would let me travel today, but in future if I wanted to leave the country I'd need to get a new passport. I had intended to pace myself, but after that little encounter I greedily guzzled my first beer at 8am in the airport lounge.

…

(Cont'd)

The Istanbul flight was uneventful. From Attaturk airport I took a cab to Taksim Square where I was meeting John Mackin, Paul Stewart and other members of our ten man strong crew, with the plan of bunking into their Flight Options hotel. If the flight had been uneventful, the taxi ride wasn't. My Turkish taxi driver was sinister. He had a six-inch knife scar down one cheek, looked as though he could handle himself and threw his car round corners. At times we were on two wheels. He was a Fernabahce supporter, but didn't seem too happy about his side's weekend league triumph. He was in fact morose. Or at least he was until the sight of a Ford destination, 'champions league' football, courtesy car wrapped around a tree reduced him to hysterics. 'Football, football' he roared, slapping his steering wheel. I was glad to arrive in Taksim Square in one piece ...

The sight that greeted me was of messy and very drunk reds massed around the square. At that point, about 11.00pm on Tuesday evening there was an element of tension in the air, or at the very least some electricity. Young Turks were entering the square flying flags from car windows. Some of them were trying to be provocative and gesturing at Liverpool supporters. But in the hours that followed, I think the Turks themselves came to realize that Liverpool supporters were interested only in drinking and singing. And what was more there were thousands of these red pilgrims. They were good for business and they were very good at drinking and singing ...

...

The Turks wanted to know why we were just stood on the street in the early hours of the morning and what time we were planning to go to bed. Some of them had stopped to have a bevy with reds on their way home from a shift at a bar or a restaurant. They seemed puzzled by the mass open-air drinking festival going on around them, but they were keen to join in. I tried explaining that what they were witnessing was a big religious pilgrimage, in which tens of thousands had come from disparate locations to pay homage to the Redmen, to our glorious past and to renew our relationship with the European cup.

When I went to bed in the early hours of Wednesday, the streets around Taksim Square, although quietening down, were still abuzz. The next day Taksim was chokka again by 10.30am and there was a discernible electricity in the air that grew throughout the day. Taksim Square was an assault on the senses; delicious wafts of kebab, crazy taxi drivers weaving their way past pedestrians and a dull buzz of excited chatter and singing from tens of thousands of scousers. It was the perfect setting for a European Cup Final featuring Liverpool. The square was bedecked in red and white. It was a bright sunny day and there was a mass red and white throng creating a carnival on the streets of Istanbul. That was certainly the mood amongst our little crew as we strolled the streets around Taksim taking in the sun and heading down to the river on Wednesday lunch time.

We never made the river, but we were entertained by some Kurdish shoe shine lads, who clearly didn't go to school, but spoke better English than most of our party. For an hour or so we idled away our time in the sun on a large terrace with stunning views down to the river and over the city. The sight of numerous mosques and some shabby neighbourhoods, that made Kensington look like the height of middle class affluence, indicated that we were indeed on the very edge of Europe, with Asia but an afternoon's stroll away. By the standards of European trips we were having a quiet and uneventful day. We were taking it easy. At some point, Mackin and I sloped off to the Galatasaray Fish Market for a feast of Sardines, Squid and Octopus, but whereas normally we'd have polished off a bottle or two of wine, this was not the occasion for that. Steady as she goes – cold leisurely beers were the order of the day. This was not a time to be rip-roaring drunk.

...

AFTER THE MATCH

... What do you do when you've just seen your team stage the most incredible, dramatic, against the odds European cup victory of all time? That was the dilemma that now faced us. We had to do justice to what we had just seen, but first of all we had to get back into town, but we had no chance of finding our minibus in the chaos outside. We met Simon Morris and boarded one of the public buses and headed back for Taksim. It was packed to the rafters and it was desperate. People were on the verge of passing out and were forcing the doors open and alighting for a spot of fresh air, before re-boarding. Over two hours later we finally hit some clear road and moved above snail's pace. Then within a couple of minutes the bus made a strange noise and ground to a shuddering halt, pulling onto the hard shoulder. Thick black acrid smoke poured out of the back. Our bus was on fire in the middle of nowhere.

After what we had just witnessed and the emotional roller coaster ride we'd experienced, we looked and felt like acid casualties. But now it was time for champagne, kebabs, more champagne and Efes. At 7.00am we ventured out into Taksim Square for a dance – a fitting tribute to the red men. Morris was back to his apache ways, had acquired a red head dress and was doing some sort of rain dance. At 8.00 we waved Nico, founder of the Keep Belgium Scouse movement, into a cab to the airport and I promised him we'd continue the celebrations in Antwerp, which was where I was headed straight after the final to play football. At 9am I made it to bed. By 11 I was checking out ...

For a while afterwards, I began to think that I'd caught a chill in the Attaturk Stadium. After all the temperature had dropped at night fall and it had been draughty at the top of those steps. For the next week, every time I thought back to the events inside that stadium, I got the most incredible shiver and goose pimple inducing rush. Ordinarily only heavy duty narcotics can produce such a feeling.

Glossary:

Reds	Liverpool supporters/fans
Scouser	Person from Liverpool
Bevy	A drink, normally of beer
Chokka	Short for chock-a-block: very crowded
Efes	A Turkish brand of beer
Kensington	A suburb of Liverpool
Acid	A drug

Perspectives on interactions and relationships

The account in Exhibit 1.5 demonstrates most clearly that interactions and relationships play a large part in consumer experiences, and that the value of the experience is a subtle mix between an occasion created by the achievements of players and staff of LFC, and the processes and activities of the fan concerned in contributing to the occasion. It exemplifies the notion of co-creation of value that will be re-visited in Chapter 4.

At the start of the chapter we looked at some of the relationships that LFC enter into in order to engender trust and commitment of their fans, so that the fans have a close affinity with the club, and remain loyal advocates of LFC. In addition to the relationships with their customers (the fans) they have many other relationships. The LFC website lists Setanta Sports (ESPN), the Premier League, Carlsberg (their sponsors), Adidas (the kit manufacturers), Unibet (a betting company) and EA Sports (a developer of interactive and video games) as their partners, and clearly they have many other B2B interactions with mobile/ cell phone operators, credit card companies, caterers, and so on. It must be remembered, however, that these are interactions and relationships that are viewed from *the perspective of an organization* to achieve organizational objectives.

When we examine the narrative in Exhibit 1.5, we can readily observe that consumer experiences (that contribute to the co-creation of value) also involve many interactions and relationships. For example, the fan concerned interacted with other fans; those he knew (his crew of ten) and others (the 'thousands of reds' in Istanbul). He also interacted with Turkish waiters, taxi and bus drivers, and various other Turks (the shoe-shine boys). He interacted with other employees, at check-in desks, shops and bars. He interacted with various air services, and with a number of destinations – Belfast, Amsterdam, Istanbul, Antwerp – and with technology to share his experience with others on the fanzine website. In the latter case, he was clearly identifying himself with *a consumer community*.

A feature of this book is that we explore relationships from *the consumer experience perspective* as well as from the organizational perspective. We do not do this simply out of interest but with a conviction that a real understanding of consumers' interactions and relationships provides knowledge that organizations currently lack to a large extent; knowledge that could improve their competitive advantage.

Structure and features of the book

The book is organized in two main parts. In the remainder of Part I, we examine interactions and relationships from an organizational perspective. In Chapter 2, we explore the main themes in RM that have been researched and practised over the past thirty years. The underlying principle of customer retention is the basis of the discussions of market-based RM. The external and internal relationship networks that organizations work within are then presented under the heading of network-based RM. Chapter 3 is entirely devoted to the concept of customer loyalty, including discussions of loyalty schemes (programmes) and the relationship between customer loyalty and profitability. In Chapter 4, the changing environment in the twenty-first century, with a concentration on the information and communication technology (ICT) advances that have contributed to current consumer experiences, is outlined. Here, details of the S-D logic of marketing are first outlined (Vargo and Lusch 2004, 2008).

In Part II, interactions and relationships from a consumer experience perspective are examined. Chapter 5 contextualizes this approach by developing further the debate and ideas on the S-D logic of marketing. To our knowledge, a consumer experience perspective has not been presented systematically elsewhere, and therefore constitutes a novel feature of the book. Chapter 6 focuses on how consumers (as well as organizations) use and integrate their resources. The approach adopted in Chapters 7 and 8 synthesizes experiences of many individual consumers in an experience domain, through their interactions and relationships, with a view to identifying value-enhancing and value-inhibiting features of their experience. The process has been labelled 'consumer experience modelling' (CEM). The approach adopted in Chapters 9 and 10 focuses on communities of consumers, with a particular emphasis (in Chapter 10) on social networks and C2C exchanges.

Finally, in the conclusion, after a brief summary of the book's contents, we outline some of the research directions that RM is likely to take in the next five years, as well as pedagogic issues associated with the approach adopted in Part II.

We intend that this book is not just a textbook, but also a tool for facilitating active student learning. With that in mind, the following features have been incorporated:

- discussion questions and activities;
- case studies;
- learning objectives, learning outcomes and learning propositions.

Discussion questions and activities

Discussion questions and/or activities are provided at the end of each chapter. Given the variety of readership of this book, some of the questions may be more appropriate for students on undergraduate programmes/MSc/MA programmes, while others are really aimed at students on MBA/Executive programmes. In the latter case, we assume that students have two to three years' managerial experience or are currently in a management position.

In the former case, we assume that students are on an academic route. Some questions can clearly apply to all students.

Case studies

In Part I, there is a case study at the end of each chapter. The purpose of the case study, related to the chapter content, is clearly stated. These case studies offer opportunities for student activities, and for further discussions which are guided by a series of questions that encourage active student participation. In Part II, Chapters 6–9 are written around case scenarios (e.g. the British Library, gap-year travel experience, save-the-cinema campaign), and Chapter 10 offers personal and organizational accounts of social-network usage, and so, instead of offering a pre-written case study at the end of these chapters, guidelines are given for students to engage in their own case scenarios by employing the concepts for understanding consumer experiences that are outlined in the chapters.

Learning objectives, learning outcomes and learning propositions

Each chapter in Parts I and II, from Chapter 2 onwards, will have learning objectives specified at the start of the chapter, so that the purpose of the chapter is known in advance. Chapters 2–4, in Part I, will have conventional learning outcomes at the end of the chapter, outlining what students should be able to do having read and understood the chapter content. However, in Part II, learning propositions will be stated instead of learning outcomes. This is not simply a matter of semantics. The notion of a learning outcome has with it an assumption that the teacher knows what are desirable goals, and monitors progress against those goals. In the chapters in Part II, the aim is that the students co-create the value of the learning, and the outcomes of such a process are not known in advance of the learning experience. The learning propositions, therefore, provide debating points based on the material presented in the chapter. As such they provide ideas for seminars/tutorials. We as teachers/writers, according to this view, provide learning propositions that act as potential building blocks for students to develop their own outcomes.

Case Study 1	Political marketing then and now: a focus on Barack Obama's 2008 presidential campaign

Purpose: To demonstrate how information and communication technology (ICT) mediates marketing activity, interactions and relationship-building.

Case Study

Background

Political marketing is a sub-discipline of marketing that has received greater attention in the marketing literature since a special issue of the *European Journal of Marketing* was devoted to it in 1996. The joint editors of the special issue then referred to political marketing as at a 'craft' stage; a discipline that needed to develop its own underpinning frameworks.[1] It was, however, argued in 1996, that:

Marketing has been extended to include all organizations and their relationships. Relationships are with any public not just commercial customers, and, therefore, include exchanges of value between any social entities ... Politics falls within marketing's extended domain centrally because an exchange takes place when a voter casts his or her vote for a particular candidate. They are engaged in a transaction and exchange time and support (their vote) for the services the candidate offers after election through better government.[2]

And that:

Marketing offers political parties the ability to address diverse voter concerns and needs through marketing analyses, planning, implementation and control of political and electoral campaigns.[3]

It was felt that electioneering had evolved from propaganda to media campaigning to political marketing in an analogous way to that which traces business practices from a production orientation to a selling orientation to a marketing orientation.[4] The main political marketing tools used to connect with voters consisted of polls and focus groups that were devised to establish voters' needs and deliver voter satisfaction.[5]

Features of the Obama presidential campaign of 2008

According to ABC News in the USA on 23 August, 2008, at 3.25 a.m., Eastern Time (ET):

Sen. Barack Obama has sent his vice presidential text message: were you awake to read it? At 3.04 ET, and just after midnight on the west coast, the Obama campaign sent the following message to anyone who signed up to find out who the presumptive Democratic nominee had picked: 'Barack has chosen Senator Joe Biden to be our VP nominee. Watch the first Obama–Biden rally live at 3pm ET on www.barackobama.com. Spread the word!'

This may be seen as political marketing 2008-style. Remember, in 1996, text messaging was simply not available in the USA, the World Wide Web had only a very small number of users and 'search engine' was a phrase only understood by technical folk.

In 2008, Obama's campaign team communicated with potential voters by text message. How did this come about? Very simply, anyone who accessed Obama's personal website (easily found through Google) was invited to 'Join Obama Mobile' by filling in details of their mobile phone number and zip-code (both required), email address, first name, last name and address (all optional). By joining, they signed up to the right to receive text messages (from Obama) on their phone or to text GO to 62262 (the digital equivalent of OBAMA on the mobile handset). The intention of the Obama campaign team was to text the members of Obama Mobile with the news of

Case Study

the vice-presidential nominee before the mass media knew about it, thus giving the members advanced, privileged information. Those who received the message at 3.04 a.m. heard the news 20 minutes in advance of the media. However, such was the number of text messages that were sent (estimated 3 million) that some members did not receive the text message until 12 hours after it was sent. However, such recipients did not seem upset. One person observed:

> Whatever you think of when it was sent, you have to admit this was a really smart way for a campaign to get thousands, if not millions of numbers. Texting is a huge new tool.[6]

The last part of the text message said 'Spread the word!' There is recognition of the power of social networking, not just through text messaging, but also through the most popular social networking sites. Barack Obama has a page on Facebook (see http://en-gb.facebook.com/barackobama), and uploads videos of his addresses to YouTube. It is hardly surprising that observers claim that:

> Obama's contact list is one many marketers would pay dearly for. Obama fans are young, politically passionate and digitally savvy, with the means to access millions like them via word-of-mouth.[7]

Barack Obama polled over 69 million votes (53 per cent of the popular vote) on 4 November 2008, and was inaugurated as President of the United States on 20 January 2009.

Notes

1 Lock, A. and Harris, P. (1996) 'Political Marketing – Vive La Difference!', *European Journal of Marketing*, 30(10/11): 14–24.
2 O'Cass, A. (1996) 'Political Marketing and the Marketing Concept', *European Journal of Marketing*, 30(10/11): 37–53, quotation on p. 38.
3 Ibid., quotation on p. 40.
4 Wring, D. (1996) 'Political Marketing and Party Development in Britain', *European Journal of Marketing*, 30(10/11): 92–103.
5 O'Cass, A. 'Political Marketing and the Marketing Concept', *European Journal of Marketing*, 30(10/11): 37–53.
6 http://www.marketingvox.com/obama-adds-biden-to-text-message-dictionary-040581/ (accessed on 6 February 2009).
7 Ibid.

Activities and discussion questions

Log in to Barack Obama's website (www.barackobama.com) and critically examine the features:

- What are the features that encourage website visitors to engage with Barack Obama?
- Do you think the website and its related links helps create trust with, and commitment to Barack Obama? Provide evidence for your views.

- How much do website users (voters) need to use their own knowledge, skills and capabilities to interact with Barack Obama and what he stands for?
- Briefly summarize the changes in ICT between 1996 and 2008, and how this affects interactions and relationships between organizations and consumers.

Social network usage:

- It is estimated that (in 2008) about one-third of internet users are members of a social networking site. List the social networking sites that you and/or your friends use and/or are aware of.
- Should organizations tap into social networking sites? What are the potential pros and cons?

Barack Obama and the Fox News Network have opted for having a page on Facebook.

- Has your organization done a similar thing or thought about it? Would you consider it a relationship marketing or customer relationship management initiative?
- Under what conditions do you think it is effective for an organization to tap into a social networking website? What might be the disadvantages?
- What does your organization do to further understand consumer/customer experiences?

References

Ballantyne, D., Christopher, M. and Payne, A. (2003) 'Relationship Marketing: Looking Back, Looking Forward', *Marketing Theory*, 3(1): 159–166.

Berry, L.L. (1983) 'Relationship Marketing', in L.L. Berry, G.L. Shostack and G.D. Upah (eds), *Emerging Perspectives on Services Marketing*, Chicago, IL: American Marketing Association; 25–28.

Bourassa, M.A., Cunningham, P.H. and Handelman, J.M. (2007) 'How Philip Kotler has helped to Shape the Field of Marketing', *European Business Review*, 19(2): 174–192.

Christopher, M., Payne, A. and Ballantyne, D. (1991) *Relationship Marketing: Bringing Quality, Customer Service and Marketing Together*, Oxford: Butterworth Heinemann.

Grönroos, C. (1994) 'Quo Vadis Marketing? Towards a Relationship Marketing Paradigm', *Journal of Marketing Management*, 10(5): 347–360.

Grönroos, C. (1997) 'From Marketing Mix to Relationship Marketing – Towards a Paradigm Shift in Marketing', *Management Decision*, 35(4): 322–329.

Grönroos, C. (2004) 'The Relationship Marketing Process: Communication, Interaction, Dialogue, Value', *Journal of Business and Industrial Marketing*, 19(2): 99–113.

Gummesson, E. (2002) 'Relationship Marketing and a New Economy: It's Time for De-programming', *Journal of Services Marketing*, 16(7): 585–589.

Harker, M.J. (1999) 'Relationship Marketing Defined? An Examination of Current Relationship Marketing Definitions', *Marketing Intelligence and Planning*, 17(1): 13–20.

Harris, L.C. and Ogbonna, E. (2008) 'The Dynamics Underlying Service Firm–Customer Relationships', *Journal of Service Research*, 10, May: 382–399.

Harwood, T., Garry, T. and Broderick, A. (2008) *Relationship Marketing: Perspectives, Dimensions and Contexts*, Maidenhead, UK: McGraw-Hill.

Jackson, B.B. (1985) 'Build Customer Relationships that Last', *Harvard Business Review*, 63, November/December: 120–128.

Kotler, P., Keller, K.L., Brady, M., Goodman, M. and Hansen, T. (2009) *Marketing Management*, Harlow, UK: Pearson Education Limited.

Kuhn, T.S. (1970) *The Structure of Scientific Revolutions*, Chicago, IL: Chicago University Press.

Morgan, R.M. and Hunt, S.D. (1994) 'The Commitment-Trust Theory of Relationship Marketing', *Journal of Marketing*, 58, July: 20–38.

O'Malley, L. and Tynan, C. (1998) 'Relationship Marketing in Consumer Markets: Rhetoric or Reality?', *European Journal of Marketing*, 34(7): 797–815.

Parvatiyar, A. and Sheth, J.N. (1999) 'The Domain and Conceptual Foundations of Relationship Marketing', in J.N. Sheth and A. Parvatiyar (eds), *Handbook of Relationship Marketing*, Thousand Oaks, CA: Sage Publications.

Pine, B.J. and Gilmore, J.H. (1999) *The Experience Economy: Work is Theater and Every Business a Stage*, Boston, PA: Harvard Business School Press.

Sheth, J.N. (2002) 'The Future of Relationship Marketing', *Journal of Services Marketing*, 16(7): 590–592.

Vargo, S.L. and Lusch, R.F. (2004) 'Evolving to a New Dominant Logic of Marketing', *Journal of Marketing*, 68, January: 1–17.

Vargo, S.L. and Lusch, R.F. (2008) 'Service-Dominant Logic: Continuing the Evolution', *Journal of the Academy of Marketing Science*, 36: 1–10.

Voss, C. and Zomerdijk, L. (2007) 'Innovation in Experiential Services – An Empirical View', in DTI (ed.) *Innovation in Services*, London: DTI; 97–134.

2 Relationship Marketing Themes

Learning objectives

- To outline the key features of Relationship Marketing (RM).
- To highlight some common themes from the academic literature.
- To evaluate the main concepts and models that relate to these themes.

Introduction

In this and the following chapter we consider and discuss the key aspects and themes of RM. The traditional view of RM has focused on the supplier's perspective and therefore these chapters will tend to follow the same approach.

In the past, when you, as a customer, made a decision to purchase a product or a service, your supplier would only really be interested in persuading you to choose, and subsequently buy, their product or service. Once the sale was made, the supplier would probably then be more interested in seeking out a new customer. In recent years, however, supplying organizations are now not only interested in making the sale but also in establishing, developing and maintaining a relationship with you, the customer. Why is there this change in focus? What has caused these changes to take place and what are the benefits gained by the parties concerned?

This chapter reviews the concept of RM (the development and maintenance of mutually beneficial relationships), its key features and its themes that have been researched and practised over the past three decades.

There has been the development of a perspective where knowledge of individual customers is used to guide highly focused marketing strategies leading to 'personalized' marketing. As long-term relationships with customers cannot be duplicated by the competition, such relationships offer a unique and sustainable competitive advantage.

To successfully apply this approach, a company needs to have a high degree of knowledge of the technology in which it competes, an understanding of its competitors, customers and of its internal organization. RM also requires an emphasis on dialogue and creativity that ensures greater customer involvement with the company in the creation and maintenance of a relationship. Such marketing strategies, however, may not be appropriate to all buyer–seller relationships. The extent to which the development of ongoing relationships is desirable depends on the degree of uncertainty on the part of the buyer and whether the market environment is turbulent. The greater these are, the higher the likelihood of customers seeking a relationship (Zeithaml 1981; Berry 1983; Lovelock 1983).

The trend towards service orientation and the adoption of information technology within a global context has led to change and complexity (Mulki and Stock 2003). Companies need a degree of stability in which to work and establishing more open relationships with key customers and other partners/stakeholders can help (Ballantyne et al. 2003). Levels of product quality have also improved dramatically, forcing companies to seek competitive advantage in other ways. In addition, changes in legal developments resulting from increasing public pressure have led to greater emphasis on customer relationships.

The current academic literature on RM tends to fall into a number of categories or 'themes':

- RM as a new type of marketing
- Relationships in networks
- The benefits of RM
- What is meant by a 'relationship' and what are the components of a successful one?
- In what contexts is RM practised?
- Stages of relationship
- Relationship marketing for all?

We now explore each one of these in more detail.

Theme 1: RM as a new type of marketing

RM is often seen as a new type of marketing. Trading through strong relationships occurred years ago when owners of small businesses knew and understood the needs of their customers. However, as the size of firms increased over the years, it became difficult to maintain such contacts. Today, new technology and the development of sophisticated databases have made this possible once again.

In its simplest form, after-sales service can be considered as RM but many companies do this quite reactively rather than as a planned strategy. More pro-actively, organizations gather information about their customers and then decide with whom they can communicate so that buyers and sellers can work together to mutual benefit.

Some have argued that RM can emphasize a whole offering that includes a number of services as well as the product itself. Indeed some (e.g. Grönroos 1996) see it as redefining the business as a service business (incorporating both product and service elements), making the key competitive elements part of service competition (this has more recently been developed as the service-dominant logic [S-D Logic] which we discuss in more detail later).

Grönroos redefines marketing as follows: 'Marketing is to establish, maintain and enhance relationships with customers and other partners, at a profit, so that the objectives of the parties involved are met. This is achieved by a mutual exchange and fulfilment of promises' (1996: 13). Grönroos sees this redefinition of the business as an important strategic role for RM together with the need to look at the organization from a process management perspective rather than seeing marketing simply as one of a number of organizational functions. This, of course, requires a significant change in business philosophy. Similarly, as RM focuses on developing a continuous relationship between buyers and sellers and marketing through relationships as compared to transactional marketing, participants may become interdependent over time as they continue to interact (Boedeker 1997; Holmlund and Törnroos 1997).

According to Grönroos, all marketing strategies lie between the extremes of transactional and relational. He sees the relational strategy as focusing on interactive marketing with the 'marketing mix' performing a supporting role. Rather than employing market share as a measure of marketing success, this approach uses customer retention.

Christopher et al. (1991) see RM as a synthesis of three complementary perspectives:

- The shifting of emphasis from a transactional to a relationship focus.
- A broader view of the markets with which the company interacts. In addition to customer markets, there is the development and enhancement of relationships with other markets such as supplier and internal markets.
- A recognition that quality, customer service and marketing activities need to be brought together.

Christopher et al. (1991) see all three of these perspectives being linked to customer retention. The second perspective above implies relationships with others, not just customers, and particularly internal markets. This is a very important market as there seems to be a strong linkage between employee satisfaction, employee retention and customer retention (Reichheld and Kenny 1990). The third perspective is concerned with improving service quality through the integration of quality, customer service and marketing. All these together should lead to improved customer retention.

All the above imply a change, not only in terms of marketing practices but also in terms of the development of a new marketing theory. Möller and Halinen (2000), however, argue that RM does not form a general theory of marketing as it involves two types of relationship theory: first, one that is 'market based' which is consumer oriented and, second, one that is 'network based' which is more inter-organizationally oriented. They see the former as being low in relational complexity and the latter as being high. Table 2.1 displays the managerial challenges each type of RM produces.

Table 2.1 Managerial challenges of the two types of relationship theory

Market-based	Network-based
Developing and managing customer relationships	Managing the firm from a broader resource perspective where there is a focus on exchange relationships
Applying different marketing tools to different customer segments	Managing a portfolio of exchange relationships
Managing individual customer relationships Managing multiple contact channels	Managing networks Managing individual relationships
Importance of information systems/ databases	Establishing, developing and maintaining strategic partnerships
	Constructing supplier and customer networks

Source: Adapted from Möller, K. and Halinen, A. (2000) 'Relationship Marketing Theory: Its Roots and Directions', *Journal of Marketing Management*, 16 (1–3): 40–47. Reprinted with permission of Taylor & Francis Ltd http://www.informaworld.com

The above implies the need for different approaches depending on the particular focus: the consumer or the organization. However, as it is unlikely that building and maintaining relationships with customers alone will be successful, other stakeholders need to be considered. Therefore, it is more likely that the network-based relationship theory is appropriate for all RM situations.

Theme 2: Relationships in networks

As we note above, and in Chapter 1, RM is often seen as involving more than just relationships between buyer and seller but also suppliers and other infrastructure partners (Sheth and Parvatiyar 1995) involved in exchanging something of value (Aijo 1996).

RM shares with a number of other disciplines a concern over strategic alliances, partnerships and strategic networks. It embraces intra- and inter-organizational relationships as well as relationships between organizations and individuals (Eiriz and Wilson 2006).

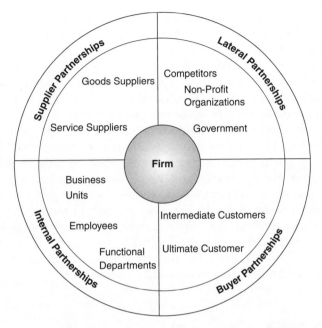

Figure 2.1   Forms of relational exchange

Source: Adapted from Morgan, R.M. and Hunt, S.D. (1994) 'The Commitment–Trust Theory of Relationship Marketing', *Journal of Marketing*, 54, July: 21. Reprinted with permission from the *Journal of Marketing*, published by the American Marketing Association

Some identify the importance of relationships with a number of additional 'customer' types: supplier, recruitment, referral, influence and internal markets (Christopher et al. 1991, 2002; Peck et al. 1999). Gummesson (1999) goes further and identifies thirty relationship types all of which have the potential values of long-term collaboration producing mutual benefits.

Morgan and Hunt (1994) identify ten forms of relational exchange which can exist within four types of partnerships: supplier partnerships, lateral partnerships, internal partnerships and buyer partnerships (Figure 2.1).

Are all these relationships within networks of equal importance and value? Martin and Clark (1996), distinguish between first-, second- and third-order relationships. First-order relationships are those which the focal firm experiences directly with other stakeholders in the marketplace. Second-order relationships are the networks of relationships that take place between the various participants, and third-order relationships are the internal relationships in the participants' organizations, and include customer-to-customer interactions. A theatre, for example, would have first-order relationships with its audience (customers), with the providers of the script, stage props, etc. (its suppliers), the Arts Council, local authority or media (its regulators) and with other theatres and other entertainment providers (competitors). Its second-order relationships could include, for example, those between the Arts

Council and other theatres and other arts providers, and examples of third-order interactions could include interaction between competing theatres or between different audience members.

In a similar vein, Boedeker (1997) believes that RM can be put to use on various levels, depending on the type and number of bonds used by the company to increase customer loyalty. At the lowest level, price incentives are used to increase the value of the customer experience, but as price is the most easily imitated tool, this seldom offers long-term competitive advantage. At the second level, therefore, in addition to price, social bonds are developed by offering unexpected services. This can only be achieved by learning about clients' wants and needs and customizing the service. Eventually a third level is established, where bonds that provide clients with value-adding systems and which are not available from other sources are institutionalized within the organizational structure. Boedeker (1997) believes that this approach can be applied to various kinds of relationship such as the company network, between two individual companies, between the company and other stakeholders and also internally.

Theme 3: The benefits of RM

From a firm's perspective, relationship marketing is based on two arguments:

- It is more expensive to win a new customer than it is to retain an existing one.
- The longer the association, the more profitable the relationship for the firm.

Whilst it would depend on the individual, it is claimed that getting a new customer is five to ten times more expensive than retaining one. This is not only because of the direct costs that are incurred but also the costs of unsuccessful prospecting that can be saved. Furthermore, as customers become more satisfied with the service they receive, the more they buy (Reichheld and Sasser 1990). As purchases increase, operating costs fall due to increased efficiency.

Reducing customer-defection rates is obviously critical for retention. As defection rates fall, the average customer-relationship lifespan increases. When customers defect they take profits away from current transactions *and* future profits *and* negative word-of-mouth comments. Therefore, RM stresses the following as key to profitability:

- loyalty
- customer retention
- long-term relationships.

Indeed, 'customer share' is more important than market share (Gummesson 1999) although the relationship must be win–win if it is to be long-term and constructive and the initiative must come from all parties to produce equal and respectful interactions. The share of the customer refers to the percentage of an individual's lifetime purchases. In addition, 'economies of scope' can occur which refer to the cost savings resulting from the complementarities of products. 'Customer loyalty' is now being used instead of 'brand loyalty' and this emphasizes the interactive nature of the commitment of the customer to the firm and/or its employees. Brand loyalty, in contrast, suggests that the commitment is to the product.

Another key benefit is that long-term service customers become better co-producers and this helps production and delivery and therefore improves quality. This also means that service providers can gradually build up knowledge about their customers. In addition, customers tend to become less price sensitive as the relationship becomes more important to them than price alone. Thus RM improves security and makes outcomes more predictable.

Theme 4: What is meant by a 'relationship' and what are the components of a successful one?

A relationship implies interaction (Sheaves and Barnes 1996), and Duck (1991) sees relationships as providing reciprocal support with the nature of this support helping to define the degree and type of relationship. Although 'relationship' implies interaction it is not necessarily a cooperative one as relationships can also involve conflicts and can exist between enemies. Of equal importance is the fact that interaction does not necessarily mean that there is a relationship. There is therefore a need to outline what activities and exchanges relationships involve (Holmund and Törnroos 1997).

Social relationships can range from more formal interactions which are unlikely to be characterized by much feeling or emotion, to the much more personal relationships which resemble what psychologists refer to as close relationships (McCall 1970). There are exchange relationships where there is the expectation of receiving a benefit and, on the other hand, 'communal' relationships where both parties are concerned with the welfare of the other. In the latter case, benefits are based on the needs of the other and would seem to be more long term than exchange relationships (Clark and Mills 1979).

Although many factors have been identified in the literature as being particularly important for successful relationships, five seem to be the most commonly noted (Conway and Swift 2000):

- commitment
- trust
- seller's customer orientation/empathy
- experience/satisfaction
- communication.

Commitment

Commitment is an intention to continue a course of action or activity (Hocutt 1998) and is a long-term concept. Some believe that the level of commitment a partner feels towards a relationship is of major importance in relationship development and subsequent success (Morgan and Hunt 1994; Wilson 1995). Commitment can also be viewed as the desire to maintain a relationship (Hocutt 1998) and is often indicated by an ongoing 'investment' into activities which are expected to maintain the relationship (Blois 1998).

Commitment is also likely to be influenced by social bonding. Buyers and sellers who have a strong personal relationship are more committed to maintaining the relationship than less socially bonded partners (Wilson and Mummalaneni 1986).

Trust

Trust is expectation that the word of another can be relied upon and implies honesty in negotiations. Trust is the precondition for increased commitment (Mietilla and Möller 1990) and like commitment is often stated as a vital factor in successful relationships.

Ford sees trust as an important consideration as 'many aspects of relations between customers and suppliers cannot be formalised or based on legal criteria. Instead relationships have to be based on mutual trust' (1984: 18).

Promises must be kept in order to maintain relationships, with mutual trust being a main factor in long-term relationships (Takala and Uusitalo 1996). The challenge for relationship marketing is to inculcate trust in the partner. Trust is established where the perceived performance matches promised performance.

Some link trust to commitment (Morgan and Hunt 1994; Liljander and Strandvik 1995; Wilson 1995). Morgan and Hunt (1994), for example, argue that both trust and commitment are 'key' elements in a relationship as they encourage marketers to work at preserving relationship investments, by cooperating with exchange partners. Trust and commitment also help in resisting attractive short-term alternatives, in favour of staying with existing partners.

Trust can be influenced by satisfaction and experience (Ganesan 1994) as trust is unlikely to be built where no (or very little) experience exists. Similarly, others see rapport as an important influence (Macintosh 2009).

Some distinguish between trust and trusting behaviour (Cowles 1997; Ali and Birley 1998). Ali and Birley (1998) distinguish between trust based on the personalities involved and trust based on actual behaviour with the latter being more rational. Cowles (1997), however, believes that trust and trusting behaviour are linked to risk. A customer relationship therefore does not always involve trust (if there is no risk, trust is not relevant). For example, if there are contractual safeguards, there is no risk and therefore no trusting behaviour.

Trust can also influence the development of customer orientation/empathy. The greater the level of trust, the more the chance of a positive attitude being developed and this in turn can lead to a heightened level of customer orientation/empathy.

Customer orientation/empathy

The word 'empathy' refers to the ability to see a situation from someone else's point of view and the greater the degree of empathy between the parties concerned, the fewer the barriers to relationship development. Indeed, even where service delivery has failed, the ability to empathize with the customer can help build a relationship. For example, if a hotel guest complains about a room and the complaint handler clearly understands what the complainant is experiencing, service recovery leading to future bookings is more likely. Customer orientation/empathy, therefore, encourages trust and increases the chance of developing a long-term relationship and thus more sales. It requires the whole firm to satisfy customer needs more successfully than the competition.

Experience/satisfaction

The success of a relationship depends on the degree to which relationship expectations meet with relationship performance. Also, the last experience is usually remembered best (this is known as the 'recency effect'): thus if the last experience is positive, this may overcome any negative experiences encountered previously and vice versa. Experience, therefore, has an important influence on customer satisfaction (Rosen and Suprenant 1998) and, of course, the more satisfied the customer, the more likely that the relationship will last.

Relationship satisfaction can be seen to be needed for relationship quality and Storbacka et al. (1994) propose a sequential conceptual framework with the links between the various stages being important for analysis (Figure 2.2). They propose that the dissatisfied customer will defect and the relationship will end but this may be too simplistic, in that there may be a zone of tolerance. For example, the experience of poor restaurant service may be suffered on a few occasions if the quality of food was still good. Customer satisfaction, however, doesn't automatically lead to retention as large numbers of customers who defect say they are satisfied (Reichheld 1993). Indeed, a customer could rate a service highly and yet not be satisfied with the experience.

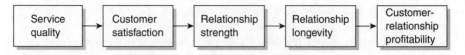

Figure 2.2   Stages in the development of relationship profitability
Source: Adapted from Storbacka, K., Strandvik, T. and Grönroos, C. (1994)
'Managing Customer Relationships for Profit: The Dynamics of Relationship
Quality', *International Journal of Service Industry Management*, 5 (5): 23.
Reprinted with permission from the *International Journal of Service Industry
Management*, published by Emerald Group Publishing Limited, all rights reserved.
Permission cleared through rightslink

Satisfaction, as well as being an important component of relationships, can
also influence other components. For example, the relationship between
trust and commitment is mediated by satisfaction (Hocutt 1998).

Communication

As all relationship components are experienced through communication, this
is a vital component in its own right. In the business context, communication
should involve two-way dialogue (Grönroos 2004). Indeed, at its basic level,
the communicator (or sender of the message) needs 'feedback' on the communication and this is only possible if there is a two-way flow of information.

There are two main categories of communication for an organization –
internal and external. Communication is particularly important when a new
business relationship is being established and communication is essential in
relationships as it implies dependence and commitment (Takala and
Uusitalo 1996). It also has the propensity to influence levels of trust between
buyer and seller (Selnes 1998).

Theme 5: In what contexts is RM practised?

In Chapter 1 we indicate a number of contexts in which RM has developed:

- service markets
- channel management
- business-to-business markets
- not-for-profit organizations
- consumer markets.

RM is widely practised in service markets. This is due to the fact that normally both the service provider and consumer are required to be present for
the service to take place (getting a haircut, going to the dentist, for example).
As a result, some form of relationship must exist during service provision

(Palmer 1997). RM is used in channel management and relationships between members of the marketing channel have been examined. (Dwyer et al. 1987; Anderson and Narus 1990). RM is also found in business-to-business (B2B) marketing and it is in this area that a good deal of the initial thinking on RM occurred. Indeed, a particular approach, the 'interaction model', can be regarded as a forerunner of RM. The interaction perspective looked specifically at the interaction between suppliers and purchasers and developed out of research undertaken by the IMP (International Marketing and Purchasing) Group which specifically considered such interactions in an international context. The perspective places the emphasis on processes and relationships. Buyers and sellers are seen as active participants in long-term relationships with marketers and purchasers supporting and maintaining relationships rather than merely buying and selling. The links between the two parties can eventually become institutionalized.

Håkansson (1982) gives three sets of variables to be taken into consideration when assessing the importance and influence of interaction:

- the environment in which the interaction takes place
- the 'atmosphere' surrounding the interaction
- the elements and process of the interaction itself.

These relationships go through two basic stages of development, the first of which Håkansson calls the 'episodes' stage, which consists of an exchange of products/services, information, etc. between companies. Once this stage has been achieved to the mutual satisfaction of concerned parties, they progress to the next stage, termed 'adaptations and institutionalization' which is largely based on the concept of developing relationships. A crucial element in both achieving and developing each stage of the relationship is the establishment of a degree of mutual trust. Clear expectations about roles and responsibilities on the part of both parties develop over time and eventually these expectations become 'institutionalized' and form part of the traditional way of operating.

Jackson (1985) is often quoted as being one of the first people to apply an RM perspective in the B2B marketing context. She distinguishes between two extreme types of situation. At one extreme there is the 'always a share' situation where a buying organization, by the very nature of the market it is in, can share out the business to various suppliers. In this situation, building a long-term relationship with one supplier would be inappropriate. The other extreme case is what Jackson terms the 'lost for good' situation. Although the term seems to sound a negative, this scenario is positive for a supplier where there is an ongoing relationship with a buyer. The business, however, is likely to be 'lost for good' if it is lost at all. Jackson (1985) believes that RM is valuable in the latter situation and 'transaction' marketing more appropriate in the former case. Of course, she accepts that there are intermediary types. The key to the approach is that a supplying firm needs to understand the customer's position to gain a benefit and a key issue on the part of the buyer is the possible cost of change, especially if there has been a long-term relationship.

Another sector where RM may be important is the not-for-profit sector (McCort 1994; Conway 1997; Brennan and Brady 1999). McCort (1994) believes that organizations in this sector match well with an RM strategy because of the dual nature of their customers – those who fund the service and those who use the service may not necessarily be the same people but where mutual benefit is required (taxpayers paying for healthcare, for example). Brennan and Brady (1999) also believe that not-for-profit organizations are well suited to RM due to the increasing requirements to measure and monitor customer satisfaction and of the growing importance of internal marketing in this sector. RM can overcome a short-term, tactical emphasis that can exist with not-for-profit organizations (Conway 1997). In not-for-profit organizations, because 'consumers' do not pay directly for the service, there is pressure for marketing to take on a 'selling' function in order to attract funds and this tends to be of a tactical, short-term nature. There is a need for a more long-term marketing perspective and in order to ensure that not-for-profit organizations have a more strategic, planning perspective, the development of long-term relationships with a variety of 'customers' becomes important.

For consumer markets, Shani and Chalasani consider RM as 'an integrated effort to identify, maintain and build up a network with individual consumers and to continuously strengthen the network for the mutual benefit of both sides, through interactive, individualised and value added contacts over a long period of time' (Shani and Chalasani 1992: 44). They believe RM to be based on the identification, building and continuous updating of a database to store relevant information about current and potential customers. These strategies also require the use of innovative media to target the customer and communicate with him/her on a one-to-one basis. Tracking and monitoring of the relationship with each customer over time is needed and the lifetime value for the organization calculated.

Theme 6: Stages of relationship

Some use a marriage metaphor to describe the various stages through which a relationship can develop (Dwyer et al. 1987; Grossman 1998). The marriage analogy may not be an appropriate approach, however. Tynan (1997), for example, argues that the marriage analogy may now be less than helpful as it does not help in the understanding of timescales, the number, nature and willingness of the parties involved, nor does it offer the possibility of a consideration of dysfunctional relationships (although Dwyer et al. use a divorce metaphor within their scheme).

Duck (1991) states that building a relationship involves four key elements:

- awareness of the opportunities for friendship
- the ability to encourage and entice likeable persons into a relationship
- skills and knowledge about the ways in which relationships are helped to develop and grow
- skills that help to maintain and repair relationships.

Waddock (1989) presents a process comprising recognition of the need/use of partnership, initiation of the partnership, establishment and maturity. Scanzoni (1979), on the other hand, sees three stages of involvement: exploration, expansion and commitment.

Christopher et al. (2002) present a different five-stage model, which they term 'a ladder of customer loyalty' At the bottom rung of the ladder, customers are viewed as 'prospects'. At the top rung of the ladder they become true 'partners', having climbed intermediate rungs, labelled, in turn, as 'purchaser', 'client', 'supporter' and 'advocate'. The role of RM here is to advance relationships up the ladder. Partners work together for mutual benefit and advocates are so deeply involved in the organization that they are very loyal long-term purchasers but they also influence others through positive word-of-mouth. Moving customers up the ladder, however, is not a simple task. Organizations need to know exactly what each customer is buying and as every customer is different, they need to know how they can continue to offer additional value and satisfaction that will differentiate their offering. Essentially this is through exceeding expectations.

Similarly, Cross (1992) talks of the 'five degrees of customer bonding' which are awareness, identity, relationship, community and advocacy. All of these have different levels of trust and interaction in the relationships with customers. It is the final three stages which are considered to be the key ones relating to RM as they emphasize two-way interaction.

Theme 7: Relationship marketing for all?

Successful RM would seem to require a supportive culture which involves effective internal marketing. Organizational structures and rewards schemes geared to an understanding of customer expectations using a sophisticated customer database are also likely to be required. However, there may still be additional factors that make RM less attractive (Sharland 1997). For example, it is important to note that costs are incurred when building and maintaining relationships (Blois 1998). Relationships have positive and negative aspects, their value being determined by the relative importance of each. From the point of view of a specific customer, the balance between the positive and the negative may vary between suppliers for a whole variety of reasons. For example, a customer's view of the desirability of entering into a relationship will be affected by perceptions of the likely size of the transaction costs involved.

Summary

This chapter has presented a review of the literature dealing with the growing interest in the philosophy of RM. The chapter has considered the implications of its philosophy and its benefits to the parties concerned. The application of RM can be found in a variety of contexts, particularly in service and business-to-business markets due to the importance of personal interaction within these areas. A case has also been put forward for its application within a not-for-profit context. The chapter also delves a little more deeply into what is meant by the term 'relationship', identifying types of relationship and the various components that a successful relationship requires. In addition, various stages in the development of a relationship have been highlighted and circumstances where RM may not be so appropriate have been noted. In discussing the common themes, a good deal of literature has been referred to. Such an extensive list of references presented at the end of the chapter offers the reader a wide variety of sources offering the opportunity for further reading.

Learning outcomes

After reading this chapter you will:

- be able to outline the key features of RM;
- identify common themes from the academic literature;
- be able to evaluate the main concepts and models that relate to these themes;
- have an extensive list of further reading on the subject of RM.

Activities and discussion questions

- Think of an organization that pursues an RM approach with you as the customer. What are the key features that you have used to help you identify such an organization and why?

- Consider *one* business relationship: how would you describe the degree/stage of the relationship you have and why? What are the advantages and disadvantages of having this relationship?
- To what extent do you think RM can be considered as a 'new' type of marketing? Justify such a decision.

Case Study 2	Contact Theatre: a successful 'relationship-focused' subsidized theatre

Purpose: To demonstrate how a broader view of customer and the building of mutually beneficial relationships with such different customer types can enhance the strategic effectiveness and success of an organization.

Situated just outside Manchester City Centre, UK, the Contact Theatre (known as 'Contact') was originally a university theatre predominantly funded and controlled by the local university. As a result of an overall review, Contact was established as a pioneering theatre venue in Manchester. It receives the largest source of its finance from the North West Arts Board (NWAB). In addition, the Association of Greater Manchester Authorities (AGMA) and Manchester City Council provide funds for specific types of work. There is still, however, some support from the university (cash and in kind).

The theatre was totally refurbished and re-opened in 1998 with a different mission and governance structure. The building includes three theatre spaces – Space 1, a 350-seat end-on theatre; Space 2, an 80-seat flexible studio, and Space 3, a rehearsal, workshop and performance space. It also creates performances and events in its 'lounge' area, which has a stage, a bar and room to dance. The theatre's website is a space for debate, artistic showcases, insight into artistic processes and sharing of ideas.

The theatre's programme combines a mix of productions and touring projects ranging from theatre, dance, participatory projects, education initiatives, music and clubs. It is seen as a space where new kinds of theatre are created, a place where artists can meet, develop, explore and take risks. It claims to be constantly 'exploring new ways to develop, to learn and to create exciting theatre, bringing together passions, fashions, moods, moves, sounds, networks, anger, engagement, words, rhythms, visions and visuals in the theatre'.[1] A wide range of development opportunities for artists is available with a particular focus on emerging artists. It runs residencies, training courses, and provides a lot of support and advice. Many of the artists at Contact have developed through its participatory projects, but artists are welcomed at all stages in their lives. International collaboration is also seen as very important. Artists are regularly invited from across the world to perform at Contact, and programmes of theatre exchange help to develop new kinds of artistic understanding. The theatre embraces music and the cultures surrounding music, a full range of visual media, and writers who are poetic, experimental and collaborative. The vision of the theatre is that of a 'young people's theatre' where young people can grow, learn and make decisions as a young artist, audience member, organizer or leader. Although the majority of the theatre's audiences come from these age groups, the theatre also welcomes audiences and artists of all ages.

The motives for a theatre's existence can be very different depending on whose views are being sought: management, artists, audience, funders, regulators, sponsors, etc. Indeed, the measurement of 'success' of a subsidized theatre could be considered problematic because of ambiguous goals and objectives and the difficulty in measuring outputs.[2] The attraction of revenue needs to match the organization's objectives such as the covering of costs, meeting funding body targets or reaching both core and new audiences. In addition to box-office revenue, funds could be from business support through sponsorship, donations/gifts in kind, corporate entertainment, trusts and individuals. There does, however, seem to be a general consistency amongst employees within Contact of what the key indicators of success are. All see quality of work and quality of experience as important. The theatre has won many awards for its work, including, in recent years the Art 04 and Breakthrough awards from the Arts Council, plus many awards for its artists, writers and shows. The Chief Executive/Artistic Director believes that quality of work attracts the best artists. He also sees the importance of audience satisfaction, of evaluation and of acquiring feedback. Indeed, audience forums take place monthly with more than 20 participants attending each. Although all staff understand the importance of the box office, all feel that this should not be the only indicator. External stakeholders also believe that the theatre is successful in terms of what it sets out to do and the representatives of its major funders, the North West Arts Board (NWAB) and the Association of Greater Manchester Authorities (AGMA) view the theatre's Board as being effective in helping to achieve this. As a representative of AGMA says, 'The theatre impacts on the community through outreach and education. They talk of collaboration and this is exactly the direction that AGMA wants'.

It is the Artistic Director who provided the strategic direction for a theatre as well as being the creative driving force behind the organization. Of particular importance, therefore, are the relationships that exist between the Artistic Director and those involved in revenue generation, regulation, usage and staff members. Relationships that are effective should be clearly of a two-way, mutually beneficial nature. The theatre believes that it is important to collaborate with people in order to achieve the best results. Its partners range from local, national and international arts organizations which come to Contact to present or make work, to specialist agencies working with particular communities. All speak of two-way relationships and the importance of evaluation and feedback from the audience (forums and informal feedback via staff and evaluation of publicity). The general view is that the theatre should be seen as a quality theatre for young people by young people. The fact that the term 'for' rather than 'to' is used reinforces the two-way perspective that is communicated. All employees believe in the importance of building relationships with the audience and others who deal with this audience, e.g. teachers and youth workers. They also acknowledge the existence of important other beneficiaries with whom there is a need to build relationships, such as emerging artists, companies, other theatres, funding bodies and the theatre's board. Due to the vast array of activities, the building of relationships and increasing collaboration are considered as vital:

'We need to build relationships with a variety of customer types: audiences, artists, staff, funding bodies. It is only through collaboration with these that we can achieve what we have set out to do. Everything is audience development. Relationship development and collaboration with other organisations so that the whole community can become involved are important aspects of this'. (John McGrath: Chief Executive)

Participation is at the heart of the theatre's work, and it runs a huge range of activities in which young people and artists can join, learn and develop. These activities range from outreach projects with a wide range of communities, to drop-in sessions, to intensive artistic-development programmes such as Young Actors and Young Writers groups. Young people are also encouraged to become involved in planning and decision making at Contact through a range of opportunities including its Open Contact forum and its Action Contact groups.

In terms of staff as the 'internal' customer, there seems to be a general consistency of perceptions. Even though there is a clear hierarchy on paper, employees see the organization as open with collaboration existing between departments and with external bodies. This results in high levels of satisfaction on the part of staff, high levels of mutual trust/commitment and two-way communication.

External stakeholders also have a positive relationship with the theatre. The NWAB has a positive view of its relationships with Contact's Board which is seen as being very representative of other groups, e.g. black members and youth. Similar views are displayed by AGMA: 'Contact is always responsive to a variety of requests from a variety of stakeholders' (representative of AGMA).

Notes

1 www.contact-theatre.org (accessed 18/7/09).
2 Hill, E., O'Sullivan, C. and O'Sullivan, T. (1997) *Creative Arts Marketing*, Oxford: Butterworth Heinemann.

Activities and discussion questions

- What does Contact use as a measure of 'success' when it assesses its performance? Why do you think this is the case?
- Who does the theatre consider as its customers and are all such customers considered as equally as important? Justify your answer.
- Using examples from your own experiences, to what extent do you think RM could help not-for-profit organizations fulfil their mission?

References

Aijo, T.S. (1996) 'The Theoretical and Philosophical Underpinnings of Relationship Marketing: Environmental Factors Behind the Changing Marketing Paradigm', *European Journal of Marketing*, 30(2): 8–18.

Ali, H. and Birley, S. (1998) 'The Role of Trust in the Marketing Activities of Entrepreneurs Establishing New Ventures', *Journal of Marketing Management*, 14(7): 749–763.

Anderson, E. and Narus, J.A. (1990) 'A Model of Distributor Firm and Manufacturer Firm Working Partnerships', *Journal of Marketing*, 54, January: 42–58.

Ballantyne, D., Christopher, M. and Payne, A. (2003) 'Relationship Marketing: Looking Back, Looking Forward', *Marketing Theory*, 3(1): 159–166.

Berry, L.L. (1983) 'Relationship Marketing', in L.L. Berry, G.L. Shostak and G.D. Upah (eds), *Emerging Perspectives of Services Marketing*, Chicago, IL: American Marketing Association.

Blois, K.J. (1998) 'Don't all Firms have Relationships?', *Journal of Business and Industrial Marketing*, 13(3): 256–270.

Boedeker, M. (1997) 'Relationship Marketing and Regular Customer Cards: Daily Product Retailing in Finland', *Marketing Intelligence and Planning*, 15(6): 249–257.

Brennan, L. and Brady, E. (1999) 'Related to Marketing? Why Relationship Marketing Works for Not-For-Profit Organisations', *International Journal of Nonprofit and Voluntary Sector Marketing*, 4(4): 327–337.

Christopher, M., Payne, A. and Ballantyne, D. (1991) *Relationship Marketing*, Oxford: Butterworth-Heinemann.

Christopher, M., Payne, A. and Ballantyne, D. (2002) *Relationship Marketing: Creating Stakeholder Value*, Oxford: Butterworth-Heinemann.

Clark, M.S. and Mills, J. (1979) 'Interpersonal Attraction in Exchange and Communal Relationships', *Journal of Personality and Social Psychology*, 37(1): 12–24.

Conway, A. (1997) 'Strategy versus Tactics in the Not-for-Profit Sector: A Role for Relationship Marketing?', *Journal of Non-Profit and Voluntary Sector Marketing*, 2(1): 42–51.

Conway, A. and Swift, J.S. (2000) 'International Relationship Marketing: The Importance of Psychic Distance', *European Journal of Marketing*, 34(11/12): 1391–1414.

Cowles, D.L. (1997) 'The Role of Trust in Customer Relationships: Asking the Right Questions', *Management Decision*, 35(3–4): 273–283.

Cross, R.H. (1992) 'The Five Degrees of Customer Bonding', *Direct Marketing*, October: 33–58.

Duck, S. (1991) *Understanding Relationships*, New York: Guilford Press.

Dwyer, E.P., Schurr, P.H. and Oh, S. (1987) 'Developing Buyer–Seller Relationships', *Journal of Marketing*, 51(2): 11–27.

Eiriz, E. and Wilson, D. (2006) 'Research in Relationship Marketing: Antecedents, Traditions and Integration', *European Journal of Marketing*, 40(3/4): 275–291.

Ford, D. (1984) 'Buyer/Seller Relationships in International Industrial Markets', *Industrial Marketing Management*, 13(2): 101–113.

Ganesan, S. (1994) 'Determinants of Long-term Orientation in Buyer–Seller Relationships', *Journal of Marketing*, 58, April: 1–19.

Grönroos, C. (1996) 'Relationship Marketing: Strategic and Tactical Implications', *Management Decision*, 34(3): 5–15.

Grönroos, C. (2004) 'The Relationship Marketing Process: Communication, Interaction, Dialogue, Value', *Journal of Business and Industrial Marketing*, 19(2): 99–113.

Grossman, R.P. (1998) 'Developing and Managing Effective Consumer Relationships', *Journal of Product and Brand Management*, 7(1): 27–40.

Gummesson, E. (1999) *Total Relationship Marketing: From 4Ps to 30Rs*, Oxford: Butterworth-Heinemann.

Håkansson, H. (ed.) (1982) *International Marketing and Purchasing of Industrial Goods*, Chichester: John Wiley & Sons.

Hocutt, M.A. (1998) 'Relationship Dissolution Model: Antecedents of Relationship Commitment and the Likelihood of Dissolving a Relationship', *International Journal of Service Industry Management*, 9(2): 189–200.

Holmlund, M. and Törnroos, J.A. (1997) 'What are Relationships in Business Networks?', *Management Decision*, 35(4): 304–309.

Jackson, B.B. (1985) *Winning and Keeping International Customers*, Lexington, MA: Lexington Books.

Liljander, V. and Strandvik, T. (1995) 'The Nature of Customer Relationships in Services', in T.A. Swartz, D.E. Bowen and S.W. Brown (eds), *Advances in Services Marketing and Management*, Vol. 4, London: JAI Press; 141–167.

Lovelock, C.H. (1983) 'Classifying Services to Gain Strategic Marketing Insight', *Journal of Marketing*, 47, Summer: 9–20.

Macintosh, G. (2009) 'Examining the Antecedents of Trust and Rapport in Services: Discovering New Interrelationships', *Journal of Retailing and Consumer Services*, 16(4): 298–305.

Martin, C.L. and Clark, T. (1996) 'Networks of Customer-to-customer Relationships in Marketing', in D. Iaccobucci (ed.), *Networks in Marketing*, Thousand Oaks, CA: Sage Publications; 342–366.

McCall, C.J. (1970) 'The Social Organisation of Relationships', in G.J. McCall, N.K. Danzin, G.D. Suttes and S.B. Kurth (eds), *Social Relationships*, Chicago, IL: Aldine Publishing; 3–34.

McCort, D.J. (1994) 'A Framework for Evaluating the Relational Extent of a Relationship Marketing Strategy: The Case of Nonprofit Organisations', *Journal of Direct Marketing*, 8(2): 53–65.

Miettila, A. and Möller, K. (1990) 'Interaction Perspective into Professional Business Services: A Conceptual Analysis', in R. Fiocca and I. Snehota (eds), *Research Developments in International Industrial Marketing and Purchasing*, Proceedings of the 6th IMP Conference, University of Bocconi, Milan, Italy.

Möller, K. and Halinen, A. (2000) 'Relationship Marketing Theory: Its Roots and Directions', *Journal of Marketing Management*, 16(1–3): 29–54.

Morgan, R.M. and Hunt, S.D. (1994) 'The Commitment–Trust Theory of Relationship Marketing', *Journal of Marketing*, 54, July: 43–48.

Mulki, J.P. and Stock, J. (2003) 'Evolution of Relationship Marketing', in H.S. Eric (ed.), *Proceedings of Conference on Historical Analysis and Research in Marketing (CHARM)*, East Lansing, MI, May 15–18; 52.

Palmer, A. (1997) 'Defining Relationship Marketing: An International Perspective', *Management Decision*, 35(3/4): 319–322.

Peck, H., Payne, A., Christopher, M. and Clark, M. (1999) *Relationship Marketing: Strategy and Implementation*, Oxford: Butterworth-Heinemann.

Reichheld, F.F. (1993) 'Loyalty Based Management', *Harvard Business Review*, 71(2): 64–73.

Reichheld, F.F. and Kenny, D.W. (1990) 'The Hidden Advantages of Customer Retention', *Journal of Retail Banking*, 13(4): 19–23.

Reichheld, F.F. and Sasser Jr., W.E. (1990) 'Zero Defections: Quality Comes to Services', *Harvard Business Review*, 68(5): 105–111.

Rosen, D.E. and Suprenant, C. (1998) 'Evaluating Relationships: Are Satisfaction and Quality Enough?', *International Journal of Service Industry Management*, 9(2): 103–125.

Scanzoni, J. (1979) 'Social Exchange and Behavioral Independence', in R.L. Burgess and T.L. Hudson (eds), *Social Exchange in Developing Relationships*, New York: Academic Press; 61–99.

Selnes, F. (1998) 'Antecedents and Consequences of Trust and Satisfaction in Buyer–Seller Relationships', *European Journal of Marketing*, 32(3/4): 305–322.

Shani, D. and Chalasani, S. (1992) 'Exploiting Niches Using Relationship Marketing', *Journal of Services Marketing*, 6(4): 43–52.

Sharland, A. (1997) 'Sourcing Strategy: The Impact of Costs on Relationship Outcomes', *International Journal of Physical Distribution and Logistics Management*, 27(7): 395–409.

Sheaves, D.E. and Barnes, J.G. (1996) 'The Fundamentals of Relationships: An Exploration of the Concept to Guide Marketing Implementation', in T.A. Swartz, D.E. Bowen and S.W. Brown (eds), *Advances in Services Marketing and Management: Research and Practice*, Vol. 5, Greenwich, CT: JAI Press.

Sheth, J.N. and Parvatiyar, A. (1995) 'Relationship Marketing in Consumer Markets: Antecedents and Consequences', *Journal of the Academy of Marketing Science*, 23(4): 255–271.

Storbacka, K., Strandvik, T. and Grönroos, C. (1994) 'Managing Customer Relationships for Profit: The Dynamics of Relationship Quality', *International Journal of Service Industry Management*, 5(5): 21–38.

Takala, T. and Uusitalo, O. (1996) 'An Alternative View of Relationship Marketing: A Framework for Ethical Analysis', *European Journal of Marketing*, 30(2): 45–60.

Tynan, C. (1997) 'A Review of the Marriage Analogy in Relationship Marketing', *Journal of Marketing Management*, 13(7): 695–703.

Waddock, S.A. (1989) 'Understanding Social Partnerships: An Evolutionary Model of Partner Organisations', *Administration and Society*, 21(1): 78–100.

Wilson, D.T. (1995) 'An Integrated Model of Buyer–Seller Relationships', *Journal of the Academy of Marketing Science*, 23(4): 335–345.

Wilson, D.T. and Mummalaneni, V. (1986) 'Bonding and Commitment in Supplier Relationship: A Preliminary Conceptualization', *Industrial Marketing and Purchasing*, 1(3): 44–58.

Zeithaml, V.A. (1981) 'How Consumers' Evaluation Processes Differ Between Goods and Services', in J.H. Donnelly and W.R. George (eds), *Marketing of Services*, Chicago, IL: American Marketing Association; 186–190.

3 Customer Retention and Loyalty

Learning objectives

- To outline the key features of customer retention and particularly customer loyalty.
- To highlight the variety of influences on this loyalty and the practical implications of these for reward schemes.
- To outline and evaluate the concept of 'customer equity'.

Introduction

The previous chapter highlighted the change in focus from transactional marketing to a more long-term, on-going relational approach that produced mutual benefit to the participants. The key benefit to the organization was that as long-term relationships with customers could not be duplicated by the competition, unique and sustainable competitive differentiation could be produced. Pursuing a retention strategy allows the firm to gain the benefits of it being cheaper to retain an existing customer than it is to acquire a new one and to experience a more profitable relationship as a result of a longer association (Reichheld and Sasser 1990). This is what can be considered to be the 'loyalty ripple effect' (Gremler and Brown 1996). Customer retention, therefore, becomes a measure of marketing success (Christopher et al. 1991; Grönroos 1996). Relationship Marketing (RM) places a good deal of stress on loyalty as reducing customer defection rates is critical to retention and 'customer loyalty' is now being used as well as 'brand loyalty' to emphasize the interactive nature of the commitment of the customer to the firm and/or its employees. As marketing is increasingly being defined in relationship terms, there is clearly a need for the effective management of loyalty (Fournier and Yao 1997).

We hear of loyalty and commitment as being important for relationships and we now have a variety of loyalty cards in use, but what is actually meant by the term 'loyalty'? This chapter will look at the various attempts at defining the term and the attempts at operationalizing it within an RM context.

Loyalty: a behavioural or attitudinal concept or both?

Over the years, *brand* loyalty has tended to be defined and measured in either behavioural or attitudinal terms (Mellens et al. 1996). At first glance, loyalty can be considered to be a behavioural concept being seen in terms of actual purchase behaviour. Therefore, behavioural definitions were built on proportions of purchase (share of purchase, share of visits, share of wallet) or patterns of purchase (frequency, probability of purchase/re-purchase, repeat purchase behaviour or a combination of various aspects of purchase behaviour). These were all then assumed to imply preference towards a particular brand.

Most loyalty programmes use these types of measures to reward 'loyalty' so that the more that is spent, the more rewards there are. However, evidence indicates that this does not necessarily mean that customers become loyal to a particular brand but more to a loyalty scheme (Dowling and Uncles 1997). Indeed, there is some evidence that the so-called key links between loyalty and profitability (Reichheld 1996) such as loyal customers costing less to service, being less price sensitive, spending more time with the company and passing on positive word-of-mouth recommendations may not be the case (Dowling and Uncles 1997; Neal 2005). There is clearly a need to therefore look more deeply into the behavioural measure of loyalty.

Loyalty programmes must also consider profitability when rewarding customer behaviour. Kumar and Shah (2004), for example, note that many frequent-flyer airline loyalty schemes reward on the basis of distance travelled rather than on the price paid. Therefore someone who could get a good price deal for a long-haul flight could gain the same reward as someone who had paid full price.

Another difficulty is the fact that such schemes reward past and present behaviour (Neal 2005) but what of future loyalty? (Reinartz and Kumar 2003). This indicates that behaviour alone is not enough in defining what we mean by 'loyalty'.

Oliver (1999) sees loyalty as a deeply held commitment to re-buy or re-patronize a preferred product or service in the future and Shoemaker and Lewis (1999) consider truly loyal customers as those who feel so strongly that their company can best meet their needs and that any competitors rarely need to be considered.

Based on the above, attitudes are clearly involved in the concept of loyalty. An attitude is a psychological tendency that is expressed by evaluating a particular entity with some degree of favour or disfavour (Eagly and Chaiken 1993). Attitudes comprise cognitive and affective 'elements' or 'domains'. People need to know that something exists before they can have

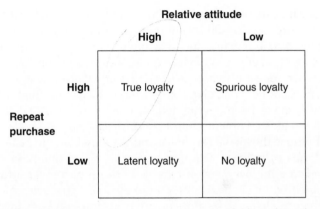

Figure 3.1   Types of loyalty

Source: Adapted from Dick, A.S. and Basu, K. (1994) 'Customer Loyalty: Towards an Integrated Conceptual Framework', *Journal of the Academy of Marketing Science*, 22 (2): 101. With kind permission from Springer Science + Business Media

an attitude towards it and this is known as the cognitive element. The 'favour' or 'disfavour' noted above refers to 'liking' or 'disliking' and this is that element of an attitude that most people consider. Such an attitudinal component allows for a higher-order or long-term commitment that cannot be inferred by simply observing customers repeat purchasing behaviour. This attitudinal aspect of loyalty is believed to be linked to *future* usage and positive word of mouth (WOM) to friends/colleagues.

In reality, most academics agree that neither behavioural nor attitudinal measures *on their own* are sufficient to explain or define customer loyalty.

Dick and Basu (1994) bring the two variables of behaviour and attitude together and produce a typology of loyal behaviour. By using the dimensions of relative attitude and repeat purchase (patronage), they distinguish between:

- true loyalty
- spurious loyalty
- latent loyalty
- no loyalty.

Figure 3.1 presents this. *True loyalty* occurs when repeat purchase is *high* and relative attitude is *high*. This would be the most preferred category for an organization although there should be no complacency. Both attitude and behaviour need to be constantly reinforced.

Spurious loyalty occurs when repeat purchase is *high*, but relative attitude is *low*. In this context, customers may display behavioural loyalty in the short term, probably because of promotions, deals and special offers ('double points' on loyalty cards, for example). However, these people are often susceptible to even better offers from competitors and therefore there is a danger of a continual spiral of promotions.

When repeat purchase is *low*, but relative attitude is *high*, *latent loyalty* is the result. Here customers would like to purchase from an organization, but find it difficult to do so in practice due to inconvenient locations, difficult opening times, etc. Clearly an organizational response should be to remove such barriers.

Finally, when repeat purchase is *low* and relative attitude is *low*, there is *no loyalty*. Here customers perceive competing offers as undifferentiated.

True loyals have been segmented further (Rowley 2005) into captive, convenience seekers, contented and committed. Captive loyals continue to purchase because they have no choice and they are likely to be neutral to the brand in terms of attitude. Convenience seekers are often associated with routine and low-involvement purchases with no particular attitude to the brand. Contented loyal customers tend to evaluate products on their merits and here there are likely to be more positive attitudes towards the brand. The final category, committed loyal customers, hardly ever consider alternative brands and tend to offer verbal word of mouth recommendation.

Some consider attitudinal and behavioural loyalty as not enough in terms of measuring loyalty. These other approaches can be considered to be 'contingency approaches' (Uncles et al. 2003). Rundle-Thiele and Bennett (2001), for example, believe that the type of market will have an important influence. They found that the degree to which behavioural or attitudinal measurements are appropriate depends a great deal on whether the market is a consumable goods market, a durable goods market or a service market. In a similar vein, some note differences in customer motivations (Neal 2005) and others see loyalty depending a good deal on different type and strength of relationships a customer has with the brand itself (Fournier and Yao 1997).

Rewarding loyalty: a conceptual framework

RM's focus on developing and maintaining long-term mutually beneficial relationships has led to the development of loyalty programmes/schemes. However, we have already noted that there may be potential problems with these, such as being too focused on the past, being linked to spending or frequency of usage and not profitability, and thus there being a weak correlation between customer (behavioural) loyalty and profitability (Reinartz and Kumar 2002). In addition, customer loyalty tends to be managed *at the aggregate level* and therefore individual customer level differences may get ignored (Kumar and Shah 2004).

Like Dick and Basu (1994), Kumar and Shah (2004) reinforce the position that 'true', sustainable loyalty requires both behavioural loyalty (high patronage behaviour) and attitudinal loyalty (high relative attitude) from customers. They present a conceptual framework which incorporates a two-tier method of customer rewards, based on this premise. The conceptual framework is presented here in stages.

Stage 1: Capturing customer data

Kumar and Shah's model begins with the importance of *both* behavioural and attitudinal elements of loyalty. Data regarding both of these (survey and behavioural data) need to be captured in the organization's central data 'warehouse'. Figure 3.2 displays this.

Figure 3.2   Capturing customer data

Source: Adapted from Kumar and Shah (2004: 320)

Stage 2: Building loyalty amongst all customers

It is clearly important for an organization to build behavioural loyalty. Favourable attitudinal loyalty is of no real financial value until there is actual action (i.e. this would be classified as Dick and Basu's 'latent loyalty') and although different customers may have different spending in terms of value, these may differ in terms of purchase behaviour and profitability. There is therefore a need to handle and analyse the behavioural data that is housed within the central data 'warehouse'. Such analysis could involve the relationships between purchase behaviour and profitability and produce potential plans of action to enhance the building of loyalty (see Figure 3.3).

		Profitability	
		Low	High
Purchase behaviour	High	Habit purchase of one type of product/service, for example	Purchases a number of the organization's products/services on a frequent basis
	Low	Infrequent purchase of any of the organization's products/services	Infrequent purchase of a range the organization's products/services

Figure 3.3   Behaviour analysis: linking purchase behaviour to profitability

Source: Adapted from Kumar, V. and Shah, D. (2004) 'Building and Sustaining Profitable Customer Loyalty for the 21st Century', *Journal of Retailing*, 80: 321. Reproduced with permission of Elsevier. Permission conveyed through Copyright Centre Inc.

- Top-left cell: high-purchase behaviour/low profitability – this implies habit purchase of one type of product/service rather than commitment and positive attitude towards the supplier. The proposal here is to identify and target such people to produce a positive attitude towards the provider in order to develop possibilities of 'upselling' (selling of higher priced variants) and/or cross-selling (selling of related products/services).
- Bottom-left cell: low-purchase behaviour/low profitability – this indicates low purchase frequency generally and thus low profitability. This could be a new customer and therefore actions that could lead to increased purchase frequency would be appropriate here.
- Top-right cell: high-purchase behaviour/high profitability – behaviour in this cell implies the successful development of upselling and cross-selling on a regular basis. This behaviour needs to be reinforced over a long period.
- Bottom-right cell: low-purchase behaviour/high profitability – behaviour in this cell implies the successful development of upselling and cross-selling but on an infrequent basis. Actions that could lead to increased purchase frequency would be appropriate here.

From this behavioural analysis, Kumar and Shah (2004) offer a reward strategy geared to all customers for their present and past purchases irrespective of their attitude or purchase pattern. This will also enable the organization to capture transactional data. These are 'Tier 1 rewards' and would serve as an incentive for all customers to record their transactions with the firm whenever a purchase takes place (e.g. through scanned loyalty cards). Such a system would reward customers in proportion to their spending and it ensures that all (including new) customers are aware of a rewards programme. This aims to contribute to the building of behavioural loyalty (see Figure 3.4).

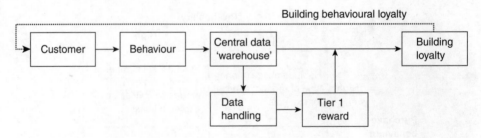

Figure 3.4   Building loyalty amongst all customers
Source: Adapted from Kumar and Shah (2004: 320)

Stage 3: The customer selection process

In addition to treating all customers in the same way through Tier 1 rewards, firms also need to identify those customers who have the potential for high profitability and treat these particular customers at an *individual* level. To do this, customers need to be selected on the basis of four measures:

- attitude analysis
- behaviour analyses
- customer profile information
- customer lifetime value (CLV) measures.

Kumar and Shah adapt the Dick and Basu (1994) framework and produce an attitude analysis based on the dimensions of attitude strength and attitudinal differentiation (see Figure 3.5).

Attitudinal differentiation

		Low	High
	High	Strong positive attitude towards both the organization and its competitors	Strong positive attitude towards the organization but not towards its competitors
Attitude strength	**Low**	Weak attitude to the organization's products/services. Not perceived as different from those of competitors	Weak attitude to the organization's products/services despite them being seen as better than those of competitors

Figure 3.5   Attitude analysis: for which customers should attitudinal loyalty be cultivated?

Source: Adapted from Kumar and Shah (2004: 321). Reproduced with permission of Elsevier. Permission conveyed through Copyright Centre Inc.

- Top-left cell: high attitude strength/low attitudinal differentiation – this implies that although there is a strong positive attitude to the organization's products/services, this doesn't give a competitive advantage as there is also likely to be a strong positive attitude towards competitors' products/services. The aim here is to increasingly differentiate the offering from the competition.
- Bottom-left cell: low attitude strength/low attitudinal differentiation – this indicates weak attitude to the organization's products/services which are not perceived as different from those of competitors. There is a need to cultivate attitudinal loyalty but it may not worth the effort.
- Top-right cell: high attitude strength/high attitudinal differentiation – behaviour in this cell implies a strong positive attitude to the organization's products/services, which are seen extremely favourably compared with those of its competitors. The aim here would be to continue to cultivate this attitudinal loyalty.

- Bottom-right cell: low attitude strength/high attitudinal differentiation – behaviour in this cell implies that customers perceive the organization's products/services as better than the competition s but even despite this, there is not a particularly strong positive attitude towards the organization and/or its products/services. There is therefore a need to invest in the cultivation of attitudinal loyalty here.

Depending upon the circumstance, different plans of action are proposed in terms of attitudinal loyalty. This, along with decisions stemming from the behaviour analysis already noted above (Figure 3.3), have an influence on the choice with whom to develop a relationship. Whilst behavioural loyalty is important to an organizations for profit generation, attitudinal loyalty helps in the building of exit barriers and the cultivation of attitudinal loyalty requires effective selection of customers. Whereas Tier 1 rewards are available to all, there is a need for a firm to sustain the loyalty of particular selected customers (identified via the 'customer selection process'). Therefore, there is also the need for accurate customer profile information about customers in terms of psychographic and demographic characteristics *beyond their purchase histories*. These are important in helping to predict future customer profitability (Reinartz and Kumar 2003) and, for this reason, the model also includes a consideration of the Customer Lifetime Value (CLV) which is the measure of expected value of profit to a firm resulting from a customer relationship that exists over a time period (Reinartz and Kumar 2003; Rust et al. 2004).

The resultant composite framework developed so far is presented in Figure 3.6 below.

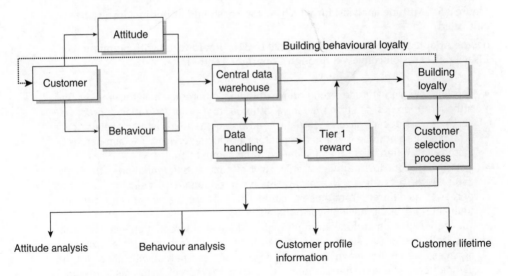

Figure 3.6   Customer selection process

Source: Adapted from Kumar and Shah (2004: 320)

Stage 4: Sustaining loyalty for selected customers

Tier 1 rewards are based on past and present behaviour. In contrast, another set of rewards are proposed. 'Tier 2' rewards have the dual objectives of influencing customer attitude *and/or* behaviour in the *future*. Firms can select which customers would be eligible for such rewards, can decide what the type of reward should be and its value.

The customer selection process measures the CLV and those customers with high and medium CLV are then extracted. Data regarding these customers are further analysed with the behaviour and attitude analyses helping to determine what the firm wants the Tier 2 rewards to do. The customer profile information along with CLV measurement then helps to determine the type and value of the rewards. Although both Tier 1 and Tier 2 rewards run concurrently, Tier 2 rewards should be considered as 'bonus' rewards for specific customers. They are not explicitly divulged to customers with discretion being given on the part of the company on a customer-by-customer basis. Such rewards are invisible to the competition and thus offer another key differentiating feature.

The final composite framework is shown in Figure 3.7. Exhibit 3.1 displays Tier 1 and Tier 2 rewards in action.

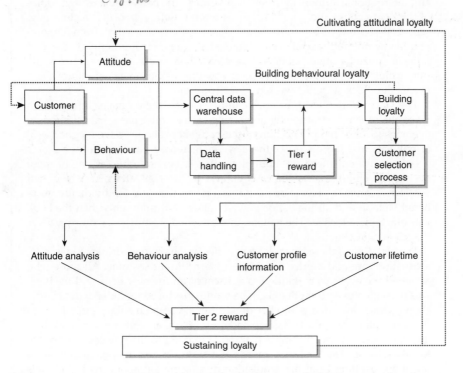

Figure: 3.7   Framework for building and sustaining profitable customer loyalty

Source: Adapted from Kumar, V. and Shah, D. (2004) 'Building and Sustaining Profitable Customer Loyalty for the 21st Century', *Journal of Retailing*, 80: 320. Reproduced with permission of Elsevier. Permission conveyed through Copyright Centre Inc.

Exhibit 3.1 Sweetens Bookshop

Sweetens Bookshop is a small independent bookshop in Bolton, an industrial town north of Manchester in the UK. It has become known locally for its personal friendly service and its ability to order books that are not in stock and subsequently deliver these books faster than the competition.

Over the years, times have become particularly hard for independent bookshops generally, having to compete with large multiple bookshops and supermarkets which can discount books to levels which would be impossible for the smaller competitor. Sweetens is no exception and indeed could be said to be in a more precarious position than most, given that a major bookseller, Waterstones, is less than half a mile away on the same street and that the local council has made major changes to the local shopping environment, adversely affecting passing trade.

In order to survive, Sweetens has had to pursue a niche strategy and, because of its history (it is claimed that paranormal activities have occurred on the premises), in addition to offering a full range of adult's and children's books in competition with all others, has developed a reputation for its expertise in books and authors focusing on local history and on topics linked to spirituality and 'body and mind'. It also organizes 'signings' where local, national and international authors in these fields come to the bookshop and sign copies of their new books and give talks. In addition to selling books, Sweetens now sells related products linked to the above and differentiates itself from the competition by holding special events targeted at the local community. These tend to be organized around public festivals (e.g. Halloween), or in response to the publication of a specific new book. It was the establishment of one of these events that 'kick-started' Sweetens' loyalty scheme.

The Harry Potter series of books and films has been a major influence on Sweetens' survival strategy. By organizing Harry Potter parties at the shop on evenings prior to the publication of these, the bookshop received a good deal of publicity and the success of these events increased awareness of the shop's existence and enhanced its reputation overall. For example, at one of these events, all children received a balloon with a label attached which had Sweetens' contact details. Each child was given their own individually numbered balloon and all the balloons were released at midnight when the book was officially launched. The balloon that travelled the furthest won a prize for that particular child.

The very first of these Harry Potter parties involved food, drinks, a magician, a treasure hunt and a prize for the best Harry Potter costume. All those who attended the event were entitled to a discount on the new book and the book was presented in a promotional gift bag (only produced for independent bookshops) which included a number of additional complementary gifts. Prior to this particular event, the bookshop had organized many other events and signings. However, it was this particular event that led to the development of the loyalty scheme. The bookshop owner and staff realized the potential open to the shop resulting from the acquisition of information about the individuals and families that had attended this first Harry Potter activity. Future events related to other activities and led to the acquisition of customer data and the Sweetens' loyalty scheme was established.

The bookshop initially had a simple loyalty system logging customer information in a book but it then linked with the Association of Independent Book Sellers who provided a loyalty card. The scheme offers 'members' 1 point for every £10 spent with 10 points leading to a £5 gift voucher. There are also periods of time when 'double points' can be acquired. The card allows the bookshop to acquire information about the membership and of members' purchasing habits. In this sense, this points system could be seen to be an example of *Tier 1 rewards*.

However, this has been taken further and the acquisition of data from the loyalty card provides the bookshop with the opportunity to contact specific members about special/key events where these members have priority status. More specifically, the bookshop also holds 'evenings' specifically for these people. The shop can now target different membership segments for signings, new book launches, the presentation of children's authors (as the data held includes whether there are any children) and other different events. In this way, *Tier 2 rewards* are being offered.

Customer switching: the antithesis of loyalty

Rather than looking at what makes people loyal to a brand or an organization, it may be worthwhile looking at those factors that would influence the opposite to loyalty – switching behaviour. Perhaps an understanding of the factors that can lead to switching can help organizations ensure that this is kept to a minimum.

Customer switching has been considered by academics in a number of contexts. For example, linked to perceptions of quality in the banking industry (Rust and Zahorik 1993), linked to dissatisfaction in the insurance context (Crosby and Stephens 1987) and related to service-encounter failure in retailing (Kelley et al. 1993). Staying within a servicecontext generally, there seems to be evidence that intention to switch is influenced by satisfaction and service quality. However, a major difficulty here is that most of the work looking at these relationships did not have the consideration of switching as an objective (Keaveney 1995) and, as a result, dissatisfaction and poor service quality do not account for *all* switching behaviour. Other influences could be time or money constraints, lack of alternatives and switching costs (Bitner 1990) or convenience, price and availability (Cronin and Taylor 1992). Indeed, in undertaking critical incident research amongst over 500 service firms, Keaveney (1995) identifies 800 critical behaviours observed of service firms that caused customers to switch. She categorized these into eight main headings: pricing, inconvenience, core service failures, failed service encounters, response to failed service, competition, ethical problems and involuntary switching (e.g. where the provider has moved).

Similarly, Reichheld and Sasser (1990) note different types of customer defection that need to be overcome:

- price: when customers move to a lower-price alternative
- product: when customers move to superior product
- service: when customers move because of poor service
- market: when customers leave the market but not to a competitor
- technology: when customers move to products outside the industry
- organizational: when customers move due to internal/external political considerations.

Consequently, organizations should pursue 'strategic customer retention management' policies (Ahmad and Buttle 2001) where long-term plans aimed at ensuring that these types of customer defection are kept to a minimum. These require the effective acquisition and analysis of ongoing research data on competitor pricing, competitor product development, technological development, market development, customer expectations, etc.

In a slightly different approach, Rowley (2005) identifies different triggers to switching amongst the loyalty segments previously noted (captive, convenience-seeker, contented and committed). *Captives* could switch in response to alternative offerings and/or new entrants to the market or if there were changes in their personal financial circumstances, whereas *convenience seekers* may be more likely to be influenced to switch in response to special promotions. *Contented* loyal customers would only be likely to switch in response to poor service delivery or product failure, whereas this would have to happen regularly for a *committed* loyal customer to switch.

Linking retention and loyalty to profitability: the 'service-profit chain' and related work

There has been a good deal of research into the linkage between customer loyalty, employee loyalty, productivity and profit. Evidence from a number of service organizations seemed to confirm that there were such relationships and Heskett et al. (1994, 1997) propose a conceptual model known as the 'service–profit chain' (see Figure 3.8). The authors believe that there are direct and strong relationships between profit growth, customer loyalty, customer satisfaction, value of service, employee satisfaction and productivity and service quality. The model presents a series of *propositions* (P1–P4, as shown in Figure 3.8) that are the links in the chain and are derived from a synthesis of case study material collected from many companies. Each link in the chain, therefore, requires testing/ verification.

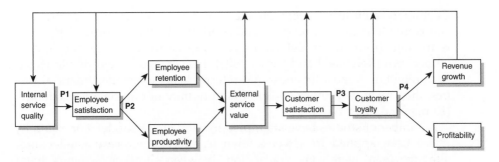

Figure 3.8   The service-profit chain

Source: Adapted from Hesket, J.L., Jones, T.O., Loveman, G.W., Sasser Jr., W.E. and Schlesinger, L.A. (1994) 'Putting the Service Profit Chain to Work', *Harvard Business Review*, March/April: 164–174. Reproduced with permission

Proposition 1: Internal service quality drives employee satisfaction

Internal service quality consists of elements such as workplace and job design, employee selection and development, employee rewards and recognition and tools for serving the customer. Whether this proposition holds true depends a good deal on the particular situation. For example, there could be large differences even within the same industry. Feelings of job satisfaction can differ a great deal between employees who work in a fast food restaurant compared with those who work in a hotel, for example.

Proposition 2: Employee satisfaction drives employee retention and employee productivity

There would seem to be mixed empirical support for this proposition. There seems to be a significant positive relationship between employee satisfaction and employee commitment in US banking, for example, but not with employee tenure. There may even be situations where satisfied employees are not necessarily productive.

Proposition 3: Customer satisfaction drives customer loyalty

If a service is designed and delivered to meet targeted customers' needs, it should lead to greater customer loyalty. This can be seen for professional services, e.g. consultants and accountants. However, a counterexample is that 13 per cent of British Airway's 'completely satisfied' customers did not intend to fly BA again according to a survey carried out in 1995.

Proposition 4: Customer loyalty drives revenue growth and profitability

Customer retention, repeat business and referral are all believed to contribute to increased revenue and profitability. For example, 5 per cent reduction in customer defections can boost profits by 25 per cent to 85 per cent (Reichheld and Sasser 1990). However, as noted previously, if such retention, repeat business and referral leads to smaller financial values, then revenue growth and profitability may not automatically follow (Kumar and Shah 2004).

A number of studies have attempted to validate the model. For example, it has been applied to a well-known leading UK grocery retailer and, although there were some correlations between all other elements, there was little linkage to employee satisfaction and loyalty (Silvestro and Cross 2000). In a similar study by Pritchard and Silvestro (2005), little evidence was found for the link between customer loyalty and financial performance and, in fact, a number of other variables were found to be coming into play that were not within the service–profit chain model at all. Similarly, there may be problems with the link between service quality and profitability (Kamakura et al. 2002).

On a more positive note, studies by Parasuraman and Grewal (2000) in their development of a service 'quality–value–loyalty chain' reinforce some of the links in the service–profit chain by developing an approach where service quality enhances perceived value which contributes to customer loyalty. For Parasuraman and Grewal, 'Service Quality' comprises the key elements of reliability, responsiveness, assurance, tangibles and empathy and 'Value' comprises four different types of value: acquisition, transaction, redemption and 'in-use'. Similarly, there is some evidence that the link between customer satisfaction and profitability is also sound (Anderson and Mittal 2000).

Customer equity

We have already highlighted a change in focus from share of the market to share of the customer. This, in conjunction, with the need to be 'customer focused' has led to the consideration of the possible value each individual customer is worth (CLV as discussed in the Kumar and Shah framework). As a result there has been a shift away from the product-focused 'brand equity' to that of 'customer equity'.

This approach stems from direct/database marketing, RM, service quality and brand equity literature. It has developed out of the need for increased accountability to shareholders, the need for the development of a new approach to decision making resulting from the masses of customer data and the fact that, in general, customer expectations have increased overall.

Brand equity was developed as a concept to refer to a brand's long-term financial value (Barwise 1993). A large number of loyal customers is an asset for a brand and is a major determinant of brand equity (Dekimpe et al. 1997) but there has been a great deal of confusion as to how brand equity can actually be measured. Customer equity as a concept arose from the work of a number of authors (Blattberg and Deighton 1996; Dorsch and Carlson, 1996; Pitt et al. 2000). Blattberg and Deighton (1996) believe that there is a need to understand the value of an organization's customer base and then to use this to determine the most effective investment in both customer acquisition and retention. Rust et al. (2000) explain customer equity as the total of the discounted lifetime values summed over all of the firm's customers. They distinguish between three 'drivers' of customer equity:

- value equity: the end customer's perception of value
- brand equity: the end customer's emotional and subjective assessment above the perception of value
- retention equity: the end-customer's repeat purchase intention and loyalty.

This customer-equity approach has developed out of the research that has been undertaken about the value of relational and experiential aspects of branding. In the relational context, the organization rather than the product is the main influence of brand equity (Berry 2000; Grönroos 2000) and therefore the reputation and identity of the organization becomes important.

Blattberg and Deighton (1996) see the importance of 'customer equity' over decisions on how many new customers to acquire or how many to retain? The goal should be to maximize customer equity by balancing acquisition and retention efforts effectively. They suggest that to do this, there is a need to first invest in the highest value customers through a customer-focused approach that considers how add-on sales and cross-selling can increase such equity. Ways to reduce acquisition costs need to be considered and then customer equity gains and losses need to be tracked against marketing programmes. Of particular importance is their view that it may be worth pursuing the writing of separate marketing plans for acquisition and retention.

Some have highlighted the various factors that influence customer equity (Rust et al. 2000, 2001) and others (Blattberg et al. 2001) have produced a model that provide insights as to how managers can manage investments in acquisition, retention and in customer add-on selling. An important area for research has been the influence that relationships have played in the development of customer equity (Bolton et al. 2001; Gupta et al. 2001; Reinartz and Thomas 2001; Hogan et al. 2002).

Hogan et al. (2002) argue that there is a hierarchy of firm's assets. Tangible and intangible assets are only valuable if they enhance the combined value of the firm's customer equity. In other words, customer equity is a combination of the value of a firm's current customer assets (present customers) and the value of the firm's potential customer assets (those customers who may switch from a competitor or who have not as yet entered the market). How these assets influence customer equity depends on the firm's customer-equity management skills. How this is undertaken, relies a good deal on the ability to collect and analyse market information.

For Hogan et al. (2002), marketing expenditure should now be seen as a long-term investment in customer assets. This creates long-term value to the organization and, where appropriate, its shareholders. The management of this is 'customer equity management' which they define as 'a comprehensive management approach that focuses the efforts of the firm on increasing the lifetime value of individual customers (i.e. the firm's customer assets) in a way that maximises customer equity' (Hogan et al. 2002: 5).

Summary

RM has customer retention as its long-term focus and this chapter deals particularly with that aspect of customer retention known as customer loyalty. Issues relating to its definition were discussed with particular reference to the need to consider past and present behaviour along with future intentions which are attitudinal in nature. Different types of loyalty were described and a model for rewarding loyal behaviour explained. Switching behaviour could be considered to be the antithesis of loyalty and therefore some consideration was given to the factors that could influence such behaviour as well as there being a discussion about the ways to reduce defections. Finally, 'customer equity' – a relatively new area of research – was identified and highlighted. This is defined and explained and the need to measure the value of both customer acquisition and retention was emphasized. The chapter concluded with a discussion on the requirement for a strategic management response to this.

Learning outcomes

After reading this chapter you will:

- be able to outline the key features of customer retention and particularly customer loyalty;
- highlight the variety of influences on this loyalty and the practical implications of these for reward schemes;
- be able to outline and evaluate the concept of 'customer equity'.

Activities and discussion questions

- Think of an organization for whom you would consider yourself to be a 'loyal customer'. What are the key factors that make you loyal and why?
- Consider a loyalty scheme of which you are aware. How successful is it? What criteria would be used to measure this 'success' and why?
- To what extent do you think customer-equity management is likely to become important in the future?

Case Study 3   The Royal Exchange Theatre season ticket scheme

Purpose: To demonstrate the potential difficulties that can be experienced when trying to develop a loyalty scheme that satisfies one group of customers whilst at the same time possibly alienating others.

The Royal Exchange was originally established in 1968 as one of three live theatres in Manchester and established itself as one of the most important regional theatres in the UK over the next thirty years. During the early 1970s the Royal Exchange Company staged numerous productions at a variety of temporary locations until 1976 when a permanent theatre was officially opened. Over the next 25 years, the theatre established itself as one of the most important regional theatres in the UK. It has produced over 200 productions in Manchester, with many being transferred to London. The theatre also presents touring productions throughout the UK in its mobile theatre.

Major productions are presented 'in the round' in the 'theatre module'. This is a seven-sided steel and glass module that sits within the hall of the Manchester Royal Exchange building. The stage area is surrounded on all sides, and above, by seating and this means all seats are less than nine metres from the circular stage giving views from all angles and in this context, it can be seen that the audience co-creates the experience in an even more intimate way than would normally be the case where the audience views the performance from the front. Indeed, observations of those people who are new to the theatre highlight this as a particular feature of their experience. The module itself is housed within one of Manchester's most prestigious historic buildings – the former Cotton Exchange which was once acknowledged as the largest room for commerce in the world. The module is suspended from four massive columns that also carry the hall's central dome because the floor of the building would not be able to take the weight of the theatre and its audience. In fact, only the stage area and ground-level seating rest on the floor of the hall itself. In this context, the audience experience includes the presentation of the theatre itself: its architecture where the modern mixes with the traditional. The theatre can seat up to 700 people on three levels, making it the largest theatre in the round in Britain; 400 seats are at ground level above which lie two galleries, each with 150 seats set in two rows.

Theatre Module [1]

The theatre is predominantly funded by the Arts Council, although other fund-ing is received from the Association of Greater Manchester Authorities (AGMA). Other revenue comes from box-office receipts, catering and sponsorship. As a result, 60 per cent of revenue is earned income with 40 per cent coming from various subsidies.

An Education Department also coordinates a year-round programme of work-shops, projects and learning resources for all ages. The theatre's mission involves innovation and new art. The theatre has a commitment to new writing and produc-ing world premieres. In 1998 it opened a studio as a space for experiment, training and innovation for writers, directors, actors and designers.

Although the Royal Exchange's mission involves innovation and new art, the gen-eral public's image of the theatre seems to be that of performing the 'classics' well and a great deal of effort is expended in ensuring that season ticket holders (who are predominantly middle-aged professionals) are satisfied. Season ticket holders gain a saving of 25 per cent on tickets when they book the season ticket and the scheme includes a ticket for each Royal Exchange Studio production. A season ticket also offers priority booking and flexibility in that the theatre reserves some of the best seats for season ticket holders, and that holders can change their date or seats (free of charge) at any time, as long as the seats are available and there is time for the original tickets to be sent in. A loyalty card gives discounts in the theatre's craft shop, costume-hire shop, bar and restaurant.

The theatre undertook quantitative and qualitative research relating to attender and non-attender attitudes to the image of the theatre. This research first comprised a postal survey using a random sample of single ticket and season ticket attenders using patron data from the box-office computer to give quantitative data from current attenders. Questionnaires were mailed to attenders producing a representative sample of season ticket holders and single ticket buyers of which 31 per cent were season ticket holders (154 respondents). Second, interviews were held with selected samples from different audience segments exploring perceptions, attitudes and motivations and one of these groups was of regular attenders.

In addition, the theatre undertook research focused specifically on its season ticket holder audience group and specifically the season ticket scheme. The research was aimed at understanding the sales and trends associated with the season ticket scheme. It also aimed to analyse the strengths and weaknesses of the scheme being offered to the public. In terms of respondent characteristics, 53 per cent were female and 47 per cent were male, 13 per cent were aged below 44, 64.7 per cent were between 45 and 64 and 21.9 per cent were aged over 65 and 42.9 per cent had retired.

Ninety-three per cent of these respondents had renewed and 6.6 per cent were new season ticket holders (STHs). Of new STHs, approximately half responded to information from the theatre's brochure, a third joined as a result of word-of-mouth recommendation with the rest joining the scheme in response to other sources such as the box office. Of those respondents who were renewing, over 80 per cent had been with the theatre since 1996.

When asked about the main reason for purchasing a season ticket that year, the largest category of reason given was that it was seen as a way of ensuring discipline to attend (27.6 per cent; 10.5 per cent considered themselves as regulars and attended out of habit; 12.4 per cent saw reduced price as a motivator and only 10.6 per cent saw the programme as a motivator.

In terms of perceptions of the various aspects of the scheme, a very large proportion of respondents (92.6 per cent) were satisfied overall (gave a good/very good rating) with there being high scores (those rated good/very good) for value for money (95.1 per cent), ease of booking (89.5 per cent), level of service (83.1 per cent), quality of information (82.5 per cent) and quantity of information (79.1 per cent).

The most popular benefits that scored highly were discount price (61.5 per cent), guaranteed seats (55.6 per cent), not missing shows (49.7 per cent), priority booking (48.4 per cent) and encourages advanced planning (45.3 per cent).

When asked whether they had any improvements to offer on the season ticket scheme, 66.2 per cent were able to do so producing 447 responses. The most popular topic was the Actual Production itself (19 per cent of suggestions) with the majority of these (70.6 per cent) referring to type of play offered. The next most popular topic for suggestions related to the support activities (17 per cent). Of these, choice and availability accounted for 20 per cent, service delivery (25 per cent) and quality of food/drink (20 per cent) as areas for improvement.

The Executive Director of the theatre believes that the Royal Exchange is funded to 'push out the envelope' and therefore sees audience development as attempting to reach a younger audience: 'Audience Development involves linking up with schools and other educational institutions' (Executive Director).

However, there is evidence from the research that there is still a resistance to change on behalf of the theatre's regular audience who are more likely to be 50–60 year-old professionals. The acquisition of the younger, 19–25 age group is particularly difficult: 'Older audiences are getting older and younger audiences don't see the theatre as a leisure option' (Artistic Director). The Artistic Director believes that there is a need to at least get new audiences to try the theatre. A combination of a mixed repertoire, different ways of performing the classics and the right type of marketing may be the way forward. Indeed, the theatre now publicizes its electronic information and social networking sites (e.g. email list, Facebook, Twitter and latest podcast) with such new media communications being specifically geared and targeted to their appropriate audiences. Most recently, the Arts Council England in association with the *Metro* newspaper is providing 618,000 free theatre tickets to anyone under 26 in more than 200 venues across England. The Royal Exchange is one of those theatres selected and is making 10,000 free tickets available over two years to under-26-year-olds as part of this national scheme to increase cultural opportunities for young people. The theatre aims to give away 50 tickets for each Friday to the first young people (known as the Friday Fifty) who apply for each performance. Combined with its free early-evening entertainment in the Great Hall, and 'happy hour' in the bar and craft shop, this is seen as a way of enticing new young attenders to try out the Royal Exchange experience. Another part of the Arts Council initiative is 'the Guest List'. The theatre offers membership which is targeted at people already interested in the Royal Exchange and who want to learn more about what goes on as well as seeing a range of different shows; 100 season tickets are offered per season, including a package of events such as tours, workshops and talks.

Note

1   http://www.royalexchangetheatre.org.uk (accessed 30 June 2009).

Activities and discussion questions

- There is an indication that there may be a conflict between the mission of the Royal Exchange and what is actually perceived by its customers. What is this potential conflict? Offer an example of another organization where there is a conflict of organization mission and what is in fact perceived.
- How does the above example show the need for a sensible balance between customer acquisition and customer retention?
- Offer another example of where difficulties are experienced when trying to develop a loyalty scheme that satisfies one group of customers whilst at the same time possibly alienating others.

References

Ahmad, R. and Buttle, F. (2001) 'Retaining Business Customers through Adaptation and Bonding', *Journal of Business and Industrial Marketing*, 16(7): 553–573.

Anderson, E.W. and Mittal, V. (2000) 'Strengthening the Satisfaction–Profit Chain', *Journal of Service Research*, 3(2): 107–120.

Borwise, P. (1993) 'Brand Equity: Snark or Boojum?', *International Journal of Research in Marketing*, 10(1): 93–104.

Berry, L.L. (2000) 'Cultivating Service Brand Equity', *Journal of the Academy of Marketing Science*, 28(1): 128–137.

Bitner, M.J. (1990) 'Evaluating Service Encounters: The Effects of Physical Surroundings and Employee Responses', *Journal of Marketing*, 54(1): 69–82.

Blattberg, R.C. and Deighton, J. (1996) 'Managing Marketing by the Customer Equity Test', *Harvard Business Review*, 74, July–August: 136–144.

Blattberg, R.C., Getz G. and Thomas, J.S. (2001) *Customer Equity: Building and Managing Relationships as Valuable Assets*, Boston, MA: Harvard Business School Press.

Bolton, R.N., Lemon, K.N. and Verhoef, P. (2001) 'CUSAMS: A Decision Support Model for Customer Asset Management in Service Industries', *Working Paper Carroll School of Management*, Boston.

Christopher, M., Payne, A. and Ballantyne, D. (1991) *Relationship Marketing*, Oxford: Butterworth-Heinemann.

Cronin Jr., J.J. and Taylor, S.A. (1992) 'Measuring Service Quality: A Re-examination and Extension', *Journal of Marketing*, 56(3): 55–68.

Crosby, L.A. and Stephens, N. (1987) 'Effects of Relationship Marketing on Satisfaction, Retention and Prices in the Life Insurance Industry', *Journal of Marketing Research*, 24, November: 404–411.

Dekimpe, M.G., Steenkamp, J.E.M., Mellens, M. and Abeele, P.V. (1997) 'Decline and Variability in Brand Loyalty', *International Journal of Research in Marketing*, 14: 405–420.

Dick, A.S. and Basu, K. (1994) 'Customer Loyalty: Towards an Integrated Conceptual Framework', *Journal of the Academy of Marketing Science*, 22(2): 99–113.

Dorsch, M. and Carlson, L. (1996) 'A Transaction Approach to Understanding and Managing Customer Equity', *Journal of Business Research*, 35: 253–264.

Dowling, G.R. and Uncles, M. (1997) 'Do Customer Loyalty Programmes Really Work?', *Sloan Management Review*, 38(4): 71–82.

Eagly, A.H. and Chaiken, S. (1993) 'The Nature of Attitudes', in A.H. Eagly and S. Chaike, *The Psychology of Attitudes*, Fort Worth, TX: Harcourt Brace Jovanovich College Publishers.

Fournier, S. and Yao, J.L. (1997) 'Reviving Brand Loyalty: A Re-conceptualization within the Framework of Consumer–Brand Relationships', *International Journal of Research in Marketing*, 14: 451–472.

Gremler, D.D. and Brown, S.W. (1996) 'The Loyalty Ripple Effect: Appreciating the Full Value of Customers', *International Journal of Service Industry Management*, 10(3): 271–291.

Grönroos, C. (1996) 'Relationship Marketing: Strategic and Tactical Implications', *Management Decision*, 34(3): 5–15.

Grönroos, C. (2000) *Service Management and Marketing: A Customer Relationship Management Approach*, Chichester: Wiley.

Gupta, S., Lehmann, D.R. and Stuart, J.A. (2001) 'Valuing Customers', *Marketing Science Institute Report*: 1–119.

Heskett, J.L., Jones, T.O., Loveman, G.W., Sasser Jr., W.E. and Schlesinger, L.A. (1994) 'Putting the Service Profit Chain to Work', *Harvard Business Review*, March/April: 164–174.

Heskett, J.L., Sasser Jr., W.E. and Schlesinger, L.A. (1997) *The Service Profit Chain: How Leading Companies Link Profit and Growth to Loyalty, Satisfaction and Value*, New York: Free Press.

Hogan, J., Lemon, K. and Rust, R. (2002) 'CE Management: Charting New Directions for the Future of Marketing', *Journal of Service Research*, 5(4): 4–12.

Kamakura, W.A., Mittal, V., deRosa, F. and Mazzon, J.A. (2002) 'Assessing the Service Profit Chain', *Marketing Science*, 21(3): 294–317.

Keaveney, S.M. (1995) 'Customer Switching Behaviour in Service Industries: An Exploratory Study', *Journal of Marketing*, 59(2): 71–82.

Kelley, S.W., Hoffman, K.D. and Davies, M.A. (1993) 'A Typology of Retail Failures and Recoveries', *Journal of Retailing*, 69, Winter: 429–452.

Kumar, V. and Shah, D. (2004) 'Building and Sustaining Profitable Customer Loyalty for the 21st Century', *Journal of Retailing*, 80: 317–330.

Mellens, M., Dekimpe, M.G. and Steenkamp, J.B.E.M. (1996) 'A Review of Brand Loyalty Measures in Marketing', *Tijdschrift voor Economie en Management*, 41: 507–533.

Neal, B. (2005) 'The Trouble with Loyalty Schemes', *The Wise Marketer*, April: 61.

Oliver, R.L. (1999) 'Whence Consumer Loyalty?', *Journal of Marketing*, 63: 33–45.

Parasuraman, A. and Grewal, D. (2000) 'The Impact of Technology on the Quality–Value–Loyalty Chain: A Research Agenda', *Journal of the Academy of Marketing Science*, 28(1): 168–174.

Pitt, L.F., Ewing, M.T. and Berthon, P. (2000) 'Turning Competitive Advantage into Customer Equity', *Business Horizons*, 43(5): 11–18.

Pritchard, M. and Silvestro, R. (2005) 'Applying the Service Profit Chain to Analyse Retail Performance: The Case of the Managerial Strait-jacket', *International Journal of Service Industry Management*, 16(4): 337–356.

Reichheld, F.F. (1996) *The Loyalty Effect: The Hidden Force behind Growth, Profits and Lasting Value*, Boston, MA: Harvard Business School Press.

Reichheld, F.F. and Sasser Jr., W.E. (1990) 'Zero Defections: Quality Comes to Services', *Harvard Business Review*, 68(5): 105–111.

Reinartz, W.J. and Kumar, V. (2002) 'The Mismanagement of Customer Loyalty', *Harvard Business Review*, 80(7): 86.

Reinartz, W.J. and Kumar, V. (2003) 'The Impact of Customer Relationship Characteristics on Profitable Lifetime Duration', *Journal of Marketing*, 67(1): 77–99.

Reinartz, W.J. and Thomas, J. (2001) 'Modelling the Customer–Firm Relationship', *Working Paper, INSEAD*, Fontainebleau, France.

Rowley, J. (2005) 'The Four Cs of Customer Loyalty', *Marketing Intelligence and Planning*, 23(6): 574–581.

Rundle-Thiele, S. and Bennett, R. (2001) 'A Brand for All Seasons? A Discussion of Brand Loyalty Approaches and their Applicability for Different Markets', *Journal of Product and Brand Management*, 10(1): 25–37.

Rust, R.T. and Zahorik, A.J. (1993) 'Customer Satisfaction, Customer Retention, and Market Share', *Journal of Retailing*, 69(2): 193–215.

Rust, R.T., Zeithaml, V.A. and Lemon, K. (2000) *Driving Customer Equity: How Customer Lifetime Value is Reshaping Corporate Strategy*, New York: Free Press.

Rust, R.T., Lemon, K. and Zeithaml, V.A. (2001) 'Modelling Customer Equity', *Marketing Science Institute Working Paper Series*: 1–108.

Rust, R.T., Lemon, K. and Zeithaml, V.A. (2004) 'Return on Marketing: Using Customer Equity to Focus Marketing Strategy', *Journal of Marketing*, 68(1): 109–127.

Shoemaker, S. and Lewis, R. (1999) 'Customer Loyalty: The Future of Hospitality Marketing', *Hospitality Management*, 18: 349.

Silvestro, R. and Cross, S. (2000) 'Applying the Service Profit Chain in a Retail Environment: Challenging the "Satisfaction Mirror"', *International Journal of Service Industry Management*, 11(3): 244–268.

Uncles, M.D., Dowling, G.R. and Hammond, K. (2003) 'Customer Loyalty and Customer Loyalty Programs', *Journal of Consumer Marketing*, 20(4/5): 294–316.

4　Relationship Marketing: A Change in Perspective?

Learning objectives

- To outline the key influences on the changing nature of marketing as a discipline.
- To highlight the main academic, theoretical tenets of the service-dominant logic and related perspectives.
- To critically evaluate the main concepts and models used.

Introduction

This chapter builds on the previous chapters and looks at the future development of relationship marketing (RM) and of marketing as a discipline itself. It describes a number of radical changes in marketing thought which have implications for both marketer and consumer.

History of marketing thought

Chapter 1 briefly chronicled some of the key historical developments in RM. This chapter, however, deals with broader, more encompassing changes in marketing theory and to do this there is a need to look more deeply at the history of marketing from its early beginnings to marketing thought as it is at present.

The 'birth' of marketing can be seen to have taken place in the late eighteenth century when the foundations of modern economics were created (Sargeant 2005). As a function, marketing focused mainly on the facilitation of distribution and exchange of commodities (Pine and Gilmore 1999; Vargo and Lusch 2004). Of particular importance in this was the improvement of production effectiveness and the advantages gained from economies of scale. As such, the standardization of the physical product was the central theme. As stocks of physical goods increased as well as competition, a selling function then developed.

The 1950s saw the development of new inventions and improvements in communications. This resulted in a growth in international exchange and improved consumer choice. Business success now depended on understanding clients' needs and meeting them better than the competition. Marketing management as such had developed focusing on the management of marketing functions and which had a key focus on the customer. In 1960, McCarthy proposed the '4P' framework which reinforced the linkage to economics and which has been used since. This became known as the marketing concept which whilst having an 'outside-in' perspective, focused on the coordination of all activities to satisfy customers.

As noted in Chapter 1, modern western society experienced a growth in the 'service economy' producing in turn, a growing interest in the marketing of 'services'. This interest led to an acceptance that the marketing of services was different from the marketing of physical goods. This was due to services' specific characteristics, namely intangibility, inseparability, heterogeneity and perishability (Shostack 1977). Services marketing became a sub-discipline which identified some deficiencies in the dominant goods-based marketing approach and a 'broader' concept of marketing became more acceptable. This in turn led to a wider role for marketing. For example, it became increasingly used in public sector and other not-for-profit organizations. The 1980s saw an increasing demand for a move away from mass-marketing and market-segmentation techniques, to a more individualized style, congruent with customers needs. In response to this, marketing research developed new frames of reference including RM (Duncan and Moriarty 1998) and services marketing (Grönroos 1994). These, and other developments in marketing and allied disciplines to differing degrees, were moving away from the 4Ps framework and its micro-economic links including the move from a transactional- to a more relationship-oriented view: the focus of this book.

This move towards a service-dominant perspective is focused on exchange processes and relationships as opposed to the traditional exchange of goods (Vargo and Lusch 2004) and this is also reflective of the consumer culture theory that addresses the dynamic relationships between customer actions, the marketplace and cultural meanings (Arnould and Thompson 2005). Today's customers are increasingly demanding and discerning, not only wanting mutually beneficial relationships and excellent goods or services, but also positive experiences (Pine and Gilmore 1999). Schmitt (1999) further asserts that in contrast to the traditional marketing view of consumers as rational decision makers, who care only about functional features and benefits, consumers can be viewed as both rational *and* emotional human beings who are concerned with achieving pleasurable experiences. The need to add customer experience to the existing complex elements of marketing is considered to be an illustration of a change in the social and cultural factors that influence consumption (Arnould and Thompson 2005).

A different perspective and a changing role for the customer?

The 1990s and 2000s has seen a number of proposals for a paradigm shift in marketing thought with many authors (Grönroos 1994; Gummesson 1995; Rust 1998; Oliver et al. 1998; Pine and Gilmore 1999; Vargo and Lusch 2004) specifically seeing the need to redefine marketing by moving away from the goods-centred view.

Grönroos (1994) suggested a shift was taking place from a marketing mix paradigm to that of relationship marketing and that indeed it had already taken place in services marketing. Research into both industrial and services marketing highlighted the importance of 'interactions' and 'networks' and this had in turn led to a relationship perspective. This requires a movement away from a focus on a single transaction as the exchange to an ongoing relationship-exchange process (Kotler 1992). Rather than the marketing mix (the 4Ps) as the central focus Grönroos saw this as just one of a number of tools which can work together with 'interactive marketing' to enhance the development and maintenance of effective mutually beneficial relationships. Pursuing an RM strategy rather than merely providing a physical product creates more value (Grönroos 1997). Oliver et al. (1998) similarly see the integrating of relationship marketing as a new marketing paradigm but also emphasize the important role for customization to ensure that the unique needs of customers are met.

There have been other claims for a paradigm shift in marketing theory. For some (Holbrook and Hirschman 1982; Pine and Gilmore 1999; Schmitt 1999; Edvarddson et al. 2005) experiential marketing is the next big development.

Vargo and Lusch (2004), however, would seem to have gone further. They bring all these views together and identify the need to shift to a totally new dominant logic: a 'service-dominant' logic (S-D logic). Here the exchange of tangible goods needs to shift to the exchange of intangibles such as skills and knowledge and processes and where doing things 'for' and 'with' and relationships, are more important than doing things 'to' (Vargo and Lusch 2004).

A new logic

Services are not seen as something that helps to differentiate a good nor are they merely seen as what is produced in a service industry, e.g. hairdressing, healthcare, education. For Vargo and Lusch, services are defined as 'application of specialized competences (knowledge and skills) through deeds, processes and performances for the benefit of another entity or the entity itself' (2004: 2). Goods are therefore integrated with services rather than being seen as separate entities. S-D logic rejects the traditional distinction between goods and services, but rather focuses on the relationships between the two. In this perspective, goods, organizations or money involved in the exchange are seen *as vehicles for service provision* (Lusch and Vargo 2006). Similarly, Pine and Gilmore (1999) see their 'experience economy' as being characterized by goods producers delivering services wrapped around products in order to provide a high level of customization which they believe automatically turns goods into a service. For example, providers of digital cameras such as Kodak are providing digital cameras (physical products) developed through organizational competencies, skills, etc., that offer consumers the opportunities to customize their photographic experiences, using their skills, competencies, etc., in ways that were not possible with the older artifacts (35mm films and cameras).

Vargo and Lusch (2004) believe that marketing had previously inherited a model of exchange from economics. This 'goods-dominant' logic is based on tangible goods with embedded value and transactions. The S-D logic, in contrast, has a focus on intangible resources and the co-creation of value and relationships.

Operand and operant resources

A major influence on this thinking towards this new dominant logic is the distinction between different types of resource.

Originally, the term 'resources' meant natural resources that humans draw on for support. According to Pine and Gilmore (1999), these resources were originally those that were extracted from the natural world and were commodities. The industrial revolution then led to the use of commodities as raw materials to produce goods. From the latter part of the twentieth century, however, there has been a growing acceptance that 'resources' can now include intangibles including human behaviour and thought processes.

Constantin and Lusch (1994) distinguish between 'operand' and 'operant' resources. Operand resources are those *on which* an operation or act is performed to produce an effect. For example, operand resources are the physical resources which come together in such a way as to *produce* physical goods and, in this context, 'the customer' is also an operand resource as actions take place *to* him/her. Operant resources, however, are those that are employed to act on operand resources. For example, specialist knowledge and skills are used to transform physical goods into beneficial services that produce perceived value.

Originally, production took place using natural resources and if a society had many of these resources it was considered wealthy. Wealth creation therefore led to a goods-dominant logic where a firm or a society focused on its factors of production. Although technology (an operant resource) was an important resource, greater emphasis was placed on those 'wealth-creating' natural resources which in fact were *operand*. Value was produced through the conversion of these operand resources into outputs at a low cost. Success was achieved through having a share of the operand resources and operand market with customers being something to be acted upon, i.e. 'segment', 'target', 'promote to'.

The late twentieth century saw the realization that skills and knowledge (*operant* resources) were more important. Operant resources are often invisible, intangible, dynamic and infinite and are often core competences or organizational processes (Vargo and Lusch 2004). Knowledge is the foundation of competitive advantage and economic growth and the key source of wealth. Not only are mental skills the fundamental source of competitive advantage but competition also enhances mental skills and learning in society. The main flow is information and *service* is the provision of information to a consumer who desires it. The S-D logic perceives operant resources as primary precisely because they produce effects.

This logic is grounded in the Resource Advantage (R-A) theory which, according to Clulow et al. (2007), identifies key resources as being intangible assets and capabilities that create competitive advantage and superior performance. Hunt and Madhavaram (2006) note that R-A theory assumes both consumer and firm information is imperfect and costly. Demand is therefore heterogeneous across and within industries. The firm's resources (both tangible and intangible) are heterogeneous and imperfectly mobile. It is assumed that in pursuing the firm's objective of superior financial performance, competitive dynamics will tend to produce disequilibrium which in turn should produce innovation. Each economic stage, therefore, rather than being seen as a logical sequence (from agriculture to goods and then to services) should be seen as different applications of different types of competence, i.e. operant resource that could be exchanged. The central influence therefore, being knowledge/skills.

Key resources will enable the company to implement strategies that will meet customers' needs better (Clulow et al. 2007). With this approach a company will become a learning organization which strives to constantly improve its services. Many academics agree that learning and recognizing the key advantages of the company is a survival necessity. Lusch and Vargo (2006) give the example of Toyota where its position in the marketplace is based more on the intangible resource of people's skills and expertise developed over time than necessarily on the quality of its cars.

For Vargo and Lusch (2004) the distinction between operand and operant resources has implications for how exchange processes, markets and customers are perceived and approached which differ from the goods-centred perspective.

Different exchange process

In the goods-centred dominant logic, people are exchanged for physical goods (operand resources and end products). The customer is the recipient of the goods and marketers 'do' things to them; for example, segment and target them (Vargo and Lusch 2004). As such, customers are seen as operand resources. In the S-D logic, however, people exchange to acquire the benefits of competences or services (operant resources). In this service-based logic, the application of these specialized skills and knowledge is the fundamental unit of exchange. However, as a result of the division of labour, producers rarely saw the final, total good that was produced and this, coupled with the increasing length of distribution channels, reduced the potential for interaction with customers.

Goods are now used by other operant resources (customers) in the value creation process. They are no longer considered as a common focus of exchange, the central theme is the application of specialized knowledge and skills (mainly mental). Knowledge and skills can be transferred directly through education or training or indirectly by incorporating them in objects. For example, the mobile phone can be seen as an *appliance* (Vargo and Lusch 2004) for the performance of a communication service. These 'appliances' serve as the basis for meeting higher-order needs (esteem and status, for example). These are the artefacts around which customers have experiences (Pine and Gilmore 1999).

Value

The original goods-centred view assumed that the aim was to make and distribute physical goods to be sold. Firms focused on maximizing profit from the sale of standardized goods which are produced away from the market and subsequently stored until delivery is required. These goods had to incorporate utility and value during the production and distribution process so that the consumer would buy these instead of the competition. These concepts of utility and value which were incorporated into the goods were inherited from economics. In this context, value is 'value-in-exchange' (Beckman 1957; Dixon 1990) and is the value added to the selling value of the good. Value is determined by the producer.

The services-dominant view, however, sees marketing as primarily involved with operant resources which are a firm's core competences (knowledge and skills that can give a firm competitive advantage through better 'value propositions' to present and potential customers than its competitors). The aim is to ultimately develop relationships that involve the customers in the production of customized, competitive-value propositions that meet specific needs. In this context, value is *'value-in-use'* (Alderson 1957). Value should be on the *use* made of tangible goods not the goods themselves.

For example, a computer has no actual value in itself. What it can be 'used for' is what is important. In fact, services are exchanged for services, i.e. value is *in use*. Value is therefore perceived and determined by the consumer. If a consumer is the focal point then value creation is only possible when a good or service is consumed. The enterprise can therefore only offer value propositions; the consumer must determine value and participate in creating it through the process of co-production.

The customer as co-creator

In the service-centred view the focus is on the customer and the relationship. Production is no longer 'to' or even 'for' but 'with' the customer. In services, the customer is always involved in the production of value. Vargo and Lusch (2004) claim that, regardless of the organization type, the common denominators for exchange are specialized knowledge, mental skills or physical labour. People exchange skills for the skills of others, whereas goods are viewed as embodied knowledge and activities. The importance does not lie in the owning of a physical good but rather in the service it provides (Vargo and Lusch 2004). Indeed, even with tangible goods, the customer must still learn to use them, maintaining, repairing and adapting them to his or her unique circumstances. The different tariffs for mobile phones can be seen to be such examples here.

The service-centred view is customer-centric. This means more than orientation but also involves collaboration with and learning from. A service-centred dominant logic implies that value is defined by and co-created with the consumer, i.e. a move from 'make and sell' to 'sense and respond' (Haeckel 1999).

The customer becomes primarily an operant resource (co-producer) rather than an operand resource ('target') and therefore needs to be considered in the value-generating process. Moreover, as society is advancing, people's expectations are rising. It would not be enough to sell a physical product as people now expect satisfaction and other higher-order benefits (Vargo and Lusch 2004). They see customer co-creation of value as being produced as a result of a focus on 'operant' resources. Therefore, even though their service dominant view is closely linked to relationship marketing theory it subsumes it along with numerous other strands of thought into a view of marketing which is a 'continuous learning process (directed at improving operant resources)' (Vargo and Lusch, 2004: 5). It is 'inherently both consumer-centric and relational' (Vargo and Lusch, 2004: 12), and is focused on the application of competences (knowledge and skills) for the benefit of the receiver.

Communications

Interactivity, relationships and customer co-creation imply an important and different role for communications. New paradigms emphasize the importance of two-way communication characterized by dialogue and conversation (Vargo and Lusch 2004; Ballantyne and Varey 2006). Rather than traditional advertising, there is a need for listening. It is a common practice in Procter and Gamble where employees are observing and trying to hear what the market is saying. Their websites offer services like help and advice (Silverman 2006). It therefore not only engages customers emotionally, but also is a great source of knowledge.

The benefits of effective communication have long been understood to be a key feature of successful marketing (Adcock et al. 2001). However, as companies strive not only to meet their customers needs, but also to ensure the customer has a pleasurable experience in the process, communication becomes paramount. Schmitt (1999) describes the development of customer orientation, exemplified by innovative websites, customer entertainment, annual reports and the instigation of 'two-way communication channels' all designed to enhance customer experience. It is possible to suggest, however, that some companies simply pay 'lip service' to this concept, offering customer experience questionnaires, etc., but actually doing very little with any information obtained.

The literature on S-D logic has continued to develop and, indeed, by 2008, the S-D logic had been underpinned by ten foundational premises (FPs) (Vargo and Lusch 2008). These are as follows:

FP1:   Service is the fundamental basis of exchange.
FP2:   Indirect exchange masks the fundamental basis of exchange.
FP3:   Goods are distribution mechanisms for service provision.
FP4:   Operant resources are the fundamental source of competitive advantage.
FP5:   All economies are service economies.
FP6:   The customer is always a co-creator of value.
FP7:   The enterprise cannot deliver value, but only offer value propositions.
FP8:   A service-centred view is inherently customer oriented and relational.
FP9:   All social and economic actors are resource integrators.
FP10: Value is always uniquely and phenomenologically determined by the beneficiary.

The customer in the relationship: experiential marketing

Holbrook and Hirschman (1982) recognized that, whilst many marketers focus on the tangible features and benefits of products and services, applying a more experiential approach could reinforce the symbolic meanings of those characteristics which are subjective in nature. For example, the Apple iPod is not only offering an MP3 player, but rather the unique feel and shape of the physical product as well as the simplicity of the software. Value, therefore, comes from customer experience in addition to the values that are from within goods and services (Prahalad and Ramaswamy 2004).

Edvarddson et al. (2005) take this further and believe that value can be provided by involving customers in a unique and personalized pre-purchase experience. They use the term 'hyperreality' to denote the service experience through simulated reality. They give the example of IKEA which has 'experience rooms' where customers are encouraged to see, test and enjoy a variety of home-design solutions. Similarly, stores such as John Lewis create a 'home cinema room' whereby customers can experience the latest technology whilst sitting in comfortable surroundings. Research has indicated that 55 per cent of customers feel that the biggest single influence on purchase decision is the ability to sample or interact with a product before purchase (Williams 2006) and this could indicate that not everyone is happy to buy 'on-line' and that some may actually seek the physical experience (Hein 2007). This idea is confirmed by Cronin (2003) who believes that functional qualities are not enough and that an emotional reaction forms part of a quality and favourable experience. For Pine and Gilmore (1999) companies now need to move from just the provision of goods and services but also to 'experiences' (memorable events that engage customers in an inherently personal way) and 'transformations' (a series of experiences that change the customer in some fundamental way). People are more likely to remember an emotional experience and there is evidence that they are now more likely to be prepared to pay for this sensation.

McCole (2004) sees the need for this experiential marketing as traditional ways of building relationship and emotional attachments with the customer are not effective any more. He gives the example of Red Bull which every year invites people to build their own flying machines in line with the promotional tag line 'Red Bull Gives You Wings'.

Whilst Grönroos writes of a paradigm shift and Vargo and Lusch refer to a new dominant logic, Pine and Gilmore (1999) identify the next steps in the progression of economic value. This is based on a five-step model combining three dimensions: competitive position (from undifferentiated to differentiated), pricing (from market pricing to premium pricing) and relevance to needs of customers. The model charts the progression of economic value from extract commodities (which are the most undifferentiated, market priced and irrelevant to customer needs) through 'goods', then 'services' to 'experiences', and then finally to what they term 'transformations' (the most differentiated, premium priced and relevant to customer needs) (see Figure 4.1).

There are similarities with both Grönroos, and Vargo and Lusch in terms of the historical developments in marketing thought. For the latter, tangible goods are now seen as serving as 'appliances' through which services can be provided, rather than ends in themselves. Pine and Gilmore (1999), however, discuss the importance of experience and how it occurs when a company intentionally uses services as the stage and goods as props to produce memorable events. For them, customization is the key to development. Through this, goods can become services, services can become experiences. In other

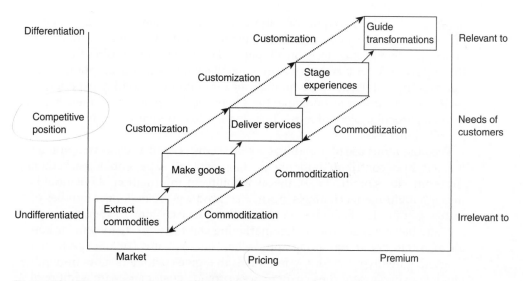

Figure 4.1   Progression of economic value

Source: Adapted from Pine, B.J.II and Gilmore, J.H. (1999: 166) *The Experience Economy: Work is Theater and Every Business a Stage*, Boston, MA: Harvard Business School Press. Reproduced with permission

words, each sequential shift occurs as a result of charging for something personal and unique that differentiates it from the competition. As well as experiences being at the centre of the entertainment business, they are now beginning to be seen in other contexts although so far most have not yet reached the stage of charging for the experience.

Pine and Gilmore also identify a final stage in economic development: 'guiding transformations'. As experience can also be commoditized ('been there, done that') this leads to *transformation* which companies create on top of experiences. This development can be seen in Figure 4.1.

In the transformation economy, the basis of success will be in understanding the aspirations of individual consumers and businesses and guiding them to fully realize these aspirations; joining a fitness centre, for example, allows an individual to have an experience which can lead to a a physical transformation. Transformations, however, can only be guided in that organizations cannot make people change.

Others have followed in their consideration of experiential marketing. Schmitt (1999) asserts that in contrast to the traditional marketing view of consumers as rational decision makers, who care about functional features and benefits, consumers can be viewed as both rational and emotional human beings who are concerned with achieving pleasurable experiences.

For Schmitt (1999) this shift towards experiential marketing has occurred as a result of three simultaneous developments: technology; the supremacy of the brand, and the ubiquity of communications and entertainment. A variety of communication media bombard customers with information that may affect their purchasing decision. Of particular interest are websites that offer the opportunity for customers to give feedback on their consumption experiences (Trip Advisor, where holiday makers rate their holiday experience, for example). Similar technologies have been used to enable customers to listen to a particular piece of music in a store, or to experience a games console prior to purchase.

The ubiquitous use of branding to what seems to be in all aspects of human life has also contributed to the development of experiential marketing. According to Schmitt (1999), the availability of information about brands through multi-media channels means that products are no longer bundles of features, but rather facilitate, provide and enhance customer experiences.

Many believe that experiential marketing can relate to customers far better than traditional marketing approaches. For Williams (2006) experiential marketing involves marketing initiatives that give customers more in-depth tangible experiences. These experiences provide customers with additional information to help inform their purchase decision making. Schmitt (1999) delves even deeper and suggests that there is a need to manage five 'strategic experiential modules' (SEMs) – sense, feel, think, act, and relate – through a variety of 'experience providers', including communications, electronic media, spatial environments and people.

Experiential marketing is not confined just to the entertainment industry. It can be seen in areas where it may not normally be expected. In the heritage sector, experiential marketing may be an effective survival strategy for struggling heritage attractions. Leighton (2007) suggests that the production of 'packaged visitor experiences' as opposed to strategies based purely on the intrinsic product, is more likely to produce positive results. Although some 'conservative' stakeholders may have concerns about the use of such experiential approaches for their particular organizations, those that have adopted such a strategy, e.g. Warwick Castle and the Scotch Whisky Heritage Centre, have increased their visitor numbers, vital to survival in the competitive heritage sector (Leighton 2007).

Another example of the value of experiential marketing can be found in healthcare. Private health care organizations, for example, including BUPA, focus on those positive experiential aspects, such as private rooms, high levels of cleanliness in unhurried environments which patients see as of major importance. These aspects are in contrast to the negative experiences of some NHS patients portrayed in the media. This strategy appeals to customers' inner feelings and emotions with the objective of creating affective experiences linked to the brand (Schmitt 1999).

Experiential marketing focuses on customer experiences rather than functional features and benefits. Functional values are replaced by sensory, emotional, cognitive, behavioural and relational values derived from experiences (Schmitt 1999). Voss (2003) suggests that this focus on customer experience engages customers and differentiates organizations. This is exemplified by airlines such as British Airways advertisements that focus on customer comfort, emphasizing space, relaxation, entertainment and food, rather than flight time or engineering specifications. Websites are also now available for potential customers to review other people's experiences of flying, providing additional knowledge to enable purchasing decisions (e.g. www.airlinequality.com). One airline's (Thomas Cook) advertising campaign utilises Schmitt's 'Think' (SEM), encouraging customers to think convergently and divergently (Schmitt 1999), by asking them which airline offers these services and providing comparisons between different airlines.

Berry et al. (2002) see the importance of managing the 'total customer experience' as does Williams (2006) who reports on UK research that found that 85 per cent of customers valued the opportunity to experience, touch, smell, taste or hear products. This reinforces Schmitt's (1999) view that sensory experiences add value to products and is vital in motivating customers and enabling them to differentiate companies and products. Customers can be both driven by rational decision making and emotions. Indeed customers may actively make decisions in the pursuit of fun and may therefore be viewed as interpretive agents rather than as passive dupes (Arnould and Thompson 2005). For example, people may choose to go to a themed restaurant such as Hard Rock Café, or Planet Hollywood, where they know what type of entertainment to expect. This is supported by well-defined and consistent themes achieved through operations, marketing communications, materials and employees (Gilmore and Pine 2002; Williams 2006). It is the skill of the marketer to translate the product or service into an 'experience', utilizing the correct environmental factors and social interactions between customers and employees (Bitner 1992; Pine and Gilmore 1999). For example, the perceived optimum conditions of calm and relaxation in a reflexology session, aided by soothing music and pleasant smelling aromatherapy, will contrast sharply with the lively, loud and colourful environments used in theme parks.

Arnould and Thompson (2005) draw on numerous works from consumer-culture theory literature and discuss 'experiential consumption activities'. Their work focuses on the involvement of the consumer in the creation of the experience. In their view, consumers are seen as 'culture producers' not as culture bearers.

This consumer creation of the experience is also highlighted by Pine and Gilmore (1999) in their model of the 'four realms' of an experience'. This model is built on two dimensions: customer participation (active or passive) and connection (absorption or immersion).

Absorption occurs when attention is occupied by bringing the experience into the mind and immersion occurs when a person becomes physically (or virtually) a part of the experience itself. The four realms are:

- entertainment (absorption and passive participation)
- educational (absorption and active participation)

- aesthetic (immersion and passive participation), e.g. going to the Rainforest CafÉ
- escapist (immersion and active participation), e.g. skydiving.

For Pine and Gilmore (1999), companies can enhance the richness of any experience by blurring the boundaries between realms. They identify the middle where the realms all come together – the 'sweet spot' – as where richest experiences occur.

The common theme amongst all the approaches in this chapter is that of customer co-creation of value. For Vargo and Lusch, 'value is defined by and co-created with the consumer rather than embedded in output' (2004: 6). For Pine and Gilmore, customer participation means the extent to which 'customers play key roles in creating the performance or event that yields the experience' (1999: 101). A similar view is held by Demangeot and Broderick (2006) who consider experiential marketing as it relates to the on-line environment. They note the critical role experience plays in shopping and in consumption generally with the acceptance that for some there is the enjoyment of the shopping experience itself. This 'hedonistic value' of shopping is also investigated and highlighted by Haytko and Baker (2004).

There are some critics of experiential marketing, however. Some highlight the lack of agreement on its definition (Johnson 2007) and others see it as merely the application of publicity stunts and glorified advertising campaigns, rather than true marketing (Kirkby 2007). There would seem, however, still to be an acknowledgement of the fact that experiential marketing strives to engage a target audience with the brand as opposed to just 'selling the product'.

Summary

There are clearly new trends developing in the marketing discipline and from the firm's perspective, companies are looking for more sophisticated tools to engage their consumers. However, S-D logic emphasizes the role of the consumer and that customer value is created through service experiences and relationships (Lusch and Vargo 2006). Experiential theory sees the important role for creating memorable sensations and emotional attachment. The focus is now rather on marketing *with* customers than *to* customers as customers are the co-creators of value. Where Lusch and Vargo (2006) claim a dramatic shift in fundamental framework, McCole (2004) sees it as a 'divergence' from the traditional view. Although there are people who do not wish to be co-producers (Kalaignanan and Varadarajan 2006) (those who wish to use a mobile phone to simply call someone for a conversation, for example), relationship marketing from the perspective of the customer and his/her role in the co-creation process is an important area for further consideration. The second part of this book looks into this in far more detail.

Learning outcomes

After reading this chapter you will:

- be able to outline the key influences on the changing nature of marketing as a discipline;
- understand the main academic, theoretical tenets of the service-dominant logic and related perspectives;
- be able to critically evaluate the main concepts and models used.

Activities and discussion questions

- Think of an organization that pursues an experiential marketing approach with you as the customer. What are the key features that you have used to help you identify such an organization? Critically evaluate their effectiveness from the customer's perspective.
- What would you consider to be the major implications of the service-dominant logic for commercial organizations? Are such implications positive and likely to enhance organizational marketing effectiveness?
- To what extent do you think experiential marketing can be considered as a 'new' type of marketing? Justify such a decision.

| Case Study 4 | Brunel's ss *Great Britain* |

Purpose: To demonstrate how an original and creative approach to producing a positive customer experience can help meet organizational and other stakeholder objectives.

Background and context

Brunel's ss *Great Britain* (Figure 4.2) is an award-winning UK heritage attraction based in Bristol. The ss *Great Britain* was designed by Isambard Kingdom Brunel and her super-sized iron hull made her the biggest, strongest ship ever built – before Brunel's last ship the *Great Eastern*. When the ss *Great Britain* was launched in 1843 she had the most powerful engines of any ship, could carry enough fuel to get to America or Australia, and also featured an innovative steam-powered propeller. Covering nearly a million miles at sea, the great ship carried emigrants from Liverpool to Melbourne in 1852 and 1875, and transported troops to the Crimean War, as well as carrying the first England cricket team to Australia in 1861. It was converted to a sailing ship, before ending her working life as a floating warehouse; she

Case Study

Figure 4.2   Brunel's ss *Great Britain* (Mandy Reynolds)

was then scuttled in the Falkland Islands in 1937 before being salvaged in 1970 and towed back to Bristol to the dry dock where she was originally built, to be welcomed by 100,000 local residents who lined the River Avon and the Floating Harbour.

The ss *Great Britain* is operated and cared for by a registered charity, the ss Great Britain Trust and receives no government support. It has three income streams – ticket sales, venue hire and fundraising – but has to cover ongoing conservation costs of over

£1 million per year. Its mission is 'to preserve the ship, the ss *Great Britain*, and her building dock for all time for the public benefit of all, and to place the same upon public display as a museum for the enhancement of public understanding and appreciation of her social, commercial, scientific and technological context and significance'.[2]

By the late 1990s it became obvious that the ship was at serious risk from corrosion and in 2001 the Heritage Lottery Fund backed the £11.3 million scheme to save the ship, conserve and restore her. The 're-launch' of the ship and dockside museum as 'Brunel's ss Great Britain' took place in 2005. Since 2005, Brunel's ss Great Britain has succeeded in attracting 170,000 visitors per year (peaking at 200,000 in 2006) and has won a staggering number of awards, including EnjoyEngland Excellence Award's Visitor Attraction of the Year 2007, the Gulbenkian Prize for Museums and Galleries 2006, Best Industrial Museum in Europe 2007 and in 2009 'Outstanding Customer Service' in the EnjoyEngland awards.

The visitor experience

The ship herself is encased in glass to conserve Brunel's iron, and the first part of the visitor experience involves going 'under water' to the dry dock beneath the great structure. Visitors are instructed 'hold your nose you're going under water' and suddenly the object is transformed into an experience. Standing beneath the bow and beneath the glass, the ship appears old but above the glass it is pristine and ready to sail. Once back above water level, visitors enter the dockyard museum where they use their 'passenger ticket' to experience a reverse chronology. The first stage involves an object-rich, product-focused learning experience featuring an interactive steering game and other interpretive devices such as video, audio and a dressing up box. Children are guided through by their own character in the form of Sinbad the ship's cat, who poses a set of tricky questions such as 'Why are propellers better than paddles?' At each of four 'timegates' the visitor can collect a unique stamp on their ticket, which effectively demarks the four time-zones into which the museum is split.

On boarding the ss *Great Britain* the visitor must choose how to make their voyage to Australia – as a first-class passenger, as a steerage-class passenger or as a marine archaeologist – and children have their own Sinbad the ship's cat audio companion. Visitors collect the appropriate audio guide and hear the announcement 'Today is a day that will change the rest of your life' as they step into the role of a Victorian passenger. This stage of the visit, which involves exploring re-created spaces such as the Promenade Deck, the Engine Room and First Class Dining Saloon, is almost entirely experiential, with audio material taken from diaries and letters of the ship's Victorian passengers and crew.

The experience is enhanced with sound (e.g. animals on deck and a mysterious talking toilet), themed aromas (newly baked bread, disinfectant in the Surgeon's Cabin, vomit in the Stewardess's Cabin) and subtle appeals to engage with the everyday lives of passengers such as a noticeboard with requests for writing paper and 'lost and found' items. The audio guide conjures up a vivid picture of life on board, from the birth of babies and the onset of serious diseases to the apparent suicide of Captain Gray. There are auto triggers at key points for the audio guide, ensuring that the most important pieces of information are not missed, but numbers arranged on the ship in the style of cabin-number plaques allow visitors to take manual control of the audio companion if they wish. The appearance of 'Isambard Kingdom Brunel' himself provides an additional dimension to the visitor experience. Providing excellent first-person interpretation, he wanders around the ship and the dockyard museum engaging visitors in conversation – which again is individualized according to nationality, age and interest – and generates even more excellent photo opportunities.

An experiential approach

Once visitors have paid for an initial visit they can revisit as often as they like during the year without charge ('Travel Back in Time Again and Again'), generating opportunity spend at each visit as well as advocacy. Events such as murder mystery dinners, Christmas lunches and parties, and the promotion of the ship as a wedding venue, have succeeded in attracting visitors from new adult and corporate market segments, alongside family events such as Vile Victorian Trails, Sinbad Sea Chest art workshops and Extreme Knotting. Over 16,000 schoolchildren visit each year and some of the children's individual interpretation of artefacts can be seen in the form of laminated panels in the Dockyard Museum.

The interpretative strategy employed by the attraction is consistent then with an engaging, experiential marketing approach. However, 'simply having an intrinsically, inherently experiential offering is very different from actively marketing that offer in an experiential manner'.[3] In terms of marketing strategy, phase one centred on the re-launch but the second phase is now clearly focused on a sustainable commercial drive and to this end current and planned marketing initiatives are aimed at broadening the visitor base and providing a rich and individualized visitor experience. Some examples of promotional activities are bus advertising, banner ads on the VisitBristol website, editorial in newspapers, voxpop interviews on local radio and bespoke ads in specialist publications for the events, corporate and education markets.

In May 2009 their marketing campaign 'A True Story' reached the finals of the Museum and Heritage Awards for Excellence. The campaign focused on the real elements of the visitor experience, with stories taken from passenger diaries, newspapers and official reports. The glamorous history of the vessel was represented in the form of a movie trailer, incorporating TV, bus and print advertising. At the same time Mr Brunel took the 'Gert Big Stink Challenge', using the ship's onboard smells, out to the streets, shopping centres and football grounds of Bristol and Bath. Costumed interpreters, introduced people to elements of a visit to the ship, challenged their preconceptions, and name-gathered. Subsequent market research demonstrated successful cut through with a high proportion of visitors reporting that advertising and leaflets had prompted their visit. Brunel's ss *Great Britain* was the first visitor attraction in the world to introduce a YouTube-style 'bolt on' to its website, enabling visitors to post their own comments, images and videos, and has plans to fully embrace Web 2.0 and incorporate experiential marketing wherever appropriate.

It is evident that the adoption of an experiential marketing approach has proved highly successful. Interpretative planning, marketing communications, pricing and visitor orientation combine to provide a compelling and absorbing experience and visitors also have the scope to co-create their own individualized experience or 'experience space'[4] to suit their own needs and level of involvement.

There are clear implications for innovative experience design in other parts of the heritage or wider tourism sectors in terms of the proven success of this integrated experiential approach.

Case Study

Notes

1 Case study based on a paper presented by Leighton, D., 'Staging the Past, Enacting the Present: Experiential Marketing in the Performing Arts and Heritage Sectors' (with Conway, A.) (2009), International Conference for Arts Management, Dallas, Texas, USA.
2 www.ssgreatbritain.org
3 Williams, A. (2006) 'Tourism and Hospitality Marketing: Fantasy, Feeling and Fun', *International Journal of Contemporary Hospitality Management*, 18(6): 482–495.
4 Prahalad, C.K. and Ramaswamy, V. (2004) *The Future of Competition: Co-creating Unique Value with Customers*, Boston, MA: Harvard Business School Press.

Activities and discussion questions

- To what extent do you think that this approach to experiential marketing can be applied to other types of goods and services?
- To what extent do you think ss *Great Britain* reinforces the key elements of Pine and Gilmore's tenets of experiential marketing?
- Under what circumstances do you feel that an experiential marketing approach would be inappropriate? Justify your answer.

References

Adcock, D., Halborg, A. and Ross, C. (2001) *Marketing Principles and Practice*, 4th edition, London: Prentice Hall/Financial Times.
Alderson, W. (1957) *Marketing Behavior and Executive Action: A Functionalist Approach to Marketing Theory*, Homeward, IL: Richard D. Irwin.
Arnould, E.J. and Thompson, C.J. (2005) 'Consumer Culture Theory (CCT): Twenty Years of Research', *Journal of Consumer Research*, 31, March: 862–882.
Ballantyne, D. and Varey, R.J. (2006) 'Introducing A Dialogical Orientation to the Service Dominant Logic of Marketing' in R.F. Lusch and S.L. Vargo (eds), *The Service Dominant Logic of Marketing: Dialog, Debate and Directions*, New York: M.E. Sharpe.
Beckman, T.N. (1957) 'The Value Added Concept as a Measurement of Output', *Advanced Management*, 22, April: 6–9.
Berry, L., Carbone, L. and Haeckel, S. (2002) 'Managing the Total Customer Experience', *MIT Sloan Management Review*, Spring: 85–89.
Bitner, M.J. (1992) 'Servicescapes: The Impact of Physical Surroundings on Customers and Employees', *Journal of Marketing*, 56, April: 57–71.
Clulow, V., Barry, C. and Gerstman, J. (2007) 'The Resource-Based View and Value: The Customer-Based View of the Firm', *Journal of European Industrial Training*, 31(1): 19–35.

Constantin, J.A. and Lusch, R.F. (1994) *Understanding Resource Management*, Oxford, OH: The Planning Forum.

Cronin, J. (2003) 'Looking Back to See Forward in Services Marketing. Some Ideas to Consider', *Managing Service Quality*, 13(5): 332–337.

Demangeot, C. and Broderick, A.J. (2006) 'Exploring the Experiential Intensity of Online Shopping Environments', *Qualitative Marketing Research: An International Journal*, 9(4): 325–351.

Dixon, D.F. (1990) 'Marketing as Production: The Development of a Concept', *Journal of the Academy of Marketing Science*, 18, Fall: 337–343.

Duncan, T. and Moriarty, S.E. (1998) 'A Communication Based Marketing Model for Managing Relationships', *Journal of Marketing*, 62, April: 1–12.

Edvarddson, B., Enquist, B. and Johnston, R. (2005) 'Cocreating Customer Value Through Hyperreality in the Prepurchase Service Experience', *Journal of Service Research*, 8(2): 149–161.

Gilmore, J.H. and Pine, J. (2002) 'Differentiating Hospitality Operations via Experiences', *Cornell Hotel and Restaurant Quarterly*, 43(3): 87–96.

Grönroos, C. (1994) 'From Marketing Mix to Relationship Marketing: Towards a Paradigm Shift in Marketing', *Management Decision*, 32(2): 4–20.

Grönroos, C. (1997) 'Value Driven Relational Marketing from Products to Resources and Competencies', *Journal of Marketing Management*, 13(5): 407–419.

Gummesson, E. (1995) 'Relationship Marketing: Its Role in the Service Economy', in W.A. Glynn and J.G. Barnes (eds), *Understanding Services Management*, New York: John Wiley and Sons.

Haeckel, S.H. (1999) *Adaptive Enterprise: Creating and Leading Sense-and-Respond Organisations*, Boston, MA: Harvard Business School.

Haytko, D.L. and Baker, J. (2004) 'It's All at the Mall: Exploring Adolescent Girls' Experiences', *Journal of Retailing*, 80(1): 67–83.

Hein, K. (2007) 'Enjoy the Experience', *Brand Week*, 48(44): 20–21.

Holbrook, M.B. and Hirschman, E.C. (1982) 'The Experiential Aspects of Consumption: Consumer Fantasies, Feelings and Fun', *Journal of Consumer Research*, 9(2): 132–140.

Hunt, S.D. and Madhavaram, S. (2006) 'Service Dominant Logic of Marketing: Theoretical Foundations, Pedagogy and Resource-Advantage Theory', in R.F. Lusch and S.L. Vargo (eds), *The Service Dominant Logic of Marketing: Dialog, Debate and Directions*, New York: M.E. Sharpe.

Johnson, M. (2007) 'Has Experiential Marketing Matured?', *Campaign (UK)*, Issue 5.

Kalaignanan, K. and Varadarajan, R. (2006) 'Customers as Co-producers: Implications for Marketing Strategy Effectiveness and Marketing Operations Efficiency', in R.F. Lusch and S.L. Vargo (eds), *The Service Dominant Logic of Marketing: Dialog, Debate and Directions*, New York: M.E. Sharpe.

Kirkby, J. (2007) 'What Art Thou Experiential Marketing?', *My Customer.com*. URL: http://www.mycustomer.com/cgi-bin/item.cgi?id=133187&d=101&h=817&f=816 (accessed 21 March 2008).

Kotler, P. (1992) 'It's Time for Total Marketing', *Business Week ADVANCE Executive Brief*, 2.

Leighton, D. (2007) '"Step back in time and live the legend": Experiential Marketing and the Heritage Sector', *International Journal of Nonprofit and Voluntary Sector Marketing*, 12, May: 117–125.

Lusch, R.F and Vargo, S.L. (eds) (2006) *The Service Dominant Logic of Marketing: Dialog, Debate and Directions*, New York: M.E. Sharpe.

McCole, P. (2004) 'Refocusing Marketing to Reflect Practice: The Changing Role of Marketing for Business', *Marketing Intelligence and Planning*, 22(5): 531–539.

Oliver, R.W., Rust. R.T. and Varki, S. (1998) 'Real-Time Management', *Marketing Management*, 7, Fall: 28–37.

Pine, B.J. II and Gilmore, J.H. (1999) *The Experience Economy: Work is Theater and Every Business a Stage*, Boston, MA: Harvard Business School Press.

Prahalad, C.K. and Ramaswamy, V. (2004) *The Future of Competition: Co-Creating Unique Value with Customers*, Boston, MA: Harvard Business School Press.

Rust, R.T. (1998) 'What is the Domain of Service Research?', *Journal of Service Research*, 1, November: 107.

Sargeant, A. (2005) *Marketing Management for Non-Profit Organisations*, Oxford: Oxford University Press.

Schmitt, B.H. (1999) *Experiential Marketing*, New York: Simon and Schuster.

Shostack, G.L. (1977) 'Breaking Free from Product Marketing', *Journal of Marketing*, 41, April: 73–80.

Silverman, G. (2006) 'How Can I Help You?', *Financial Times Magazine*, 4(5): 16–21.

Vargo, S.L. and Lusch, R.F. (2004) 'Evolving to a New Dominant Logic for Marketing', *Journal of Marketing*, 68, January: 1–17.

Vargo, S.L. and Lusch, R.F. (2008) 'Service-Dominant Logic: Continuing the Evolution', *Journal of the Academy of Marketing Science*, 36: 1–10.

Voss, C. (2003) *The Experience Profit Cycle, Research Report*. Center for Operations and Technology Management. London Business School. London. Cited in B. Edvarddson, B. Enquist and R. Johnston (2005) 'Cocreating Customer Value Through Hyperreality in the Prepurchase Service Experience', *Journal of Service Research*, 8(2): 149–161.

Williams, A. (2006) 'Tourism and Hospitality Marketing: Fantasy, Feeling and Fun', *International Journal of Contemporary Hospitality Management*, 18(6): 482–495.

Part II

Relationships from a Consumer Experience Perspective

5 Frameworks for Analysing the Consumer Experience

Learning objectives

- To outline the frameworks for analysing the consumer experience to be used in Part II.
- To briefly outline the structure of Part II.

Introduction

In Part I, the main sub-areas of relationship marketing, viewed *from the perspective of the focal firm*, have been highlighted and explained. As Grönroos emphasizes:

> The focal relationship is the one between a supplier or provider of goods or services and buyers and users of these goods or services. Relationship marketing is first and foremost geared towards the management of this relationship. (2004: 101)

As we have seen earlier, this focal relationship is embedded in a wider network of relationships. To quote Grönroos again:

> If marketing is to be successful, other suppliers, partners, distributors, financing institutions, the customers' customers, and sometimes even political decision makers may have to be included in the management of the relationship in the network of relationships. (2004: 101)

The notion of a network of relationships, viewed from a focal firm perspective, has been captured simply and effectively by Martin and Clark (1996), shown here as Figure 5.1. This represents the different 'orders' of relationships, which were briefly mentioned in Chapter 2. The first-order relationships are those which the focal firm has directly with other stakeholders

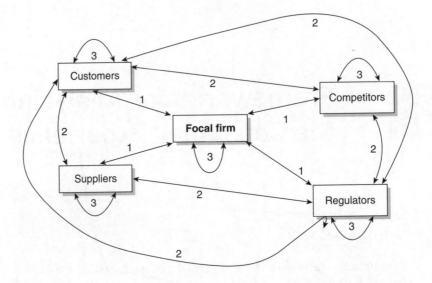

1 = first-order relationship, 2 = second-order relationship, 3 = third-order relationship

Figure 5.1   Classification of first-, second- and third-order network relationships

Source: Adapted from Martin, C.L. and Clark, T. (1996) 'Networks of Customer-to-Customer Relationships in Marketing', in D. Iaccobucci (ed.), *Networks in Marketing*, Thousand Oaks, CA: Sage Publicatons; 342–366

in the marketplace: regulators, competitors, suppliers and customers. The second-order relationships are the networks of relationships that take place between the various players. The third-order relationships are the internal relationships in the players' organizations, and include customer-to-customer interactions.

Take, for example, a multiple supermarket group as the focal firm. Its first-order relationships are those it has with regulators (such as local planning authorities and trading standards officials), with competitors (other multiple supermarket groups, together with convenience retailers, and increasingly, virtually every other type of retailer as supermarket product ranges continually expand), with the many national and international suppliers of the grocery produce and other products (and increasingly services such as insurance and banking), and with the customers (the shoppers). The second-order relationships would include, for example, those between the planning authorities and the group's competitors (a relationship of great importance where land for new store developments is scarce), or between, say, customers and regulators (for example, customer contact with trading standards officials regarding safety of products being sold in one of the supermarkets). Examples of third-order interactions could include interaction between competitors (such as buying alliances or potential mergers and acquisitions), or online consumer-discussion platforms centred on the supermarket group concerned.

The framework also provides guidance on the networks of relationships in which organizations, not normally thought of as profit-oriented firms, are embedded. Take, for example, a university as the focal organization. Its first-order relationships are those with regulators (such as the funding bodies for teaching and research and subject discipline benchmarking groups), with competitors for the provision of higher education, with suppliers (those involved with the maintenance of the physical infrastructures of the buildings/equipment, schools/colleges from where students are recruited, external catering or security service providers, etc.), and indeed with customers (both full- and part-time students, local/regional/ national/international public and private organizational users of the university's research and consultancy expertise, etc.). Second-order relationships would include, for example, those between schools/colleges and other universities, or website promotions offered by rival universities to the target student market. Third-order interactions would include those between the students at a university (such as students' unions or other university societies with varying levels of formality), or joint research projects across one or more universities.

Figure 5.1, therefore, presents a broad, comprehensive picture of the network of relationships from a focal firm/organization perspective. In so doing, it prevents the elements being treated as isolated phenomena, and also, importantly, it locates customer-to-customer interactions into the wider network of relationships. However, what differences might we expect if we develop a similar framework of relationships, but one grounded, first and foremost, in the consumers' experiences of a service domain?

In Part II, we address this question. The emphasis is on studying relationships and interactions *from a consumer experience perspective*, as opposed to a focal firm/organization perspective. It provides not only an alternative perspective to the study of relationship marketing, but also the opportunity to gain first-hand insights into consumer interactions and relationships.

Studying relationships from a consumer experience perspective offers considerable promise. A number of aspects of the changes in marketing perspectives outlined in the last chapter have direct relevance here:

- Customer and consumer experiences underpin the twenty-first century emphasis on consumer co-creation of value (see Prahalad and Ramsawamy 2004; Vargo and Lusch 2004; Edvarddson et al. 2005), which is, of course, a fundamental aspect of the service-dominant (S-D) logic of marketing discussed earlier.
- Recent research has emphasized the importance of experiential services marketing research (see Pine and Gilmore 1999; Schmitt 1999; Fitzsimmons and Fitzsimmons 2001) and experiential consumption research (Arnould and Thompson 2005), as discussed in Chapter 4.

Consumer resources

There is much agreement in the marketing and management literature that consumers can be considered as increasingly informed, networked, empowered and active (see, for example, Prahalad and Ramaswamy 2004). Indeed, one commentator has affirmed that consumers are taking over the marketplace (Szmigin 2003). A key reason behind this is the increasing availability of information, and communication technology has created much greater opportunity for consumers – individually and collectively – to offer support to, or object to, organizations and their products, and importantly, determine their own consumption experiences. The emerging S-D logic of marketing (Vargo and Lusch 2004), which we have discussed earlier, and which emphasizes consumer–firm *co-creation* of value, offers a lens through which to understand this phenomenon by, among other things, thinking about the *resources* that both consumer and firm bring to the relationship. Chapter 6 considers the issue of the resources that consumers bring to bear in their relationships with organizations in more detail.

When we think about resources in this particular context, we must consider this issue of *operand* and *operant* resources, discussed in Chapter 4. In their original discussion of the S-D logic, Vargo and Lusch (2004) describe traditional goods-dominant marketing as being focused on *operand* resources, such as physical goods (i.e. resources on which an operation or act is performed to produce an effect). From the firm's perspective, implicit in the notion of consumers as operand resources is a high level of control of marketing activities. Firms tending to view consumers as operand resources will regard them as 'things' to segment, target and carry out research on. In such circumstances the marketing landscape belongs to the providers of goods and services. However, the service-dominant logic moves the emphasis away from treating consumers as operand resources to one where consumers are treated as operant resources. *Operant* resources are resources – often invisible and intangible, such as core competences or processes – that produce effects in their own right. Such resources, according to Vargo and Lusch (2004), are likely to be dynamic and infinite, rather than static and finite (which is usually the case with operand resources). Consumers are thus considered as active participants in the co-creation of value, and it is through their experiences that 'value in use' is attained.

Thus, according to Vargo and Lusch, this service-centred view of marketing is 'customer-centric' (i.e. collaborating with and learning from customers and being adaptive to their individual and dynamic needs). This implies that value is defined by and '*co-created*' with the consumer, who brings his or her own (primarily operant) resources to bear on the process, thereby creating value-in-use. As a result, firms are in a process of continual hypothesis generation and testing, in order to constantly learn so as to try to serve customers better and improve performance. Underpinning all of this is a relationship marketing approach.

Arnould et al. (2006) identify different types of operant resources available to consumers – physical, social and cultural resources. Physical resources consist of physical and mental endowment (i.e. energy, emotion and strength). Cultural resources include specialized knowledge and skills, as well as history and imagination. Social resources incorporate family relationships, consumer communities and commercial relationships. Consumers can integrate these three types of resources together (Arnould et al. 2006; Baron and Harris 2008), both individually and collectively, through consumer-to-consumer (C2C) interactions, such as consumer campaigns on behalf of, or against, a firm and/or its products. Chapter 6 considers the issue of consumer resources (and their interaction) in more detail, with specific reference to how consumers (individually and collectively) mobilized their operant resources on behalf of an organization potentially threatened by a set of outside circumstances – a context which has been the subject of a specific research project by two of the authors. In doing this, we will highlight Arnoud et al.'s (2006) 'resource-based theory of the consumer' and draw out its implications for relationship marketing.

Experience domains

Studying relationships from a consumer experience perspective raises questions about the sorts of consumer experiences that are the most useful and interesting to explore. Or, put another way, what types of experience domains should be chosen for analysis and interpretation? We can define an experience domain as a field of knowledge, activity and discourse that stimulates consumers to engage in purposeful interactions with a network of organizations and consumer communities in the course of experiences that are collectively understood.

We have been guided, in our choice of experience domains to include in Part II, by Pine and Gilmore's (1999: 30) classification of experience realms. We have deliberately chosen those exhibiting *active consumer participation* (which, according to Pine and Gilmore, means that consumers personally affect the performance or event that yields the experience) and *consumer immersion* (which, according to Pine and Gilmore, involves the consumer becoming physically or virtually part of the experience itself). They form the bases of Chapters 7 and 8, which consider the consumer experience in terms of *consumer immersion* with specific reference to student 'gap' years (i.e. a period of time – often a year – spent between finishing high school and starting higher education – or after finishing higher education and beginning full-time employment – where individuals may travel the world, engage in voluntary work at home or overseas, etc.).

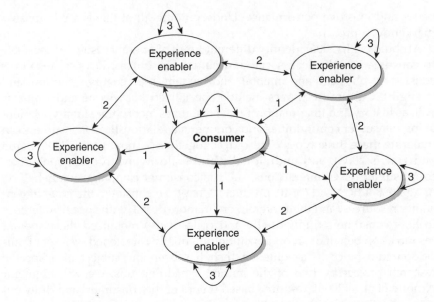

1 = first-order interaction, 2 = second-order interaction, 3 = third-order interaction

Figure 5.2   Interactions from the consumer perspective

Figure 5.2 is a visual representation of a framework of interactions that adopts the perspective of consumers within an experience domain. It is the framework that underpins the material in Chapters 7 and 8. In contrast to Figure 5.1, interactions with fellow customers (both close acquaintances and strangers) would be given high priority as *first-order interactions*. As Fournier et al. have observed, 'people maintain literally hundreds of one-to-one relationships in their personal lives – with spouses, co-workers, casual acquaintances' (1998: 44). Also important, as first-order interactions, are those with the experience enablers – inanimate entities that provide the consumers with adequate power, means or opportunity to carry out the activities that contribute to their experiences, for example organizations, facilities, technology, special events and finance. There will be variable numbers of experience enablers, depending on the experience domain. The *second-order interactions* are those that take place between the various experience enablers. *Third-order interactions* are interactions that exist within the experience enablers, as they impact the consumer experience.

Consider, for example, the adolescent girl shopping-mall experience as an example of an experience domain that represents immersion through membership of a community of practice (see Haytko and Baker 2004). Here the consumers are the adolescent girls who visit the shopping mall. The experience enablers are the mall operators, the retailers within the mall and food-courts, and less obvious ones such as the school, whose year length and day length affect mall experiences, and special events – birthdays, dances – that trigger mall visits. First-order interactions are those interactions with other consumers (those with whom they are acquainted, such as friends or parents who accompany them to the mall, and unacquainted fellow consumers, such as the boys they meet and 'scope'), and with the experience enablers. Second-order interactions are those that take place, for example, between the mall management, the retail stores and food-court operators. Third-order interactions are those, for example, between employees in a retail store insofar as they affect the shopping-mall experiences of the adolescent girls.

As we will see in Chapters 7 and 8, the identities of experience enablers will only be known properly through exploration and interpretation of *consumers' own accounts of their experiences* within the domain, and not all interactions will be of equal importance. In Chapters 7 and 8 we introduce a process for exploring interactions and relationships from a consumer experience perspective relating to gap-year experiences. We have labelled this process 'consumer experience modelling', abbreviated as CEM. We also explain the rudiments of NVivo, a qualitative data analysis software package that is used in the CEM process.

As noted above, fundamental in all of this is the notion of the *co-creation of value* as a result of the interaction between the consumer and the organization (or experience enabler in this context), and possibly also with other consumers or other entities. Caru and Cova (2007) emphasize that an individual's life is made up of consuming experiences that can occur with or without some interaction with a market relation (i.e. a business organization or other 'experience enabler'). Thus, they argue, having a meal at a friend's house is linked to a sphere outside the market, even if products from the market may be consumed (literally as well as metaphorically!) as part of the experience. They go on to outline a continuum of consuming experiences that consumers go through, relating to the extent of interaction and co-creation with market entities.

Thus, at one extreme of this continuum are experiences that are mainly constructed by consumers and which can involve company-provided products or services. Here, they argue, the firm is pursuing a traditional product or service marketing approach, and it is the consumer that organizes his or her own experience.

In the middle of the continuum are experiences that have been co-developed by companies and consumers. In these cases, the firm provides an experiential platform base on which the consumer can develop his or her own experience. Sports tourism or adventure packages, rock concerts or other cultural events could be included in this middle part of the continuum (Caru and Cova 2007).

At the other extreme of the continuum are experiences that have largely been developed by companies and in which consumers are immersed in a context that is frequently hyper-real in nature. Here, Caru and Cova argue, the firm is pursuing a total experiential marketing approach and plans all details of the experience on the consumers' behalf, and they state that many fashion and sports brands, as well as toys and other forms of entertainment, specialize in this approach.

The implications of this for *relationship* marketing are significant, in terms for example, of ascertaining the nature of the relationship between firm and consumer, and indeed, who is in the driving seat within the relationship.

Consumer-to-consumer interactions and consumer communities

In Chapters 6, 7 and 8, we primarily focus on consumers as *individuals*, and mention consumer-to-consumer interactions almost in passing, arising from the fact that consumers will obviously interact with others. However, it must be remembered that such interactions can be an integral part of a consumer experience, especially in the context of the marketing of services. The extensive literature on consumer behaviour emphasizes the importance of social influences on human consumption behaviour, and individuals will often frame their consumption choices in terms of the groups to which they belong (or aspire to belong). Thus, many consumer experiences may occur within a collective or group context, and the issue of creating and maintaining relationships in such contexts is of great interest to those responsible for relationship marketing.

Chapter 9 considers the issue of *consumer communities* and their potential influence on relationship marketing in more detail, using examples drawn from the authors' research. Various types of consumer communities – and the issues involved in attempting to develop a relationship marketing approach targeted to such communities – will be considered. In Chapter 9, we will focus on communities, defined in both *territorial* and *non-territorial* terms. A common use of the term 'community' refers to 'a group sharing a defined physical space or geographical area such as a neighbourhood, city, village or hamlet' (Azarya 1996: 114), and some marketers who are specifically responsible for the marketing of places may seek to establish relationships with members of communities defined in this sense (see for example, Warnaby et al. 2004). In order to illustrate such issues, Chapter 9 will consider the use of relationship marketing by such organizations as local public administrations and town-centre-management schemes in order to improve the experience of the users of urban places.

Azarya (1996: 114) also highlights an alternative *non-territorial* definition of community as 'a group sharing common traits, a sense of belonging and/or maintaining social ties and interactions which shape it into a distinctive social entity'. Such communities could be described in terms of ethnicity, religion, professional or academic associations. Chapter 9 will also consider such non-territorial communities with specific reference to communities of practice mentioned previously, who engage in similar activities; and also consumer communities which may be characterized in terms of their value systems, such as ethical consumption behaviour.

As noted earlier in this chapter, interactions between consumers are increasingly mediated and facilitated by recent advances in information and communication technology (ICT). The final chapter in Part II develops further the ideas in Chapter 9, to discuss the role of social networking in more detail in order to provide an indication as to *how* – in the contemporary marketing environment – such consumer-to-consumer interactions and, indeed, the development of consumer *communities* may actually be achieved, and the implications of this for marketers seeking to build relationships with consumers, both individually and collectively.

References

Arnould, E.J. and Thompson, C.J. (2005) 'Consumer Culture Theory (CCT): Twenty Years of Research', *Journal of Consumer Research*, 31(March): 868–882.

Arnould, E.J., Price L.L. and Malshe, A. (2006) 'Toward a Cultural Resource-Based Theory of the Customer', in R.F. Lusch and S.L. Vargo (eds), *The Service-Dominant Logic of Marketing: Dialog, Debate and Directions*, Armonk, NY: ME Sharpe; 320–333.

Azarya, V. (1996) 'Community', in A. Kuper and J. Kuper (eds), *The Social Science Encyclopedia* (2nd edition), London and New York: Routledge; 114–115.

Baron, S. and Harris, K. (2008) 'Consumers as Resource Integrators', *Journal of Marketing Management*, 24(1): 113–130.

Caru, A. and Cova, B. (2007) 'Consuming Experiences: An Introduction', in A. Caru and B. Cova (eds), *Consuming Experience*, London and New York: Routledge; 3–16.

Edvarddson, B., Enquist, B. and Johnston, R. (2005) 'Cocreating Customer Value Through Hyperreality in the Prepurchase Service Experience', *Journal of Service Research*, 8(2): 149–161.

Fitzsimmons, J.A. and Fitzsimmons, M.J. (2001) *Service Management: Operations, Strategy and Information Technology* (3rd edition), New York: McGraw Hill.

Fournier, S., Dobscha, S. and Mick, D.G. (1998) 'Preventing the Premature Death of Relationship Marketing', *Harvard Business Review*, January/February: 42–51.

Grönroos, C. (2004) 'The Relationship Marketing Process: Communication, Interaction, Dialogue, Value', *Journal of Business and Industrial Marketing*, 19(2): 99–113.

Haytko, D.L. and Baker, J. (2004) 'It's All at the Mall: Exploring Adolescent Girl Experiences', *Journal of Retailing*, 80: 67–83.

Martin, C.L. and Clark, T. (1996) 'Networks of Customer-to-customer Relationships in Marketing', in D. Iaccobucci (ed.), *Networks in Marketing*, Thousand Oaks, CA: Sage Publications; 342–366.

Pine, B.J. II and Gilmore, J.H. (1999) *The Experience Economy: Work is Theater and Every Business a Stage*, Boston, MA: Harvard Business School Press.

Prahalad, C.K. and Ramaswamy, V. (2004) *The Future of Competition: Co-creating Unique Value with Customers*, Boston, MA: Harvard Business School Press.

Schmitt, B.H. (1999) *Experiential Marketing*, New York: The Free Press.

Szmigin, I.T.D. (2003) *Understanding the Consumer*, London: Sage Publications.

Vargo, S.L. and Lusch, R.F. (2004) 'Evolving to a New Dominant Logic of Marketing', *Journal of Marketing*, 68(January): 1–17.

Warnaby, G., Bennison, D., Davies, B.J. and Hughes, H. (2004) 'People and Partnerships: Marketing Urban Retailing', *International Journal of Retail & Distribution Management*, 32(11): 545–556.

6 Consumer Resources: Use and Integration

Learning objectives

- To outline the nature of the resources – operand and operant – that individual customers may use in developing relationships with organizations.
- To investigate how these resources may be integrated by consumers.
- To evaluate the factors influencing customers' use and integration of resources.

Introduction: contemporary customers and resources

A number of authors writing in the marketing and management literature agree that today's consumers can be considered as informed, networked, empowered and active (see, for example, Prahalad and Ramaswamy 2004). This phenomenon is partly made possible by the increasing presence of information and communication technology (ICT), which has created much greater opportunity for consumers to act – individually or collectively – in terms of supporting, or objecting to, organizations and their products/brands. Indeed, this activity can happen with a speed that can unhinge carefully prepared organizational marketing strategies and practices. This has implications for the traditional view of relationship marketing illustrated in the last chapter in Figure 5.1, where the firm is perceived to be the focal point of a network of relationships. We have suggested that, if we take a consumer perspective on this, Figure 5.2 may be a more accurate representation of contemporary reality. Here, consumers interact with a variety of experience enablers – and of course, with each other. While customer-to-customer interactions will be considered in more detail in Chapters 9 and 10, this and the following two chapters focus more specifically on consumers as individuals, and the resources that they bring to bear within their networks of exchange relationships with experience enablers.

We can think about this consumer role through the perspective of the service-dominant (S-D) logic of marketing, first outlined by Vargo and Lusch (2004) which was discussed in Chapter 4. To briefly recap, the S-D logic focuses on intangible resources and on the co-creation of value. The S-D logic has significant implications for how we think about marketing exchange processes and relationships, and equally importantly, the resources that are brought to bear by both organizations and consumers to facilitate this. Constantin and Lusch (1994) distinguish between operand and operant resources. Operand resources are those *on which* an operation or act is performed to produce an effect, whereas operant resources are employed to *act on* operand resources (and other operant resources). Operand resources can be thought of as physical resources which come together in such a way as to produce physical goods (and, as mentioned in Chapter 4, 'the customer' may be viewed by some organizations as an operand resource as actions take place *to* him/her). By contrast, operant resources are often invisible, intangible, dynamic and infinite, and could be thought of in terms of consumers' skills and knowledge, etc., held both individually and collectively. Thus, consumers' ability to network and interact together can be thought of as creating and facilitating operant resources.

This chapter considers the use of consumer resources – both operant and operand – by consumers as *individuals*, in terms of what constitutes these different types of resources, and how they may be integrated. It begins by outlining a framework produced by Arnould et al. (2006) by which consumer resource can be considered. It moves on to look at a specific example of customer resource utilization and integration on behalf of an organization that can be thought of as an experience enabler. The organization in question is the British Library (BL), the national library of the UK, which was recently the beneficiary of much support from its users when faced with threats to services and the possibility of reduction in, and charges for, services that had always been freely provided. The chapter considers the types of resource mobilized by BL users on behalf of the organization and how these resources were integrated by individuals. As we said earlier, individual consumers may also act collectively (as indeed, was the case with the BL), and Chapters 9 and 10 consider this aspect in more detail.

Consumer resources: a framework for analysis

In considering how individuals use and integrate their resources in the course of their experiences with a particular organization, we can take, as a starting point, the framework offered by Arnould et al. (2006), which suggests that in order to enact roles and pursue life projects, consumers deploy both operand and operant resources. Operand resources constitute tangible resources, especially economic resources and goods/materials over which the consumer has *'allocative'* capabilities. In contrast, operant resources are those over which the customer has *'authoritative'* capability, and these operant resources include physical, cultural and social resources. Operant resources (and their specific configuration) – as they are often linked to cultural schema – will influence how the consumer employs their operand resources. We will consider the different kinds of operand and operant resources in more detail below.

Operand resources

Operand resources are tangible resources, especially various culturally constituted economic resources (such as income, inherited wealth, credit, etc.) and goods/raw materials over which the consumer has control – or *'allocative capability'* in Arnould et al.'s terminology. The operand resources held by a consumer may vary in quantity and quality, and, according to Arnould et al., could include objects acquired from exchanges with marketers (i.e. things they have bought), gifts, inherited special possessions, found and self-created objects, and could also include some physical spaces (such as home, workspace, garden, etc.). The amount of operand resource held by consumers will obviously affect their exchange behaviours with firms.

Operant resources

The consumer's stock of *operant* resources will affect how they employ their operand resources. For example, the operant resources – social, physical and cultural – that are held will determine which firm resources consumers are going to draw on and how they will be deployed in order to co-create value. The different types of operant resource identified by Arnould et al. are described below.

Social operant resources are:

> networks for relationships with other including traditional demographic groupings (families, ethnic groups, social class) and emergent groups (brand communities, consumer tribes and subcultures, friendship groups) over which consumers exert varying degrees of command. (Arnould et al. 2006: 93)

Physical operant resources relates to consumers' physical and mental endowments which will affect their ability to enact life roles and projects, and can include energy, emotion and strength. Arnould et al. (2006) give the example of people who are legally blind who may employ other operant physical resources (i.e. other senses) and effort to a greater degree to compensate for their lack of vision, and/or exert authority over other social operant resources during an exchange process – for example by asking a relative or friend to accompany them to offer advice and opinion in certain buying situations.

Arnould et al. state that these types of operant resources above are linked to cultural schema, such as conventions, traditions, habits of speech and gesture, and this cultural dimension will to some extent provide a broader context for their use of these other resources. *Cultural operant* resources – in which Arnould et al. include life expectations and history, imagination and specialized knowledge/skills – are likened to the notion of core competences which can be applied in or extended to a variety of situations. For example, a consumer may use the physical skills acquired to play one particular musical instrument to help in learning to play another instrument.

This chapter considers consumers' use of both operant and operand resources in order to achieve their life roles and projects, using the case study example of the British Library (BL). Here, writers, researchers (both academic and commercial), students and individual members of the public among others will use their own resources – in conjunction with those facilities and services offered by the BL – to co-create value, and in doing so achieve their individual life roles/projects, whether these be advancing knowledge through for example, academic research, trying to commercialize an entrepreneurial idea that they have, completing their undergraduate or postgraduate degree, or finding out more about their family history.

Context: the British Library

The British Library was created in 1972 through an amalgamation of existing institutions, including the library departments of the British Museum and the Patent Office Library. Its collection comprises 150 million items, including 13 million books, 7 million manuscripts (many of unique historical importance), 4.5 million maps, 56 million patents, 3.5 million sound recordings, 8 million stamps and 58 million newspaper issues, serial parts, microfilms and other formats. It is a library of legal deposit, whereby it receives a copy of every publication produced in the UK and Ireland, and in 2003 this was extended to electronic materials, including websites. The main collections are housed at St Pancras in London, in the largest public building constructed in the UK in the twentieth century, opened in June 1998. The BL also undertakes document supply and lending activities based in Boston Spa in Yorkshire, and also an increasingly important web presence (see www.bl.uk).

Until 2001 the BL had no coordinated marketing activity, with little uniformity in terms of how the organization was presented externally. As a first step to widening awareness, participation and usage, a fuller understanding of the market was sought. In 2001, following an extensive programme of research into user perceptions, etc., five main 'broad audience communities' were identified: researchers; business people; the library network; schools and young people; and the general public. For each of these communities, a Head of Marketing was appointed, reporting to the Director of Strategic Marketing and Communications. The BL has sought to meet the needs of these disparate groups by promoting, 'ready access to the British Library's collection and information experts through a range of free and priced services which are becoming increasingly integrated' (British Library 2005).

Indeed, meeting the needs of users has been explicitly articulated in marketing communications activity which, to ensure a consistency of approach, is themed around the concept of *Advancing Knowledge*. Thus, for each user community, marketing communications incorporates case studies of how the BL has helped organizations and individuals advance their own knowledge in order to achieve their business and/or personal aims and objectives – in other words, emphasizing the co-creation of value. In addition, the introduction of a new logo and brand identity has also ensured consistency of approach. All the activities described above have increased public awareness of the British Library – research carried out by MORI in the summer of 2005 indicated that 75 per cent of Britons knew about the British Library, a significant increase from under 50 per cent five years previously (British Library 2006).

External communications are also targeted at central government and other funding stakeholders. In order to highlight its efficiency and cost-effectiveness, the BL commissioned independent research to measure its economic impact. This research concluded that for the public funding it received, the BL produced a benefit–cost ratio of 4.4:1 – in other words, for every £1 of funding received £4.40 is generated for the UK economy (British Library n/d). This emphasis on cost-efficiency is ongoing – and *communicating* successes in reducing operating costs and increasing organizational efficiency is an important element of the marketing effort directed towards policymakers and related stakeholders. This is especially important when funding allocations are being decided, and such a situation provides the specific context of the case study comprising this chapter.

The British Library and the comprehensive spending review 2007

Since coming to power in 1997, the UK Labour government has initiated a series of spending reviews, whereby government-department budgets are allocated. The first spending review in 1998 was termed a 'comprehensive spending review' (CSR), and a second CSR was completed in the autumn of 2007. The aim of this second CSR was to identify the further investments and reforms needed to equip the UK for the global challenges of the coming decade. As such it represents a fundamental review of government expenditure, incorporating budget allocations through to 2010/11.

Inevitably, in the run-up to the announcement of budget allocations, speculation regarding the content of the CSR and its implications for individual government departments – and as a consequence, those other organizations/groups in receipt of funding from department allocations – was widespread. The BL falls within the remit of the Department for Culture, Media and Sport, and there was much concern among those responsible for the management of cultural amenities over reported threats of cuts in grants of up to 7 per cent a year (see Teodorczuk 2007). The potential implications and impact of such cuts for the BL were considered in a briefing document which was widely disseminated to MPs and policymakers. Here, the most relevant implication was a potential 35 per cent reduction in Reading Room opening hours and the introduction of charges for access. It caused particular consternation when news of these possible implications of cuts in funding – with reaction from a number of famous authors – was published nationally in the *Independent on Sunday* newspaper on 28 January 2007.

This story was subsequently covered by many national and local London newspapers, as items of news and editorial comment, and also by individual columnists. The basic tenor of this coverage was critical of what Liberal Democrat peer Lord Avebury termed the Government's 'cultural vandalism' (see Muir 2007). Individual MPs asked Parliamentary Questions and there was an Early Day Motion on 26 February regarding the issue. In addition, the issue was discussed on a number of newspaper-based and other 'blogs'. Such coverage served to very quickly raise and disseminate awareness of the issue among BL users, particularly academics, researchers and other regular users of the reading rooms at St Pancras, who would be the group most immediately and directly affected by these proposed actions. An online petition calling on the Prime Minister to keep the BL free of charge was started on the 10 Downing Street website.

As part of its response to this controversy, in February 2007, BL sought to elicit views from its users, and posted the following statement on its Supporters' Forum website: 'If you want to support us please let us know why the British Library is important to you'. This resulted in an overwhelming response from users, with hundred of messages. Two of the authors subjected nearly 600 of these messages to content analysis, using Arnould et al.'s framework to investigate the use of consumer resources further, and this provides the basis for the rest of the chapter.

BL user operand resources

A key theme which emerged from the analysis was the fact that BL user operand resources were very limited in many cases. The following quote highlights this:

I suspect that few of the scholars using the Library, and none of the students using it, have much in the way of financial support for their studies. Given the expense of visiting/staying in London now, any additional expense – such as the idea of charging an access fee – would be insupportable for many.

However, what did become apparent was the fact that many users were willing to use their limited operand resources to access BL facilities in order to achieve their life roles/projects. The main financial expenditure seemed to be on travel to London and staying in London – not the cheapest city in the world! – while using the BL:

I would meet scholars from all over the Third World, university lecturers from India whose salary is an average of 200 dollars a month, who had managed to get to London on a small grant, feverishly accessing records otherwise unavailable to them, in the few days that they could afford.

Various respondents emphasized that over time this expenditure could be quite substantial:

During the last thirty-six years, I have travelled to the UK at least once a year with the primary purpose of conducting research at the rare book and manuscript collections at the BL. In financial terms alone, these trips have represented a contribution in excess of £100,000 with attendant payments of VAT and so forth.

BL user operant resources

This analysis of user messages of support identified the use of *all* the types of operant resource mentioned above, which are highlighted below, using quotes from these messages.

Physical resources

The physical resources of energy and emotion of BL users was evident in most of the letters of support. User input of energy was demonstrated with respect to their use of the BL facilities, often over many years:

I cannot say how much the British Library has meant to me as a publishing scholar and teacher. Without it I could not have published books on and editions of the playwrights W B Yeats, J M Synge, Bernard Shaw, Lady Gregory, nor written the biography of Mrs W B Yeats.

... I wrote my first feature film screenplay in the British Library, with the hourly benefit of its world-class research resources. After a three-week writing and research period I sold an option on the script for £7000.

> I am an academic living in Zululand, South Africa, where scholarly resources are somewhat limited. However, I manage to do scholarly research and get my articles in international journals and books. This is possible at least partly because I have access to the British Library ...

Also evident was users' willingness to expend energy in order to provide further support to the BL:

> I have e-mailed Gordon Brown and several other MPs directly.

> I have sent the following message to the Dept of Culture Media and Sport. Please forward this message to whoever at the BL is keeping track of such letters of protest.

Emotion was evident in the language used and the sentiments expressed in the messages of support. Many users showed their strength of feeling by declaring themselves 'appalled' by the prospects of cuts. Indeed, a multitude of other expressions were used, such as: 'gravely concerned', 'scarcely believable', 'dismayed', 'alarming', 'great shame', 'latest idiocy', 'utter disgrace', 'extraordinarily sad', 'embarrassing', 'astounded', 'short-sighted', 'breathtaking', 'grave impact', 'strongly object', 'horrified', 'great anxiety', 'very disappointed', 'devastating effects', 'absolutely despicable', 'tragedy', 'deeply disturbed', 'deplorable'. The following quotations summarize the emotional impact of the BL on many of its users:

> None of my work (and thus my happiness and well-being) would have been possible without the BL.

> I was in the manuscript room of the British Library on Monday and, unaware of the gathering storm clouds, felt immensely privileged and fortunate to be there ...

Cultural resources

As would be expected with users of a research facility such as the BL reading rooms, their level of education and specialized knowledge and skills are much higher than the adult mean. Half the messages of support were from academic faculty members and postgraduate research students. The rest of the messages were from freelance and commercial researchers, authors, journalists, librarian/archivists, other (non-research) students and members of the public more generally. Given their occupations, the support letters were highly articulate, with personal titles and qualifications (e.g. Prof., Dr., etc.) often emphasized within or at the end of the letter to hopefully add weight to its contribution.

Cultural diversity was also evident, with respect to home locations and places of work, with two-thirds of the messages of support coming from the

UK, and the remainder from around the world, notably from North America, Europe and Australasia. The cultural diversity was often linked to the user's history of research work using the BL's facilities:

> It [the BL] has been a solid monumental presence for me as I have moved from Australia, to Canada, to the US with long periods in the UK. Over the years I have haunted the old reading room in Great Russell Street and used the new libraries facilities at St Pancras.

> First as a graduate student at the University of Pennsylvania, then as a visiting assistant professor at the University of Puget Sound in Washington State, and most recently as an assistant and now associate professor of English Literature at the University of Toronto, I have spent at least two months at the British Library every year but one since 1995.

Social resources

It was evident from the messages of support that family relationships, consumer communities and commercial relationships played a significant part in the experiences of BL users. Customer-to-customer interactions, mostly mediated by modern information and communication technology, were a cornerstone of the campaign, and not only via the BL website. Access to consumer communities was indicated in several of the support letters:

> I have just joined a facebook group detailing the government are proposing to cut the funding to the British Library.

> As I am sure you know, the possibility of limited funds forcing you to begin charging for use of the libraries is everywhere on the Internet.

Equally, there was evidence that work-related relationships contributed to the worldwide awareness of the potential cuts in funding. Some academic institutions had multiple contributors to the BL website, indicating the existence of networks within these locations. The quotes below demonstrate not only the importance of work-related/commercial relationships, but also the manner in which these relationships contributed to the campaign momentum:

> I am also urging my academic colleagues to write to you on their own behalf.

> In case you are unaware of it, I draw your attention to the petition mentioned in the message below ... which reached me this afternoon. It came from an academic friend who had clearly added his name and sent it on to his entire address list.

> As a member of UCU [University and College Union – the trade union for UK academics] I have been asked to email you to stress how important the British Library is to my research and to my writing.

Resource integration

The previous sections illustrate how customers can employ their physical, cultural and social resources in supporting an organization in which they believe. These resources can be *integrated* at the individual level, almost sub-consciously. The following short quotation, for example, has elements of energy and emotion (physical resources), specialized knowledge and history (cultural resources), and family (social resource):

> I am a 27-year-old doctoral student from Ireland. I have been to more libraries than most people my age. Big ones like the Bodleian in Oxford or the Library of Congress, Washington D.C., and little ones like the Ralph Vaughn Williams Library in Cecil Sharp House, London. Of all my library experiences, the British Library stands out. I have flown to London especially on a number of occasions to visit it. There, I could access material that was held nowhere else. In particular, the National Sound Archive was a revelation. I was able to listen to the recorded voice of my dead grandfather, who passed away long before I was born.

The individual customer operant resources are clearly integrated collectively, as well as individually, as evidenced by the volume of support for the BL and the speed with which it was manifested through membership of social and professional networks, which are considered in more detail in Chapters 9 and 10.

Utilization of organizational resources

As Arnould et al. (2006) state in their original discussion of the model which was used for analysis of these messages of support, the firm itself can be viewed as a resource that customers can draw on in achieving their life projects and performing their life roles. This is certainly the case in the context of the BL, with many messages of support highlighting the facilities and services offered by the BL as integral to this process. Thus, the BL's collections, the service provided by its staff in facilitating use of these collections, and the fact that all of this was accessible and freely available to all were aspects emphasized by users as being instrumental in the achievement of their life roles/projects. The following quotes relating to these aspects are typical of many messages of support:

> I write as the director of ... an international research project, whose researchers have relied heavily on the collections of the British Library for many years. The project could not function without the resources and facilities of what is, for my field, the greatest research library in the world.

> I have spent hours, nay days, in the OIOC Reading Room and simply could not have achieved as much without the wonderful freedom of access to the archives and the invaluable help of the OIOC Reading Room staff.

> There are other Copyright libraries in the UK, but there is nowhere else that is so accessible and which has such an enormous holding of printed and other materials.

This has significant implications for how users regarded the BL and, indeed, how they perceived their relationship with the institution, the strength of which being demonstrated, of course, by their willingness to expend their resources on its behalf when threatened by potential cutbacks, which were regarded by many users as a direct threat to their own values and objectives. The positive associations users felt with the BL in terms of its contribution to intellectual life, not only on a national, but also a global basis, arising from the BL's global 'reach', were evident in many messages of support:

> It is one of the great cultural institutions in Europe, and a model of the free dissemination of learning, history and cultural perspective to all.

> The British Library is not merely a UK national resource but a world resource of inestimable value to the pursuit of knowledge internationally.

> The internationalism of the BL's holdings has been fundamental and it must be the case that the only real competitors among world libraries are the Library of Congress and the Bibliothèque Nationale. From that standpoint, the BL also performs a service to the world.

Indeed, for many users the BL also had an important symbolic role which was obviously a major factor in the strength of their perceived affiliation with the institution:

> The BL is without doubt the leading flagship institution for British scholarship, and perhaps the most significant factor in the worldwide reputation of British intellectual life and cultural history for foreign scholars.

> The Library is a vital part of our national culture heritage, upholding the tradition of free access to knowledge for all. People are rightly proud of such a fantastic institution and to reduce its collections or charge for entry would hamper individuals in their research, work against meritocracy in academia and reduce British scholarly prestige.

As noted above, the potential cuts to the BL were regarded by many users as a threat to their fundamental value systems, and as such, resonated with symbolic meaning for users:

> Its very presence and (more significantly) the respect it is accorded by those in power demonstrate that I live in a civilised country that realises that knowledge, and access to knowledge, is vital to successful human existence.

> The research that is conducted in the BL is essential both for the private interest of individuals and the construction of a coherent understanding of our national history and culture. The successful and responsible maintenance of national archives is emblematic of a government's resolve to learn from history, rather than dismissing it as the concern of an interested minority.

Conclusions: implications for organizations

So what are the possible implications of this? The experience of the BL indicates the extent to which consumers can mobilize their operant resources if sufficiently motivated. If, for a particular organization, its consumers are willing to expend operant and operand resources on its behalf, then developing relationships to facilitate this is arguably a very important task, and organizations should consider the extent to which they can be proactive in this. The extent and speed of user response to the publication of news as to the potential threat to BL services was mediated by ICT, and was facilitated by the BL via the establishment of a specific Supporters' Forum on the organizational website through which messages of support were channelled and put into the public domain to indicate the strength of user protest about the potential cuts, and support for the organization. In other words, the BL tried to harness a 'grassroots' reaction to the news of potential cuts which would obviously impact negatively on the consumer's experience of the organization and, as we have seen, for many users directly undermine their fundamental beliefs and value systems with regard to free access to educational and personal development possibilities (which they regarded the BL as facilitating).

Indeed, when the BL's financial settlement as a result of the CSR was announced in November 2007, the proposed cuts did not materialize, and the BL's 'grant-in-aid' from the Government was increased in line with inflation (at 2.7 per cent per annum) until 2010/11. It was felt that the user response to the news of possible cuts obviously had an effect, although quantifying this is impossible. So while we can think of this particular initiative as successful in achieving its short-term objective of influencing the outcome of the CSR process in 2007, it does raise some more general issues for organizations in terms of how they may develop meaningful relationships with their consumers, building upon their positive experiences of, and with, the organization. One issue relates to how organizations may solicit the views of their consumers as a means of building such relationships. All this information about how users perceived the BL and the resources they used in conjunction with the organization to co-create value arose from one question posted on the Supporters' Forum section of the organization's website. This raises some interesting points relating to the development of new forms of marketing research techniques, particularly those mediated by information technology, and in particular Web 2.0 and social networks, which can turn market research into a more collaborative activity and facilitate the building of relationships between researcher and respondent (see Cooke and Buckley, 2008). This approach gave BL management the ability to gain rich data in the user's own 'voice' about their feelings towards the organization and provided many new insights. We will return to this issue later.

Admittedly, BL users could be regarded as more educated and articulate than those of many other organizations, but arguably any consumer community, when asked for its perceptions of the brand/company (especially if under threat in some way, as was the case here), could be quite eloquent in articulating their feelings. Indeed, understanding the terminology used by consumers in such circumstances may be of benefit to organizations in creating promotional and communications messages, so as to communicate in a common language. In addition, the content of the messages of support enabled a fuller understanding of the values the users associated with the BL, which again could be used in future marketing communications activity to optimize its effectiveness.

Hopefully in this case we have shown how an understanding of the different types of resources that consumers bring to bear in their relationships with organizations can be used for the benefit of all. The ability of organizations to understand the nature of their customers' resource utilization, and capitalize on this in the process of value co-creation will arguably be a major challenge – and indeed, opportunity – in the future.

Learning propositions

- Consumers will employ resources in their relationships with service providers/experience enablers.
- These resources can be classified as *operand* and *operant*.
- Operand resources are primarily economic over which the consumer has 'allocative' capability.
- Operant resources can be classified in terms of *physical*, *cultural* and *social* resources.
- These resources can be integrated by consumers both individually and collectively.

Activities and discussion questions

- Think of an organization with which you regularly engage in some form of exchange situation. What types of operand and operant resources do you deploy in your relationship with the organization?
- Thinking about the resources identified in the previous discussion question, how are they integrated?
- For your organization (or the last organization you worked for), what operand and operant resources are used to try to develop relationships with consumers?

References

Arnould, E.J., Price, L.L. and Malshe, A. (2006) 'Toward a Cultural Resource-based Theory of the Customer', in R.F. Lusch and S.L. Vargo (eds), *The Service-Dominant Logic of Marketing: Dialog, Debate and Directions*, Armonk, NY: M.E. Sharpe; 320–333.

British Library (2005) *Redefining the Library: The British Library's Strategy 2005–2008.* Available from www.bl.uk/about/strategy.html

British Library (2006) *British Library Annual Report Accounts 2005–06.* Available from www.bl.uk/about/annual/2005to2006/introduction.html

British Library (n/d) *Measuring Our Value: Results on an Independent Economic Impact Study Commissioned by the British Library to Measure the Library's Direct and Indirect Value to the UK Economy.* London: British Library.

Constantin, J.A. and Lusch, R.F. (1994) *Understanding Resource Management.* Oxford, OH: The Planning Forum.

Cooke, M. and Buckley, N. (2008) 'Web 2.0, Social Networks and the Future of Market Research', *International Journal of Market Research*, 50(2): 267–292.

Muir, H. (2007) 'Cuts Threaten Services at British Library', *Guardian*, 29 January: 7.

Prahalad, C.K. and Ramaswamy, V. (2004) 'Co-Creation Experiences: The Next Practice in Value Creation', *Journal of Interactive Marketing*, 18(3): 5–14.

Teodorczuk, T. (2007) 'Labour Cuts "Will Set Art Galleries Back a Decade"', *London Evening Standard*, 23 January: 16.

Vargo, S.L. and Lusch, R.F. (2004) 'Evolving to a New Dominant Logic of Marketing', *Journal of Marketing*, 68(January): 1–17.

7 Introducing Consumer Experience Modelling

Learning objectives

- To outline a process, Consumer Experience Modelling (CEM), that focuses on interactions and relationships from a consumer experience perspective.
- To provide detailed guidelines on the four stages of CEM with reference to the case of the gap-year travel experience domain.
- To facilitate the identification of *consumer* value enhancers and inhibitors within an experience domain.

A focus on consumer experience

This chapter explores relationship marketing from the perspective of the consumer experience. There are academic, practical and pedagogical reasons for focusing on consumer experiences. From an academic perspective, the service-dominant (S-D) logic of marketing, in FP10 (see Chapter 4), maintains that 'value is always uniquely and phenomenologically determined by the beneficiary' (Vargo and Lusch 2008). As Vargo and Lusch observe, this acknowledges the role of customer experience in value (co)-creation. Beyond the S-D logic, there is increased academic interest in consumer/customer experiences, especially those that are deemed to be memorably good or bad (see Lindgreen et al. 2009).

In practice, 'experience' and 'experiential' are two of the most-used words for describing products and services. For example, Holbrook (2009) catalogues over 180 examples of such usage to describe a whole range of products and services, within categories such as drinks, food, consumer durables, tourism, events, education, retailing and financial services. Also, the Department of Trade and Industry in the UK has published guidelines on managing customer experiences (Voss and Zomerdijk 2007), and another government department, the Department of Innovation, Universities and Skills, is producing Customer Intelligence Packs for each of its major customer groups using customer experience methods (Atwood 2009).

Regarding pedagogy, we argue that a focus on consumer experiences provides new opportunities for students/readers to engage in co-creating value in the learning process. As Palmer and Koenig-Lewis observe, 'customer experience can be very difficult to measure', and that 'relationship marketing has not adequately explored emotional antecedents and outcomes of a relationship' (2009: 91). We agree, and therefore present a process that can offer greater scope for learning about the thoughts, feelings and meanings behind consumer interactions, and the relationships that they spawn.

Introducing Consumer Experience Modelling

The main purpose of this chapter is to introduce and explain a process for collecting, coding and interpreting consumer 'voice' data relating to an experience domain. The process has been labelled 'Consumer Experience Modelling' or CEM. CEM will be explained here with reference to a particular experience domain – the *gap-year travel experience*. CEM is facilitated by the ability to use a qualitative data analysis software package.

To provide the context for the explanations in this chapter, a brief overview of the gap-year travel experience domain is provided.

The gap-year travel experience

In the UK, 'gap year' is common parlance for a year's gap between school and university (usually at 18 years of age), or between university and full-time employment (usually at 21 or 22 years of age). In either or both of the gap years it is becoming increasingly common for students to travel to other countries, often working overseas for part of the year. It is encouraged by an array of travel publications and student travel agencies that support backpacking activities (Huxley 2005). Despite having the possibility to earn money during their overseas travels, many gap-year students rely on their parents for some of the funding of the experience.

It was a growing marketplace in 2006 when the data below were collected. According to Jones (2004), the number of UK people taking gap years increased by 30 per cent over the period 1999–2003, with almost 300,000 people (mostly between the ages of 18 and 25) taking a gap year out to travel in 2003. Bowes (2005) estimated that around 29,000 students would defer a university place in September 2005 and thousands more eligible candidates would decide not to apply for university places. It is still a growing marketplace at the time of writing, with gap-year travel increasingly being undertaken by non-students; 30–50-year-olds (Spero 2009). People, committing themselves to gap-year travel, have a common understanding of the activities that comprise the gap-year travelling experience, and so it represents a clear experience domain. It is very normal for student gap-year travellers to 'share' their experiences with parents and friends via email and telephone correspondence.

Consumer Experience Modelling (CEM)[1]

In very general terms, CEM follows a qualitative research process (Figure 7.1). Qualitative data from consumers are collected, coded and retrieved, and then themes are identified from the retrieved data. What is specific to CEM, and relationship marketing, is the method of coding (and, therefore, retrieving) and of theme identification.

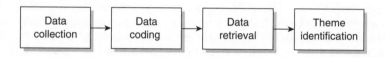

Figure 7.1   Qualitative research process

Data collection

Having chosen an experience domain, it is necessary here to collect data, *in the words of the consumers themselves*, on their experiences within the domain. There are several possibilities for obtaining consumer voice data, including:

- personal interviews
- focus groups
- consumer diaries
- blogs (weblogs).

Personal interviews

Perhaps the most familiar device for obtaining qualitative data from respondents is the one-to-one (in-depth) personal interview, where a researcher interviews a respondent about the topic of interest; in this case, the chosen experience domain. Two initial decisions need to be made when using personal interviews – the characteristics of the respondents and the structure of the interviews.

In the case of the gap-year travel experience, interviews were carried out, by second-year undergraduate students, with people who had been on a gap-year, and with some of the parents of the gap-year travellers. Although the parents are not, strictly speaking, consumers of the gap-year travel experience, it was recognized that they normally play a large part in funding (and generally supporting) the venture and gain vicarious pleasure/anxiety from their offspring's experiences. Also, in this case, the interviews were designed to be semi-structured. Two considerations led to this decision. First, highly structured interviews that produce short answers from respondents were ruled out as they were unlikely to generate the rich insights that are being sought about the interactions that make up the consumer experience. Second, although totally unstructured interviews, for example just asking the respondent to tell the interviewer about their gap-year, were considered, such a method requires experienced and confident interviewers. The majority of the student interviewers were 'first-timers'.

Bryman and Bell provide a succinct and helpful explanation of the semi-structured interview:

> The researcher has a list of questions on fairly specific topics to be covered, often referred to as an interview guide, but the interviewee has a great deal of leeway in how to reply. Questions may not follow on exactly in the way outlined in the schedule. Questions that are not included in the guide may be asked as the interviewer picks up on things said by the interviewees. But, by and large, all the questions will be asked, and a similar wording will be used from interviewee to interviewee. (2003: 343)

To apply CEM, it is essential that permission is obtained to audio-record the interviews, and also that 'word-for-word' transcripts are produced subsequently (for example in Microsoft Word).

Focus groups

The idea of focus groups is to get together a group of people so that they can discuss a focal topic of common interest and, in so doing, express their attitudes, beliefs and behaviours on the topic. Ideally, they take the form of loosely structured 'steered conversations' (Easterby-Smith et al. 2002). With CEM, there will always be a focal topic of common interest – the experience domain – and so focus groups will always be an option for collecting consumer voice data. The person(s) who runs a focus group is/are known as the moderator(s). The moderator's role is probably even more difficult than that of the interviewer in personal interviewers, as not only does he/she need to provide the loose structure to the steered conversations, but also must manage the dynamics within the focus group, so that all members of the group get the opportunity to contribute, and there are ample opportunities for members to respond to the ideas of others.

For the gap-year travel experience, focus groups, of fellow students who were interested in, or had experienced gap-year travel, were undertaken by the second-year undergraduate students. Because none of them had acted as a focus group moderator prior to the gap-year project, extensive practice was provided in tutorials. Again, it was stressed that it was essential that the focus group sessions were audio-recorded. Some groups were also video-recorded in order to capture facial expressions and other body language that aided an understanding of the group dynamics.

Consumer diaries

According to the *Concise Oxford Dictionary*, a diary is a 'daily record of events, journal'. *Consumer* diary research has often, in the past, been associated with the collection of panel data, where consumers are asked to keep diaries that detail their spending over a period of time, normally a month. In this sense, the consumer has been required to provide no more than a reliable record of daily shopping/spending events. In CEM, however, when using consumer diaries to collect consumer voice data, it is necessary to encourage consumers to go beyond the daily record of events to the creation of a *journal* that not only records events relating to the experience domain, but also contains the consumer's feelings and thoughts about the events. Such a journal provides a much richer picture of interactions and relationships within the experience domain.

Compare, for example, the two forms of diary entries written by a UK female gap-year traveller who is in Mexico:

(1) Spent 4 nights in Mexico City. Have visited an anthropology museum, had a walking tour of the Centro Historico, the Guadalope Shrine, and visited the Teotiuhacan Pyramids.

(2) Spent 4 nights in Mexico City, which isn't as scary as we thought it would be. We didn't feel unsafe at all. The locals all seem very nice, although they love to stare at us all the time. Are we being a bit paranoid? We are having difficulty in finding things to eat as it all seems to be hot dogs and taco things with a filling that we are not sure if it's meat or not. We have been eating at the hostel though for breakfast and dinner and that seems to be veggie stuff and it's free. Have visited an anthropology museum, had a walking tour of the Centro Historico, the Guadalope Shrine, and visited the Teotiuhacan Pyramids. Thought we'd get all the cultural stuff out of the way early on!

The first account provides basic factual information. The second account gives a better feel for both the person herself, and some of the issues that are important to her as part of the overall experience. Food (she is vegetarian), safety and money are clearly of paramount importance, and visiting places of historical interest is portrayed as being more of a duty than a pleasure.

Clearly, the challenge is to find consumers with both the ability and motivation to provide diary entries of the second type.

Blogs

A blog (short for weblog) is a shared online journal where people, known as bloggers, post entries about their personal experiences, interests and hobbies. Entries often contain comments that result in online discussions and may also contain photographs and other images, and links to other websites.

The variety of blogs that exist is quite staggering. A visit to the website http://www.livejournal.com shows that the range of the popular consumer interests covered by blogs covers almost nine pages! The *most* popular interests of consumers include music, movies, computers and art, but the first page also covers interests such as Harry Potter, cats and piercings. The last page – and remember these are still popular interests – includes diverse topics such as monkeys, Jimi Hendrix, pixies and bisexuality. It is probably fair to claim that blogs exist for any experience domain that is worthy of study.

The website http://www.travelblog.org, for example, contains blogs about gap-year travel. An excerpt of a blog diary from this website is shown below.

Monday 3rd of April 2006.

Yesterday, we finally arrived at the trekking mecca of El Chalten after 14 hours spent on the bus. The argentinian side of the mountains is very scenic ... for the first hour or two. After that it becomes quite boring. We thought for a while that our bus drivers were being really nice with us, stopping often to let us take some pictures or stretch our legs. But the truth is that they are instructed to bring their passengers to El Chalten as late as possible. So that we won't have the time or the energy to shop around for a place to stay and would collapse in the closest hotel to the bus stop ... which (surprise!) is owned by the same bus company! The usual gringo-milking trick you see everywhere. But that's ok because we switched to a great B&B today. Can't wait to get out on those trails but the weather isn't that good. Maybe tomorrow ...

Tuesday 4th of April 2006.

A great night sleep at our B&B. Feeling very rested and eager to go hiking. Some clouds in the sky and a bit of wind. It might be wiser to wait for the weather to clear up. Probably this afternoon. The town has a real `frontier` feeling with its unpaved roads. Lots of hotels though. And some nice restaurants too. The argentinian cuisine tastes great after three weeks spent in Chile. Looks like this area was a sacred place for the Tehuelche indians before they were crushed by the mighty white invaders (and the viruses they brought with them from Europe). According to our hosts, the land on which this hotel was built was some sort of special burial place. Strange. It all looks so peaceful now ...

On the website, there are photographs to accompany the journal account, and a space for comments from readers of the blog.

In some ways, blogs capture elements of both consumer diary writing and focus groups, and so they are potentially extremely valuable sources of consumer data. Also, there is no problem with motivating consumers to talk/write about their experiences, as they are self-motivated. However, with blogs, the researcher loses some control of the research process. There is, as yet, little advice on the efficient and effective use of blogs for marketing research purposes, and so it is probably prudent not to use blogs as the only or dominant method of collecting consumer voice data.

Overall, the data-collection stage of the CEM process should be guided by the need to encourage consumers, in their own words, not only to describe their experiences but also to convey their feelings and opinions about their experiences. It is also bound to be guided by practicalities, such as availability of suitable respondents/data. Although individuals can undertake the data collection stage, it is one which can normally be better and more quickly achieved by groups of students or other researchers. Combinations of the four methods – personal interviews, focus groups, consumer diaries, blogs – should be considered. For the gap-year travel experience, both personal interviews and focus groups were used, resulting in transcripts of 24 personal interviews and 11 focus groups. It is not unusual to have 50–100 or more pages of text at this stage, and the process of analysis of the qualitative data is a considerable challenge.

We move now to the data-coding stage. Here the process of data analysis is facilitated by:

- the application of the framework illustrated in Figure 5.2
- the use of a qualitative data analysis software package, such as NVivo.

The key word is 'facilitated'. The framework in Figure 5.2 and the NVivo software make a difficult task more manageable and understandable, but large doses of critical thinking are essential at this stage. This is another reason why it is advisable to undertake CEM in groups, as members of the group can bounce ideas off each other and, through shared learning, arrive at a robust set of codes or classifications.

Data coding

The transcripts of the 24 personal interviews and 11 focus groups associated with the gap-year travel experience are the 35 *documents* that were analysed with the help of NVivo. The data coding consists of assigning subsections (phrases, sentences, or paragraphs) of each document to appropriate classification categories. The choice of classification categories in any qualitative-analysis process is difficult and often entails many re-classifications as documents are successively scrutinised.

A starting point: a focus on first-order interactions

With CEM, a very helpful start to the coding process is provided by the framework presented in Figure 5.2. It is recommended that the first-order interactions of Figure 5.2, i.e. the interactions that consumers have with other consumers and with experience enablers, provide the basis for the initial labelling of the categories. More specifically, top-level categories should be labelled as:

- consumer-to-consumer interactions with *acquainted* other consumers, or C2CA
- consumer-to-consumer interactions with *unacquainted* other consumers, or C2CU
- consumer interactions with experience enablers, or C2EE.

Dealing with experience enablers

Prior to the analysis, the number of different experience enablers is unknown, and so a second level of the category C2EE would itemize the C2EE interactions according to the specific experience enablers, as represented by Figure 7.2.

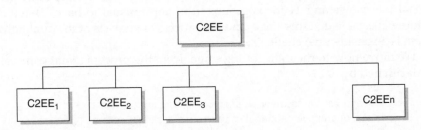

Figure 7.2   The breakdown of C2EE interactions

From the gap-year travel data, a total of $n = 17$ C2EE interactions were ultimately identified, relating to the following experience enablers (in alphabetical order): accommodation, airline, bank/money, bus, destination, email, events organizer, insurance, internet, jobs before travel, jobs in gap year, medical, rail/train, school, telephone/mobile phone, tour company, travel agent and university.

Consumer-to-consumer interactions with acquainted other consumers (C2CA)

These are interactions with people that the consumer has known for a long time (parents, siblings, children, friends, etc.) that take place in the experience domain. For example, in the gap-year travel experience domain, they include interactions with parents over the funding arrangements, or interactions with the friend(s) with whom the consumer has decided to travel.

Consumer-to-consumer interactions with unacquainted other consumers (C2CU)

Unacquainted other consumers are the previously unknown people that the consumer interacts with as a result of undertaking the experience. In the gap-year travel experience, for example, C2CU would include interactions with other gap-year travellers or backpackers who stayed in the same hostels or undertook the same activities, such as bungee jumping or paragliding.

Consumer interactions with experience enablers (C2EE)

In Chapter 5, experience enablers were defined as inanimate entities that provide the consumers with adequate power, means or opportunity to carry out the activities that contribute to their experiences, for example organizations, facilities, technology, special events finance. Identifying and labelling experience enablers are, undeniably, difficult aspects of applying CEM. The 17 experience enablers for the gap-year travel experience, listed above, were arrived at through iteration and constant refinement, and, of course, they are not definitive. Another group of researchers, faced with exactly the same documents, would produce a different list of experience enablers. While this aspect may be disconcerting, it should be remembered that CEM is a process for examining interactions from a consumer experience perspective, and, whatever the categorization of experience enablers, will provoke insights and discussions that complement those following from the study of relationships from the focal firm/organization perspective.

Dealing with negative aspects of experience

In each of C2CA, C2CU and C2EE, there will be elements of the data that refer to constraints on the experience; for example, incompatibility with travel companion, lack of money, unavailability of internet facilities. These 'negatives' will still be coded as first-order interactions, although, in the case of C2EE, they could be seen as the opposite of enablers. Difficulties with obtaining a job during the gap-year, for example, would still be coded in the second-level C2EE tree node of 'jobs during gap-year'.

An example is given now of how a document (an extract of a transcript of a personal interview with a gap-year traveller) is coded according to the CEM categories of C2CA, C2CU and the sub-categories of C2EE.

Example of data coding within CEM

What follows is an example of an interview with a former gap-year traveller. The respondent's responses are numbered and relate to the discussion on coding that follows.

Interviewer:	Hi, my name's S. and I'd like to thank you for agreeing to participate in this interview. I would just like to ask you a few questions regarding your experiences of gap-year travel and your attitudes towards it, in an attempt to understand your motivations and conclusions as to the benefits and disadvantages of this experience.
Respondent:	No problem.
Interviewer:	Where did you go on your gap year?
Respondent:	I went to Seville, which is in Spain. [1]
Interviewer:	What did you do there?
Respondent:	I worked over there as a nanny for 7 months. [2]
Interviewer:	In a nursery?
Respondent:	No, it was with a Spanish family looking after their child. I looked after the child while the mother went to work, but I stayed with the family at their house. [3]
Interviewer:	What were your reasons for going on a gap year?
Respondent:	I went because I thought it would help me to learn the language as part of my languages degree course. Plus I felt like I needed a break from proper education before starting a uni course. [4]
Interviewer:	How did you go about **organiz**ing it?
Respondent:	Well my university was the first port of call. They advised on the paths to take in order to organize the year out. It was mostly a matter of finding a family willing to hire a non-Spanish nanny, which turned out to be less of a problem than I first anticipated. The whole process was less hassle than I first thought it would be. My parents were very helpful too, they helped me in contacting the various people. [5]
Interviewer:	What influenced your decision on where to go on your gap year?
Respondent:	It was suggested by the university. But I had friends that were going on a gap year for the same purposes as me and we'd decided to go to the same place because we felt we'd be able to support each other and help one another settle more easily. [6]
Interviewer:	What sources helped you with your decision? Which didn't?
Respondent:	As I mentioned earlier my university helped me with suggestions of destinations and were excellent at offering advice about what the place was like etc. [7]

(the interview continued)

The numbered responses can be coded as follows:

1   Sentence coded in C2EE (destination)
2   Sentence coded in C2EE (job in gap-year)
3   Sentence coded in C2CU
4   Sentence coded in C2EE (university)

5 Paragraph coded in C2EE (university) and in C2CA
6 Paragraph coded in C2EE (university) and in C2CA
7 Sentence coded in C2EE (university)

Some practical issues with data coding

Even a relatively straightforward document such as the interview above raises a number of practical issues with the data coding:

- In real-time coding, not all of the C2EE sub-categories will have been identified and labelled. Identifying and labelling the C2EE sub-categories is an ongoing process. This means that with the early documents, much time is spent on determining the appropriate sub-categories. As refinements to the sub-categories are made, the early documents need to be re-visited and the coding adapted. This can be time-consuming. Once the sub-categories are agreed and specified, coding of the later documents becomes progressively quicker.
- As can be seen above, the paragraphs or sentences, uttered by the consumers (respondents), sometimes involve elements that relate to two or more categories (as with 5 and 6 above).
- Following on from the point above, the unit of analysis may be variable – sometimes a phrase, sometimes a sentence, sometimes a paragraph. If possible the unit of analysis should be as small as possible as long as it can stand on its own as a meaningful illustration of an element of the consumer experience.
- There may be responses that do not seem to fit any of the agreed categories or sub-categories at the time of the document scrutiny. To accommodate these, it may be useful to create other categories which are neither C2C or C2EE. However, it is recommended that this is done sparingly.

Overall, the data-coding process requires patience, thoroughness, ingenuity and critical thinking. It can be very rewarding, especially when undertaken by groups of students working together on the coding categories and refinements. But, of course, there need to be useful outputs from the process. So we move on to the next stage – data retrieval.

Data retrieval

By now, phrases, sentences and paragraphs from all the documents have been assigned to one or more of the categories C2CA, C2CU, $C2EE_1$, $C2EE_2$, ... $C2EE_n$. It is time to examine the totality of what is contained in each of the categories. This is referred to as data retrieval. This is where the use of NVivo or similar software is especially helpful.

From the gap-year travel data, we give an extract below (from NVivo) of what has been assigned to the category C2EE (university); a category that contains all references from the gap-year travel documents to consumers' interactions with universities.

Document 'Focus Group 11', 7 passages, 3186 characters.

Section 0, Paragraph 23, 240 characters.

D: (pensively) Yeah, well I knew I wanted to go to uni but I guess I just wanted a break as well, I mean I just thought that I had, um, spent a long time in education and I think I almost deserved to have some time off to my self as well.

Section 0, Paragraph 31, 155 characters.

D: Well I didn't really know what course I wanted to do, just that I wanted to go to uni and travel, taking a gap year was the best option for me I think.

Section 0, Paragraphs 41–49, 746 characters.

B: I thought that going to uni was more important at the time to me.
(C nods in agreement, D shakes her head)
D: (in a questioning tone but humorous tone) So if you had a gap year, did you think you wouldn't go to uni or something?
B: (laughing) Well, for me I just thought that if I went on one I might never come back! Seeing all those other cultures and stuff.
C: Yeah, that was completely the same for me. I thought that once I stopped learning then I would never want to learn again they would have had to have dragged me back kicking and screaming in to education …! Also as well I think that I wouldn't have appreciated it at all. I didn't wanna go and be ignorant about the things I'd see because that'd just be a complete waste …

Document 'interview 1', 1 passages, 453 characters.

Section 0, Paragraph 14, 453 characters.

A = I'm less apprehensive about trying new things. When you travel, you meet so many people and experience so many new things. I'm able to embrace new challenges now, for example, at university I had that self confidence to reassure myself everything would be ok and that I'd make friends quickly. I've approached my education differently too. Education used to feel like a huge burden of stress that dragged while I'm now more positive with my learning.

Document 'Interview 11', 1 passages, 270 characters.

Section 0, Paragraphs 99–101, 270 characters.

Interviewer: Claims are made that gap year interrupts the rhythm of your studies, to what extent would you agree or disagree?
Respondent: Yeah, it did kind of make me have doubts about going to university, but that was probably just the shock of coming back home too.

Document 'Interview 13', 4 passages, 1394 characters.

Section 0, Paragraphs 23–25, 262 characters.

Interviewer: What were your reasons for going on a gap year?
Respondent: I went because I thought it would help me to learn the language as part of my languages degree course. Plus I felt like I needed a break from proper education before starting a uni course.

Section 0, Paragraphs 27–29, 476 characters.

Interviewer: How did you go about organizing it?
Respondent: Well my university was the first port of call. They advised on the paths to take in order to organize the year out. It was mostly a matter of finding a family willing to hire a non-Spanish nanny, which turned out to be less of a problem than I first anticipated. The whole process was less hassle than I first thought it would be. My parents were very helpful too, they helped me in contacting the various people.

Section 0, Paragraphs 31–33, 334 characters.

Interviewer: What influenced your decision on where to go on your gap year?
Respondent: It was suggested by the university. But I had friends that were going on a gap year for the same purposes as me and we'd decided to go to the same place because we felt we'd be able to support each other and help one and other settle more easily.

Section 0, Paragraphs 85–87, 322 characters.

Interviewer: Did it prepare you for university/full time employment?
Respondent: It helped with university course due to the fact it gave me a hands on experience in Spanish culture and language. It helped me to realize more independence away from my parents and helped my confidence in approaching and meeting new people.

(and much more ...)

The above example contains extracts from both the focus groups and personal interviews (including the one used as an example of data coding), and, as yet, is very fragmented. A similar alignment of chunks of text from various sources will have been collated at each of the other categories. Despite the potentially bewildering amount of text for many of the categories, it is at this stage that an understanding of interactions and relationships within the experience domain *from the consumer perspective* begins to emerge, in the form of a *collective consumer gaze*.

Although it cannot be regarded as scientific, it is possible to obtain a 'feel' for the acuity of the various interactions by simply examining the number of separate consumer mentions in each of the categories.

What, then, might be regarded as the core interactions and relationships experienced by gap-year travellers? And what might be at the inner and outer peripheries of the collective consumer gaze? The core interactions (by the criteria of most mentions in a category) are represented in bold type in Table 7.1. Those in the inner periphery are represented in italics, and in the outer periphery in normal type.

Table 7.1   Collective customer gaze

(Sub)-category	Number of mentions in the (sub)-category
C2CA	88
C2EE (university)	49
C2EE (destination)	46
C2EE (jobs in gap-year)	31
C2CU	30
C2EE (jobs before travel)	29
C2EE (internet)	26
C2EE (tour companies)	*23*
C2EE (internet)	*21*
C2EE (email)	*16*
C2EE (school)	*16*
C2EE (banks/money)	*15*
C2EE (accommodation)	*10*
C2EE (travel agent)	9
C2EE (insurance)	7
C2EE (events organizers)	7
C2EE (telephones/mobile phones)	6
C2EE (bus/train travel)	5
C2EE (medical)	3

Even allowing for the potential lack of precision in selecting categories that fall into the core and inner and outer peripheries of the collective consumer gaze, it is instructive for organizations, such as banks, insurance companies and travel agents (all of whom see one-to-one relationships with gap-year travellers/backpackers as potentially lucrative) to recognize their 'place' in consumers' perspectives of experience enablers in the experience domain. Armed with this richer picture of the collective consumer gaze, such organizations can consider how to match more clearly their products/services to consumer values (see Chapter 8 for an elaboration). First, however, it is necessary to make sense of the fragmented chunks of text that are contained in each category. We move on now to the theme-identification stage of CEM.

Theme identification

As the extract above, from the C2EE (university) category, demonstrates, each category contains relevant material from all the documents. However, as yet, there is no pattern or structure to the data. What are the underlying themes that can be drawn out of the data that provide helpful directions to those who want to gain a greater understanding of consumers' interactions within the experience domain? Identification of the themes is not something that comes easy. It will require serious thinking, initiative, ingenuity and the ability at times to 'think outside the box'. As with the data-coding stage, theme identification is aided by discussions within a (student) group.

We believe that theme identification within CEM should be related to consumer value. This is consistent with a service-dominant logic of marketing (Vargo and Lusch 2004), and a focus on consumer experiences. Therefore, as a means of ultimately identifying the themes emerging from the data, it is helpful to examine the data in all the categories for evidence of consumer value enhancers and consumer value inhibitors. This not only provides a very useful and focused start to theme identification, but also ensures that the perspective of the consumer experience is being maintained, and that there is not a premature temptation to seek for 'managerial implications' for the organizations involved in the experience domain.

Consumer value enhancers and inhibitors

Table 7.2 shows the consumer value enhancers and inhibitors that were implied by the data in the C2EE (university) node. It should be noted that, although the value enhancers and inhibitors have emerged from the material

Table 7.2   Consumer value enhancers and inhibitors – C2EE (university)

Value enhancers	Value inhibitors
• Opportunity to get information about gap-year experiences e.g. university guild • Universities consider that gap-year students have enhanced social skills, maturity and greater level of commitment to university course • Meet new people who become life-long friends • Builds confidence and interpersonal skills • Variety of 'life-changing' experiences/adventures • Doing work enhances employability • Work that links to future career and university course is valued • Gives a clearer idea of future plan. Time to think and focus • A 'window of opportunity' which might not come along as part of normal career route • Financial and practical support from parents • Saving money for trip is a good discipline	• Takes you out of the 'learning cycle' • Takes you off the career path • Can lead to financial hardship • Top universities do not offer deferred entry • Parental concerns, e.g. negative impact on career

that relates to university as an experience enabler, not all of them refer directly to the university. For example, neither the value-enhancing idea that gap-year travel 'builds confidence and interpersonal skills' nor the value-inhibiting idea that gap-year travel involves 'parental concerns e.g. negative impact on career' is uniquely associated with university. But they have arisen out of discussions about gap-year travel and university. Indeed the same two ideas also emerged from the identification of consumer value enhancers and inhibitors associated with the C2CA category, but many other ideas also emerged (see Table 7.3). It is not necessary to worry about duplication – indeed the duplicate ideas may ultimately determine the stronger themes; ones that cut across many of the interactions/relationships.

Table 7.3   Consumer value enhancers and inhibitors – C2CA

Value enhancers	Value inhibitors
• Variety of 'life-changing' experiences/adventures • Builds confidence and interpersonal skills • Travelling with friends reduces anxiety • Financial and practical support from parents • Opportunity to emulate siblings' success and experiences • Escape from parental control • Escape from general problems, e.g. exam stress, mundane life	• Parental concerns, e.g. negative impact on career, safety • Travelling with friends makes experience too easy • Lack of financial support • Takes you out of the 'learning cycle' • Peer pressure to overspend • Homesickness • Difficulties keeping in touch with parents • Peer pressure to go

For the gap-year travel experience domain, there are a total of 19 such tables; C2CA, C2CU and 17 C2EEs. The contents of each table will be the result of reading, re-reading and discussing the material. As well as giving a comprehensive picture of consumer quality-of-life ingredients in the experience domain, they unearth contradictions and conflicts, for example 'escape from parental control' versus 'difficulties in keeping in touch with parents', or 'travelling with friends reduces anxiety' versus 'travelling with friends makes experience too easy'. Any implied paradoxes should not be regarded as a problem, but as a stimulus to 'dig deeper' and find out more.

Conclusion

This chapter has described the CEM process, using the 'gap-year travel experience' domain as an example. The process ensures a wealth of information on consumer interactions within the domain, provided through a consumer 'gaze' on interactions, and the identification of consumer value enhancers and inhibitors. But how might such information be used? How can it provide additional insights for all players within the experience domain? These questions are addressed in the next chapter.

Learning propositions

- Consumer experiences are best understood through interpreting 'voice' of consumers.
- 'Voice' of consumers is best obtained through qualitative research techniques.
- Consumer experience networks contain consumer interactions with other consumers and a range of experience enablers.
- The consumer experience modelling (CEM) process facilitates the identification of important consumer interactions in an experience domain.
- Consumer value enhancers and inhibitors can be inferred from the consumer experience data.
- We are all consumers, and so can identify more closely with consumer voice.

Activities and discussion questions

1   To practise the process of CEM in the gap-year travel domain:

   (a)   Log in to an appropriate gap year travel website (e.g. www. travelblog.com).

   (b)   Choose three reasonably lengthy blogs about gap-year activities.

   (c)   Code the accounts of the blogs into the categories C2CA, C2CU and C2EE. List your C2EE categories.

   (d)   Retrieve all entries according to C2CA, C2CU and all the C2EE sub-categories.

   (e)   Identify and list consumer value enhancers and inhibitors for each category and sub-category.

2   To gather data in a different experience domain, try one of the following:

- early parents' experience domain – interview 8 or more parents who have had their first child within the last two years.
- retired persons experience domain – interview 8 or more people who have retired from work.
- grandparents' experience domain – interview 8 or more grandparents.

In each case the data collection is achievable by groups of 3–5 students. The interviews should be recorded and transcribed into Microsoft Word. They should provide a reasonably sized data set for the application of CEM.

3   Learn how to use the latest version of NVivo sufficiently well to carry out the code and retrieve stages of CEM.

References

Atwood, R. (2009) 'DIUS Promises to Ditch the Jargon but Defends its Use of "Customer"', *Times Higher Education*, 9 April: 6–7.

Bowes, G. (2005) 'The Gap Year that Grew', *Observer*: 14 August.

Bryman, A. and Bell, E. (2003) *Business Research Methods*, Oxford: Oxford University Press.

Easterby-Smith, M., Thorpe, R. and Lowe, A. (2002) *Management Research: An Introduction*, London: Sage Publications.

Holbrook, M.B. (2009) 'Manufacturing Memorable Consumption Experiences from Ivy to Ivory: The Business Model, Customer Orientation, and Distortion of Academic Values in the Post-Millennial University', in A. Lindgreen, J. Vanhamme and M.B. Beverland (eds), *Memorable Customer Experiences: A Research Anthology*, Gower Publishing/Ashgate.

Huxley, L. (2005) 'Western Backpackers and the Global Experience: An Exploration of Young People's Interaction with Local Cultures', *Tourism, Culture and Communication*, 5(1): 37–44.

Jones, A. (2004) 'Make or Break Time', *Guardian*: 27 July.

Lindgreen, A., Vanhamme, J. and Beverland, M.B. (2009) *Memorable Customer Experiences: A Research Anthology*, Aldershot, UK: Gower Publishing/Ashgate.

Palmer, A. and Koenig-Lewis, N. (2009) 'An Extended, Community Focused, Experiential Framework for Relationship Marketing', *Journal of Customer Behaviour*, 8(1): 85–96.

Spero, R. (2009) 'Recession Funds Gap Year Boom for Redundant Workers', *Daily Mail*, 18 March.

Vargo, S.L. and Lusch, R.F. (2004) 'Evolving to a New Dominant Logic of Marketing', *Journal of Marketing*, 68(January): 1–17.

Vargo, S.L. and Lusch, R.F. (2008) 'Service-Dominant Logic: Continuing the Evolution', *Journal of the Academy of Marketing Science*, 36: 1–10.

Voss, C. and Zomerdijk, L. (2007) 'Innovation in Experiential Services – An Empirical View', in DTI (ed.), *Innovation in Services*, London: DTI; 97–134.

Note

1. This section draws heavily on Baron, S. and Harris, K. (2010) 'Toward an Understanding of Consumer Perspectives on Experiences', *Journal of Services Marketing*, 24(7).

8 Consumer Experience Modelling: Value Enhancers and Inhibitors

Learning objectives

- To identify consumer quality of life issues in an experience domain from lists of consumer value enhancers and inhibitors.
- To pose key questions relating to consumer quality of life within an experience domain.
- To demonstrate the potential for generating relationship-building options for organizations that contribute to an experience domain.
- To briefly compare quality of life from macro-marketing and CEM perspectives.

Introduction

In Chapter 7, a process for exploring interactions and relationships from a consumer experience perspective (CEM) was introduced and explained. The process generates sets of consumer value enhancers and value inhibitors originating from the consumers' accounts of first-order interactions – those with acquainted and unacquainted other consumers, and those with the range of experience enablers. In the context of the gap-year travel experience domain, 17 experience enablers were identified and so there were 19 sets of consumer value enhancers and inhibitors. So, although, through CEM, the 'raw' consumer voice data has been systematically transformed into consumer-value enhancers and inhibitors, there is still work to do with the 19 documents in order to address the implications of the findings to consumers *and to the many contributors* to the experience domain.

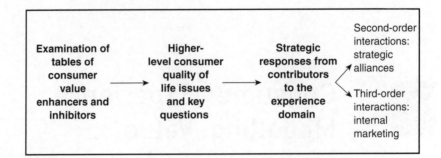

Figure 8.1   From enhancers and inhibitors to strategic responses

The latter point is very important. Although the focus is on interactions and relationships from a consumer experience perspective, the outcomes can provide organizations that contribute to the consumer experiences with strategic relationship-building options.

Implications for consumers and contributors to the experience domain

Through Figure 8.1, we suggest a process that aids the progression from tables of consumer enhancers and inhibitors to the identification of higher-level consumer issues to the potential for strategic responses from contributors to the experience domain. Again the gap-year travel experience domain data will be used to demonstrate the process.

Underlying this process is that the identification of *consumer implications* (in the form of higher-level consumer quality of life issues) *precedes* any discussion of *managerial implications* (in the form of the development of strategic responses from contributors to the experience domain).

Examination of tables of consumer value enhancers and inhibitors

Tables 7.2 and 7.3 were used as examples in Chapter 7. If we add three more tables of value enhancers and inhibitors, developed from the gap-year travel data set (Tables 8.1–8.3), we can begin to appreciate the task of deriving higher-level consumer quality of life issues and key questions. Clearly, the task would be more difficult if faced with all the (19) tables, but the five tables provide enough material to illustrate the process.

Table 8.1 Consumer value enhancers and inhibitors – C2E (email)

Value enhancers	Value inhibitors
• Way of reducing parental anxiety • Cheaper than phone call • Enables continuous communication • Helps relieve homesickness • Made possible by internet cafes • Enables you to convey excitement of the experience • Supplements telephone call • Can communicate visual experiences • Enables planned communication • Enables communication across time differences • Gives control to the sender	• Lack of email access points in remote locations • Raises parents' expectations about contact options and frequency

Table 8.2 Consumer value enhancers and inhibitors – C2E (jobs during gap year)

Value enhancers	Value inhibitors
• Having a job prior to leaving reduces anxiety • Work is easy to find • Having to find job when on year out is considered part of the leaning experience • Unpaid work is satisfying and enhances exposure to other cultures • Work gives insights into future career possibilities • All work exposes you to cultural experiences • Having a variety of jobs enhances exposure to a range of experiences • Work has a focus, i.e. pays for aspects of the trip therefore enhances commitment • Temporary work gives flexibility to change itinerary, and freedom to control work hours	• Diversity of jobs can be too stressful • Work compulsory to fund gap-year experience

Table 8.3 Consumer value enhancers and inhibitors – C2E (banks/money)

Value enhancers	Value inhibitors
• Financial support from parents • Opportunity for financial independence from parents • Overdraft support from banks • Working before travel gives finance • Financial planning by parents and student before trip can make things a lot easier • Government loans provide support	• No money to take a gap year • Fear of 'running out of money'. Not having enough to get home • Fear of bank problems, e.g. excessive overdraft or bank charges • Sorting bank problems in a foreign country • Facing overwhelming debt on return

Tables 7.2 and 7.3, and Tables 8.1–8.3, should be read and re-read in order to get 'beneath the skin' of the products/services that are currently available and offered to gap-year travellers, in order to identify the more fundamental quality of life and well-being issues that are being expressed (perhaps in different forms) within the tables. In this way, questions can be generated that challenge contributors to the gap-year experience to re-integrate their resources in ways that have potentially positive implications for the consumers concerned.

Higher-level consumer quality of life issues and key questions

The individual bullet points in Tables 7.2 and 7.3, and Tables 8.1–8.3 are useful in their own right when compared with the advice given by many agencies on the benefits and drawbacks of gap-year travelling. For example, from Tables 7.2 and 7.3, the points are made, by the consumers, that gap-year travel 'builds confidence and interpersonal skills' and offers 'a variety of life-changing experiences and adventures'. Organizations involved in the adventure travel industry, such as VentureCo, observe that gap-years can build soft skills, language skills and a sense of achievement, while Durham County Council in North East England, on their website for parents of gap-year travellers, advises that 'a gap year well spent will hone your son/daughter's communication skills, teach them how to stick to a tight budget, and broaden their social and intellectual horizons'. Here, observations *made by consumers*, on value-enhancing elements of gap-year travelling, provide confirmation of some of the benefits of gap-year travel that have been identified by organizations that are active in enabling the experience. Likewise, compare the concern expressed by the consumers, that a gap year 'takes you out of the learning cycle' (Tables 7.2 and 7.3) with the advice offered on the 'universityoptions' website that 'not all (university) courses are keen for their prospective students to disappear for a year'.

However, the purpose of adopting a consumer experience perspective to interactions and relationships is to seek insights about the experience that are not necessarily uncovered through a conventional focal firm perspective. Some consumer value enhancers and inhibitors feature in several tables. Some are clearly articulated with strength of feeling. They are often the starting point for the search for higher-level consumer issues.

Higher-level consumer quality of life issues

A detailed study of the tables of consumer value enhancers and inhibitors for the gap-year travel experience domain, for example, revealed four, interdependent issues that appear to be central to the experience:

- parental/family relationships
- life planning

- communication/keeping in touch
- financial management.

Conventionally, the *parental effect* is recognized through the provision of facts and information about gap years (as, for example, given by Durham County Council, above). The tables above, however, suggest that there are subtleties in the parental/family relationships that are not necessarily being addressed. For instance, relationships with the parents of gap-year travellers, as seen from Tables 7.2 and 7.3, and Tables 8.1–8.3, can be both value enhancing (e.g. financial and practical support from parents) and value inhibiting (dealing with parental concerns such as negative impact on career, safety). They can be apparently contradictory (escaping from parental control versus difficulties in keeping in touch with parents, and homesickness). And what about the sibling rivalries that occur, when one's brother or sister have taken a gap year, supported financially by the parents? The complexities and subtleties cut across the four issues above.

If *life planning* is taken as a starting point, it can be seen that this encompasses a range of short-, medium- and long-term issues. It was revealing how many consumers looked beyond the perceived immediate benefits and drawbacks of the gap year itself (as mentioned in the first paragraph of this section). The jobs taken before and during the gap year are seen not only as essential financial support, but as the beginning of plans to enhance future employability and gain insight into future career possibilities, and as a good learning experience with job markets. Especially with voluntary, unpaid work, there is an expectation of exposure to other cultures. The period of the gap year is not only to gain a variety of life-changing experiences/adventures, but is, importantly, a period for contemplating the future, having time to think and focus, and an escape from continual examination-related routines and stress. The value-enhancing opportunity to meet new people who can become lifelong friends is clearly weighed against the value-inhibiting drawback of facing overwhelming debt on return.

One of the tables (Table 8.1) contains consumer value and enhancers and inhibitors relating to email as an experience enabler. This is but one of the tables that highlights the significance of *communication/keeping in touch* issues of gap-year travellers (the others being internet, telephones/mobile phones and destination). Telephoning home from different countries has long been recognized as something that can vary enormously, both in terms of practicability and cost. For example, the gapyear-newzealand website offers guidance to UK gap-year visitors about how to use their mobile (cell) phones in New Zealand. However, the whole communication experience of gap-year travellers goes beyond one mode of communication. In most countries that they visit, they have a choice of communication modes – telephone, email, text messaging, MSN (at the time of writing). They can choose to communicate to individuals, or to mailing lists of friends/relatives. They can send visual images via email, phone or webcams. They can control the form and time of communication. In some, more remote destinations, they are restricted in their communication efforts. Each year, technology advances widen the scope of communication possibilities. This, in turn, presents the travellers with more decision-making about how, when and why to communicate with friends/relatives in their home country and with the people they meet on their travels. They wish to plan and control their communication to people in their home country, whilst retaining their independence and not raising too much the parental expectations of regular communication (the absence of which may inadvertently contribute to parental anxiety).

Financial management aspects of the gap-year experience are expressed in many ways and so occur not only in Table 8.3, but also, in some form or other, in most of the 19 tables, including Tables 7.2, 7.3, 8.1 and 8.2. Earning, borrowing and spending money is never far from the consciousness of gap-year travellers, and the financing of the experience affects the parents and siblings of the traveller. Although there is a great appeal of being financially independent and responsible, there are genuine concerns about overspending and accumulating debt.

Key questions

What, then, are some of the key questions that could be addressed in order to improve the quality of life and well-being of the players in the gap-year travel experience domain? Here are some that arise from the tables and discussion in this section. They are by no means exhaustive. Nor is it certain that they can be answered.

- How can the concerns about the break in education through gap-year travel be assuaged?
- How can it be ensured that support mechanisms from parents/friends do not take away the implicit challenge and make it too easy for the gap-year traveller?
- What can be done to reduce parental anxiety at various stages of the experience without sacrificing the control exercised by the gap-year traveller?

Potential for strategic responses from contributors to the experience domain

To address the higher level consumer issues, represented by the three questions above, it may require strategic responses from contributors to the experience domain. The potential for strategic responses can be developed in the context of the second- and third-order interactions within the experience domain that were identified in Figure 5.2. As a reminder, second-order interactions are those that take place between the experience enablers, and third-order interactions are interactions that exist within the experience enablers insofar as they impact on the consumer experience. Where experience enablers are organizations (such as universities, schools, banks, travel agents, insurance companies, in the gap-year travel experience domain), second-order interactions may become strategic alliances between enablers, and third-order inter-actions represent internal marketing/communications within the various enablers.

In this section the *potential* for strategic responses from contributors to the experience domain is discussed, through addressing the three questions.

How can the concerns about the break in education through gap-year travel be assuaged?

Maybe this is a question that should be addressed seriously by UK universi-ties. While some universities offer advice to students proposing to take a gap year prior to starting their university course, and some programmes (for example, foreign language and international business degrees) regard 'a year abroad' as an essential part of the programme, normally the incorpora-tion of gap-year activities means a disruption to the established university systems. There is an opportunity for a university to actively embrace gap-year travellers, encourage them to apply, and build in course activities that draw on the experiences and capabilities that the consumers have attained. Such a strategic move would involve serious revision, through internal marketing and communication, of attitudes and actions throughout the whole university, in order that it would not be seen simply as a cynical recruitment activity.

But it need not stop there. Strategic alliances could be developed with, say, employers and travel companies, and internal marketing could embrace the current student body. The university could engage itself in the entire gap-year experience as evidence of its commitment to the student. It could become involved with the 'job before travel' element – something that most gap-year students must undertake – through the university careers service. Perhaps there are alternatives to the obvious and convenient work in bars and fast-food outlets, even ones that are beneficial to the proposed course that has been selected? Most universities have student travel service organi-zations on their premises that can aid the year out, and have both under-graduate and postgraduate students from many of the destinations chosen by gap-year travellers. They could put the gap-year student applicants in touch with appropriate contacts.

Some of these ideas may appear fanciful, but they should illustrate that imagination and creativity can (should?) be employed to address a funda-mental question, relating to an experience domain, that encourages a strate-gic response. In this case, the issue is how to help incorporate the gap year into the learning cycle and career path, rather than it being perceived simply as a 'break' in education, in order to diffuse parental anxieties and contribute to the life-planning of the gap year traveller.

How can it be ensured that support mechanisms from parents/friends do not take away the implicit challenge and make it too easy for the gap year traveller?

One of the conflicts in the gap-year experience involves whether or not to do the travelling with friends. On the one hand, travelling with friends is seen to reduce anxiety both for the travellers themselves and their relatives. On the other hand, it can be perceived as making the experience too easy. Travellers can spend much of the time meeting and mixing with other UK gap-year travellers and following tourist trails in each destination that is visited. Whilst this behaviour may create lasting friendships, the authenticity aspect of learning about new cultures first-hand can be sacrificed to varying extents.

Support from parents takes many forms, but is most recognized through the financial support, which, for a majority of the gap-year travellers is essential to have as a supplement to money they have saved from taking jobs before the gap year, and money they will earn through taking jobs during the gap year. For the parents themselves, they commit to not only financing the gap-year traveller, but also younger siblings in the spirit of fairness. The penalties of running out of money and taking on excessive debt are well recognized by the travellers. Financial planning by parents and student before the trip can make things a lot easier, yet many travellers see financial independence from their parents as an important part of the experience.

There may be an opportunity, through strategic alliances between experience enablers such as travel agents, tour operators and tourist departments of popular destinations, for some further segmentation of the gap-year travel marketplace that guarantees authentic experiences for groups of two or more friends. There may be opportunities for banks to devise loan products that meet the parental needs to finance more than one offspring on gap-year travel, while allowing and encouraging the offspring themselves to manage their finances independently in a responsible way. Could banks even use their resources to offer potential employment in some of the more popular visitor destinations?

The conflict between support and independence is a very real and fundamental issue for many of the consumers, and yet not easy to resolve. Imagination and creativity are again required to provide strategic insights for contributors to the experience domain.

What can be done to reduce parental anxiety at various stages of the experience without sacrificing the control exercised by the gap-year traveller?

Parents, being parents, worry about their sons/daughters undertaking a gap year from the moment the idea is first mooted, even though they are normally supportive of the venture and can see the potential benefits. Gap-year travellers, mostly aged 18–24 years, acknowledge the parental anxieties and, yet, being 18–24 years of age, they wish to have and demonstrate control of the gap-year experience.

At the outset, parents seek as much information as they can about gap years. They can be overwhelmed by the quantity of information available in book form and electronically. Contributors to the gap-year experience domain, such as travel agents, tour operators, banks and insurance companies, collectively or individually, could seek to provide opportunities for providing *personalized* advice services to parents – parent meetings, road shows, tailored responses.

It is perhaps during the time that their offspring are travelling that parents are most anxious. Has s/he arrived OK at the latest destination? Is the accommodation OK? Is s/he well? What about the food? Is s/he OK for money? What is the weather like? Is it safe? Is it a good idea to be partying until the early hours of the morning? Of course, most of these concerns can be answered through various modes of communication. Yet, after initial full accounts of each day's events, the gap-year travellers can find it progressively more tedious to write or talk about the accommodation, food and weather, and do not really want their parents to know all about the partying activities. These stories are communicated to selected friends at home via group emails. And it takes time and money. The gap-year students acknowledge the parental concerns and will try to allay them, but they seek to control, to a large extent, who receives various communications and when they receive them. There is a danger that parental expectations may be raised through agreed regular email/telephone slots, given that not all locations have accessible internet cafés or good enough mobile (cell) phone signals. Parental anxiety is increased if the expected communication does not happen for whatever reason.

Information and communication technology is evolving all the time, and the technology will offer more and more sophisticated ways to address the question of how to reduce parental anxiety at various stages of the experience without sacrificing the control exercised by the gap-year traveller. At the time of writing, for example, GPS (Global Positioning System) technology is moving into the European mass markets through incorporation into mobile (cell) phones. This opens up the possibility that parents at home will be able to 'track' where their offspring is – but will the offspring want this? Also, peer-to-peer internet telephony network systems such as Skype are offering the opportunity for 'free' telephoning across the world. By the time you read this, there will be further technological advances. However, it is unlikely that parental anxiety will disappear, or that the gap-year travellers will wish to relinquish control of the communications. So whatever the level of technological development, strategic alliances between information and communication technology players will need to address these fundamental issues in order to contribute to consumer quality of life and well-being in the experience domain (and, most likely, other experience domains).

Consumer quality of life and well-being: comparison with macromarketing

The notions of consumer quality of life and consumer well-being have been introduced within the explanations in this chapter. In the final section, we make clear the context of these concepts in comparison with their more normal use in the macromarketing field.

Macromarketing, as represented by articles in the *Journal of Macromarketing*, 'examines social issues, how they are affected by marketing, and how society influences the conduct of marketing'. It includes 'the marketing of products, services or programs to enhance the quality of life for consumers, households, communities, countries and regions' (taken from the description of the *Journal of Macromarketing*, accessed via www.sagepub.com). Consumer quality of life issues are central to macromarketing, and consumer well-being is also seen as being worthy of enhancement (Sirgy and Lee 2006). Consumer quality-of-life and well-being are clearly not the exclusive property of marketers, and comprehensive and complementary research is published in other literatures, for example the medical journals. The purpose, here, however, is to contrast the approach to consumer quality of life and well-being that has been adopted in this chapter with the macromarketing approach.

The approach adopted in this chapter to consumer quality of life and well-being is different, yet complementary to that addressed in the macromarketing literature.

The macromarketing approach, as exemplified by Lee et. al. (2002) and Sirgy and Lee (2006), has a focus on macro measures of consumer quality of life and well-being in local geographical areas or communities that provide diagnostics that aid public policy making. It includes both consumer assessments of marketplace experiences and the assessment of experts charged with evaluating the costs and benefits of the local area marketplace experiences. The measures are derived by quantitative surveys of local area consumers, based on the premise that consumer well-being consists of being satisfied with all experiences involved with 'the acquisition, preparation, consumption, ownership, maintenance, and disposal of a variety of consumer goods and services' (Sirgy and Lee 2006: 32; the survey instrument can be seen in full in Sirgy and Lee 2006: 33–34). The survey instrument is completed by appropriate members of households in the local area under study.

This type of approach does not take a relationship marketing perspective, as the survey instrument is designed around the acquisition, preparation, consumption, ownership, maintenance and disposal of categories of goods and services that are likely to be offered in a local geographical area/community. The starting point of the research is what is available to create experiences in the area, rather than what the consumers do (and say they do) to create experiences. The CEM approach, in addition to being a contrasting methodology (qualitative rather than quantitative), and having a different territory (experience domain rather than geographical area), addresses consumer experience *relationships and interactions*; elements that are not explicitly measured through the conventional macromarketing approach. CEM acknowledges more overtly that consumers co-create value of goods and services.

Arguably, the Sirgy/Lee questionnaire survey approach should guarantee some measures that aid public policymakers responsible for the quality of life of residents in their geographical regions. We would argue strongly, however, that approaches such as CEM, that incorporate a genuinely consumer perspective on their own experiences, especially through gaining insights to the first-order interactions that consumers have, provide the potential to attain a greater understanding of what are real quality of life issues for consumers.

Conclusion

Figure 8.1 outlines a process for moving from the derivation, through CEM, of tables of consumer value enhancers and inhibitors to consideration of implications for consumers, and finally to a discussion of the potential strategic responses by contributing organizations to the experience domain. In the last stage, the second- and third-order interactions of Table 5.2 are recognized through the possibility of strategic alliances and internal marketing reorganizations. Fundamental to this progression is the identification of high-order consumer issues and key questions relating to them. How the contributors to the experience domain respond to them can require creativity and imagination. At the very least, this process, coupled with the awareness created by the collective consumer gaze (Table 7.1), provides a different perspective on relationships, one that organizations do not necessarily appreciate.

For students of relationship marketing, there are definite advantages in facilitating their active involvement in CEM.

Learning propositions

- Having carried out the CEM process, students/readers are in a position to identify higher-level consumer quality of life issues in the experience domain, and pose key questions.
- The identified quality of life issues and key questions can be used to develop strategic responses from organizations involved in an experience domain.
- Students' 'learning by doing' with CEM results in creative thinking about interactions in an experience domain.
- The CEM process provides complementary insights to macromarketing procedures on consumer quality of life.

Activity

Undertake a project on consumer interactions associated with the retirement experience. The details are given below. It is best undertaken by groups of 4 or 5 students.

Background

Every year, thousands of people experience retirement for the first time. Most will admit that it is a life-changing experience, and are capable and willing to give voice to the experience. This project is aimed at capturing the 'voice' of the retirement experience, identifying the interactions that are integral to the experience, and providing 'experience enablers' with strategic options for fostering relationships with consumers who are part of the retirement marketplace.

For the project, you will need to collect/capture real consumer voice data on the retirement experience and analyse the data by applying consumer experience modelling (CEM) as presented in Chapter 7.

Project guidelines

1 Gather qualitative data from retired people to obtain, in some detail, accounts of their day-to-day activities relating to their retirement experiences, and also their thoughts/feelings associated with the activities. Each account should be saved as a text document. It is important to gather accounts from retired people themselves and not from secondary sources, such as retirement guidebooks.
2 It is recommended that you enter your text documents into a qualitative data analysis software package such as NVivo, and use the code/retrieve facilities provided.
3 Apply the CEM process to identify themes, and formulate key questions.
4 Finally, provide some creative ideas of how one or more of the experience enablers can improve retired persons' quality of life and thereby gain strategic advantages within the experience domain.

There are various means of obtaining real 'voice' data from appropriate consumers, for example:

I by personal interview
II by asking retired people to keep a diary over a period
III combination of I and II above
IV by accessing weblogs (blogs) of people describing their retirement experiences.

In the cases of I and II above, take care that retired people can find the time to fulfil the tasks you require of them. It is recommended that you obtain at least eight documents (transcripts) from I to III, supplemented, if necessary, with documents from IV.

N.B. The activity above could be completed with other experience domains of your choice. Good alternatives to the retirement experience are new parents' experience and dog owners' experience.

References

Lee, D.-J., Sirgy, M.J., Larsen, V. and Wright, N.D. (2002) 'Developing a Subjective Measure of Consumer Well-Being', *Journal of Macromarketing*, 22(2): 158–169.

Sirgy, M.J. and Lee, D.-J. (2006) 'Macro Measures of Consumer Well-Being (CWB): A Critical Analysis and Research Agenda', *Journal of Macromarketing*, 26(1): 27–44.

9   Communities Within 'Experiential Networks'

Learning objectives

- To understand the concept of 'community' in a customer experience context, introducing the concept of 'experiential networks'.
- To identify different types of communities, using the distinction between territorial and non-territorial experience networks.

Introduction: the importance of networks

In Part II so far, we have considered consumers primarily as individuals. However, we have alluded on various occasions to the social and other networks that these individual consumers may be members of, and as a consequence, consumers may act collectively with others that they feel some affinity with, in order to co-create value and/or experience in some way. For example, in Chapter 6 we looked at the use and integration of various operant resources by individual consumers, using the example of the users of the British Library and their messages of support on behalf of the organization when faced with potential cutbacks to its funding. Here, *social* resources – arising from individual's relationships and memberships of various types of communities – were identified as important, not only in terms of disseminating the news about the possible cuts to the Library, but also in coordinating a response to this news through various professional/cultural associations, and work-related, social and family networks.

As mentioned previously, the academic framework of consumer resources we used to analyse these user messages was originally developed by Arnould et al. (2006), and this model identified three types of operant resources that could be used by consumers – physical, cultural and social. These social resources are defined in terms of 'networks of relationships with others' (2006: 93), and can be further sub-divided as follows:

- Demographic groupings – Arnould et al. describe these as more 'traditional' groupings. They could include, for example, families, ethnic groups and social class, and, indeed, many of the marketing textbooks would regard these as typical criteria for market segmentation.
- Consumer communities – this type of social resource is described by Arnould et al. as 'emergent', and could include 'brand communities' (i.e. relating to relationships with brands, such as user groups, fan clubs, etc.), 'consumer tribes and subcultures' (e.g. relating to psychographic and lifestyle attributes, such as ethically motivated/conscious consumers, skateboarders, surfers, punks, goths and other music genre followers).
- Commercial relationships – these relate to groups of individuals that interact with commercial entities. For example, like many other cultural institutions, the British Library has a 'Friends of the British Library' scheme, which individuals can join and in return for an annual subscription receive a range of financial benefits (such as concessionary prices for public talks, etc.) as well as a special programme of visits, lectures and other events. There is also a Supporters' Forum with its own dedicated website at www.bl.uk/supportus/index.html which encourages online interaction. Indeed, the messages of support analysed in Chapter 6 were solicited via a question posted on this website, which currently asks users to respond to the question 'How has the British Library helped you?', in an attempt by the organization 'to understand more about the value that we add to your research or work'.

All of this has a lot of resonance with Gummesson's (2006) concept of 'many-to-many marketing'. Gummesson emphasizes the importance and ubiquity of a wide range of relationships – private, professional and commercial – and argues that when relationships encompass more than two people or organizations, then *networks* will emerge, which he views in terms of complex patterns and contextual dimensions. He argues that 'networks are the basis of life, society and organisations, and consequently also of management and marketing' (2006: 346). Thus, networks are identified by Gummesson as a more generic, 'core variable' of marketing, with relationships and interaction postulated as two 'subcore variables' that could be incorporated within the concept of a network.

In a specific marketing context, Iacobucci defines a network as describing 'a collection of actors (persons, departments, firms, countries and so on) and their structural connections (familial, social, communicative, financial, strategic, business alliances and so on)' (1996: xiii).

Building on the network concept, Gummesson uses the expression 'many-to-many marketing' to describe, analyse and utilize the network properties of marketing. He contrasts this with 'one-to-one marketing', which he describes as largely representing mainstream relationship marketing and customer relationship management, where the target is a single supplier and a single customer relationship. Trying to capture this complexity in terms of Figure 5.2 at the beginning of Part II of the book, which considers interactions from the consumer perspective, we can perhaps re-draw the diagram to better highlight the network properties – as shown in Figure 9.1.

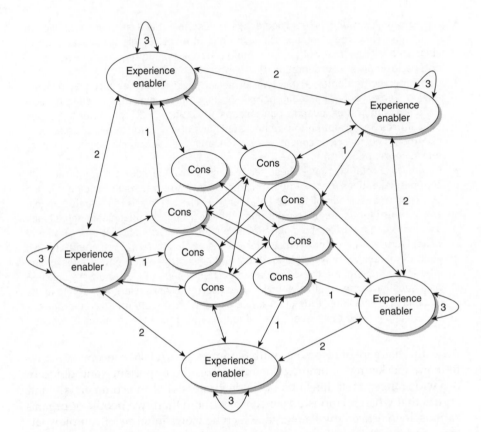

1 = first-order interaction, 2 = second-order interaction, 3 = third-order interaction

Figure 9.1   The experience network

In this re-drawn diagram, the plethora of boxes representing individual consumers (cons) and their interaction, both with each other, and with experience enablers, is an attempt to emphasize the 'many-to-many' properties in the particular context of consumer communities. Of course, the second- and third-order interactions between and within the experience enablers (identified by the numbers 2 and 3) should also be regarded as an element of this 'many-to-many' concept as experience enablers may also collectively interact and develop relationships in order to enhance the experiential aspect of the network as a whole (which we will see later in the chapter in relation to the marketing of places). Indeed, we could consider Figure 9.1 as constituting an *experience network*, and the remainder of this chapter focuses on the various elements of the experience network and how they may collectively act to co-create and enhance the value inherent in an experience. In doing this, we will look at the communal aspects of various experience networks drawn from a number of contexts within which the authors have researched in the past.

The concept of 'community'

Before looking at some examples of communities within experience networks, it is perhaps worthwhile to consider what we mean when we talk about 'communities', be they consumers or experience enablers. Azarya (1996) states that the term community can relate to a variety of phenomena and also has numerous diverse associations, and goes on to suggest that this ambiguity arises from the confusion between community as a type of *collectivity* (or social unit), and community as a type of *social relationship* (or sentiment). In the first case, community as a type of collectivity 'usually refers to a group sharing a defined physical space or geographical area such as a neighbourhood, city, village or hamlet' – this could be termed a *territorial* approach to community. The second case, community considered as a type of social relationship, could be thought of as a *non-territorial* approach. Here, community can be thought of as 'a group sharing common traits, a sense of belonging and/or maintaining social ties and interactions which shape it into a distinctive social entity, such as an ethnic, religious, academic or professional community' (Azarya 1996: 114).

These two approaches are not mutually exclusive, but can perhaps be best thought of as constituting different emphases. Azarya argues that those who think of communities primarily in territorial terms, while not dismissing totally the element of common ties, think of these ties as not sufficient in themselves to constitute a community. On the other hand, the non-territorial approaches emphasize the social ties, regarding territory as not being totally necessary for community to exist. Thus, these social ties (arising for example, from common values, interests, kinship relations, etc.) may exist between people who may be geographically dispersed, as none of them presuppose people living together. Earlier in this book, we have emphasized the mediating effect of information technology in terms of connectivity between individuals who may be widely dispersed geographically – for example the messages of support for the British Library mentioned in Chapter 6 came from all over the world. This point is emphasized by Azarya (1996) who states that, as a consequence, the non-territorial approach to thinking about community has gained force as a result of modern advances in communication which have reduced the importance of territorial proximity as a basis for human association.

This territorial/non-territorial distinction in how we think about communities can provide a useful framework for thinking about the 'many-to-many' marketing properties of networks from a consumer experience perspective. The rest of this chapter will consider various contexts within which we can think about these issues. We start with an obvious manifestation of a territorial approach to thinking about community and networks – the marketing of *places*, and here we will focus particularly on the second- and third-order interactions (i.e. between and within experience enablers – namely those responsible for the management and marketing of, particularly urban, places). We will then consider how community may be defined from a consumer experience perspective via non-territorial approaches which emphasize to social ties between individuals, in terms of, what we might term communities of practice, communities defined by value systems and issue-based communities.

Territorial experience networks: marketing places

The most obvious manifestation of communities defined in territorial terms are, of course, places. The more overt management and marketing of places – particularly urban places such as towns and cities – has become much more widespread, and professionalized, over the past 30 years (see Ashworth and Voogd 1990a; Ward 1998; Kotler et al. 1999). This in turn, has led to the subject of place marketing becoming a growing focus for researchers, not only from the management discipline, but also from disciplines such as geography and urban studies (given the explicit spatial aspect), and also public administration (given the fact that much place-marketing activity is implemented by local authorities/administrations, often in conjunction with the private sector through the mechanism of public–private partnership bodies).

Various authors researching the subject of place marketing have identified two key factors which distinguish this particular context from more 'mainstream' marketing. These are the complex and kaleidoscopic nature of the place product, and also the complexity of the organizational mechanisms for its marketing. It is this second factor that we will consider first, because of the obvious implications for the management and marketing of the place 'experience'. However, it must be recognized that these product and 'process' factors are interlinked, a factor we will return to later, when we consider the implications of all of this.

Turok describes cities as 'complex adaptive systems comprising multitudes of actors, firms and other organisations forming diverse relationships and evolving together' to develop place-based competitive advantage (2009: 14), and as noted above, one of the specific characteristics of place marketing is the complexity of organizational mechanisms and the plethora of stakeholders (often with competing agendas) that are involved in marketing activity. This is highlighted by Short and Kim (1999), who identify what they term a 'political economy' perspective on place marketing, which emphasizes recent transformations in urban governance through the involvement of business coalitions in local economic development. The most obvious manifestation of this can be seen in the proliferation of partnership agencies (comprising stakeholders from public, private and voluntary sectors) responsible for urban-place marketing, urban regeneration and economic development. Recognizing this potential complexity, van den Berg and Braun introduce the concept of the 'strategic network' in terms of locating responsibility for the place-marketing/branding effort, comprising a cooperative approach between all place-marketing actors, with interdependency of actors forming 'the backbone of the network' (1999: 995–996).

The result of all of this is the need for a consensual and inclusive approach to place-marketing strategy-making. Van den Berg and Braun stress the importance of what they call 'organizing capacity', defined as 'the ability to enlist all actors involved and, with their help, to generate new ideas and to develop and implement a policy designed to respond to fundamental developments and create conditions for sustainable development' (1999: 995).

However, this plurality of actors and perspectives can often cause strains in place-management/marketing processes in some locations. Indeed, the resulting potential for conflict is very real – Kotler et al. describe communities as potentially 'chronic battlegrounds where interest groups battle for power and push their competing agendas and strategies' (1999: 106), and there can be a real danger of certain groups dominating the management and marketing agenda, and the consequent marginalization of others (with obvious subsequent potential for tension and conflict). Acknowledging such issues, Corsico introduces the metaphor of city as *market*, reflecting the fact that an urban place is 'the milieu in which a system of trade, a network of relationships is valid' (1993: 79). The urban place and its institutions, therefore, become the forum in which the various urban stakeholders can communicate and (hopefully) reach some consensus as to its future development. This has obvious resonance with Gummesson's (2006) concept of 'many-to-many' marketing, which explicitly utilizes these network properties of marketing.

Thinking about this in the specific context of the 'experience network' framework, shown in Figure 9.1, we can think of all these interactions between the various actors in the 'strategic network' of a particular place as second- and third-order interactions (i.e. between and within experience enablers). One of the authors has researched these networks in detail (see Warnaby et al. 2002, 2004, 2005a) and has identified different types of interaction between network members in order to develop and implement marketing activities, as follows:

- formal (or structural) interaction – which could occur through membership of partnership agencies and steering groups etc.
- informal interaction – through participation in local networks and through information sharing with other agencies
- initiative-specific interaction – where agencies came together to develop and implement a particular place-marketing initiative and then disbanded (Warnaby et al., 2002, 2004).

This complexity of organizational mechanisms for place marketing is linked to the other factor characterizing place marketing – the complexity of the place 'product' itself. Ashworth and Voogd (1990a, 1990b) highlight the complex, multi-layered nature of the urban-place product, suggesting that it consists of a 'holistic' product, which in turn comprises various attributes and attractions which, following Sleipen (1988), they term 'contributory elements'. This is developed further by van den Berg and Braun (1999) who identify three levels of (urban) place marketing:

1 *individual urban goods and services*, where marketing is concerned with the marketing of one location, service, attraction, etc.
2 *clusters of related services*, such as urban tourism or port facilities

3   *the urban agglomeration as a whole*, which (unlike the previous categories) may not in itself be a well-defined product and is, as a consequence, open to various interpretations, as different *combinations* of individual urban goods/services and clusters may be promoted to distinct market segments (Ashworth and Voogd 1990b).

This complexity and possible ambiguity can create problems. Ashworth (1993) argues that the complicated nature of the urban-place product creates difficulty in identifying specific responsibility for its marketing, and suggests three possible producers of the urban-place product:

1   the assembler of the various elements in the place product 'package' (as is the case in the tourism industry)
2   governments and their agencies, who 'concern themselves with coordinating, stimulating, subsidising and occasionally even operating various facilities as well as engaging in much generalized place promotion' (1993: 645)
3   the consumers themselves, who create their own unique place product from the variety of services, amenities and other place elements available to them, with the place producer having little direct control over this process.

In considering the relative importance of these place-product producers, Ashworth implies the primacy of the consumer, as follows: 'Each consumption is an individual experience ... Thus in many logical respects the producer of the place-product is the consumer who produces an individual product by the process of assembly for consumption' (1993: 645).

This notion of the consumer as producer of his or her own unique urban 'experience' echoes one of the key foundational premises of the service-dominant logic that was discussed in Chapter 4, namely, that value is uniquely and phenomenologically determined by the beneficiary (Vargo and Lusch 2008). Referring to Figure 9.1, this brings us back to the first-order interactions between place users and urban-experience enablers, and indeed between the place users themselves.

We can consider these first-order interactions (and the growing importance of more overtly experiential aspects thereof) with specific reference to the subject of town centre management (TCM), again one of the main focuses of research for one of the authors (see Warnaby et al. 1998; Forsberg et al. 1999, 2005b; Stubbs et al. 2002). Synthesizing various definitions, Warnaby et al. define town centre management as:

the search for competitive advantage through the maintenance and/or strategic development of both public and private areas and interests within town centres, initiated and undertaken by stakeholders drawn from a combination of the public, private and voluntary sectors. (1998: 17–18)

One of the key motivations behind the setting up of TCM schemes was a response to threats to traditional urban retail areas as a consequence of the development of retail activity in 'off-centre' locations (on the edge-of-town and out-of-town), and in the 20 years or so that TCM schemes have been in operation, the objectives and activity scope of many initiatives developed under their aegis have arguably moved much more overtly towards the experiential (Warnaby, 2009).

In their early stages, the prime concerns of many TCM schemes were essentially *janitorial* (i.e. coordinating the basic service infrastructure provision such as street cleaning, refuse collection, etc.). As TCM schemes have matured, their activity scope has become more strategically-oriented in terms of trying to influence the future development of the town, in terms of focusing on managing the occupier mix within the town centre, and also promotional and marketing activities. However, whilst these janitorial and strategic aspects remain essential preconditions for success, Warnaby (2009) argues that if towns and cities are to maintain and enhance their position in an ever more competitive and hostile environment, town centres have to focus more explicitly on the *experiential*. Such views are also articulated in a recent report, *Future of Retail Property*, the British Council of Shopping Centres (BCSC), which states that, 'customer "experience" is the new battleground. Shopping must not be bland and uneventful, but rather an efficient, exiting and emotionally engaging episode' (BCSC 2007: 10–12). In seeking to achieve this, shopping places must follow the example of the retailers within them, and engage in the 're-enchantment of retailing'. This encompasses a set of practices 'that activate non-functional sources of value' during a visit to a store (Badot and Filser 2007: 167), immersing the consumer in a memorable experience.

In thinking about these experiential issues in relation to places, some frameworks from the services marketing literature have some use. Of particular applicability is the servuction model, developed by Langeard et al. (1981). This model highlights the experiential aspects of the purchases of goods or services by the consumer, emphasizing that all products deliver a 'bundle of benefits' to the consumer. According to this model, the organization providing the service comprises two elements – visible and invisible. The *visible* element constitutes both the inanimate environment within which the service experience occurs, and the contact personnel within the organization who interact with consumers during the service experience. Supporting this is the *invisible* element – namely, the support infrastructure that enables the visible part to function. The model is completed by the introduction of other consumers with whom the original customer may interact within the system.

Warnaby and Davies (1997) and Warnaby (2009) have adapted the original servuction model to the context of towns and cities. In this context, the *visible* element comprises:

- the *physical setting* – i.e. the retail venues themselves, and also venues relating to other land uses (e.g. cultural or leisure activities), as well as the general ambience of both the retail activities and the destination as a whole
- the *social milieu* – i.e. contact personnel within all the above venues, as well as the wider socio-cultural factors of the city (e.g. friendliness of the population and local

customs), which will provide a context for the behaviour of the contact personnel in the retail and other venues (Warnaby 2009).

This visible element is underpinned by the management of a range of support services and logistical operations. Some services could be regarded as *hygiene* factors in that they alone would not motivate consumers to visit a location, but their absence would cause dissatisfaction (e.g. toilets, car parking, street cleaning). Other services could be thought of more in terms of *motivating* possible visits (e.g. catering facilities and leisure facilities such as crèches and children's play areas). In addition, *logistical* services would include a basic transport infrastructure (both within the locale and between the locale and its catchment area), and also the logistics provision for specific venues within the physical setting (e.g. deliveries for retailers).

Thus, thinking about towns and cities as experiential networks both visible and invisible elements of the servuction model are incorporated, as well as seeking to influence the interactions between all users of a location – in other words, a management focus on the *totality* of the system. This highlights the importance of first-, second- and third-order interactions highlighted in Figure 9.1 if places are to be managed and marketed as holistic entities, thus ensuring the user experience is fully taken into account by the place-marketing actors responsible for individual urban places.

Non-territorial experience networks: communities of practice, value and issues

As mentioned earlier in this chapter, there is another type of community where social ties and interactions, rather than location, form the primary basis for community (although as was stated earlier, the two approaches should not be thought of as necessarily mutually exclusive, but in terms of differences in emphasis). From a customer experience perspective, we have classified these types of non-territorial communities as *communities of practice*, communities linked by *value systems* and communities arising from specific *issues*. We will consider each type in more detail below.

Communities of practice

In simple terms, we can perhaps think of communities of practice as networks linked by their behaviour. This might be particularly relevant when thinking about groups linked by work and/or professional ties. To give an example of this, we will return again to the British Library, but this time to focus on another, more specific BL user group – those supported by the organization's Business and Intellectual Property Centre (BIPC) (for further details see Baron and Warnaby 2008).

According to the 2007/08 Annual Report and Accounts, the BL's first strategic priority is to 'enrich the user's experience' (BL 2008: 16). In respect of the BIPC, the BL offers 'inspiration and support to inventors, innovators and entrepreneurs' (BL 2008: 14). The BIPC, which opened in 2006 with financial backing from the London Development Agency, was designed 'to support SMEs and entrepreneurs from that first spark of inspiration to successfully launching a business'; in this, it offers:

> a unique combination of business and IP information, including free access to more than 30 high-value subscription databases, hundreds of market research reports, and the vast resources of the UK Intellectual Property Office, including searchable databases on patents, trademarks and registered designs. (BL 2007: 2)

The aims of the centre are for its customers to be inspired, have the opportunity to network with like-minded people, get personal advice from experienced people, develop their skills and knowledge, and make good use of their time. A number of initiatives had been set in place to meet the aims, and the demand for the BIPC services had far exceeded its forecast targets since opening (detailed in BL 2007).

The profile of BIPC individual customers is different from that of the academic faculty who made up the majority of the message writers to the BL's support forum, which was mentioned in Chapter 6. Thinking back to the operant resources mentioned in this chapter – namely physical, cultural and social – then the resources available to many BIPC users differs from the more stereotypical BL user. For example, unlike academics whose cultural resources reflect regular contact with library services, many BIPC customers are unfamiliar with library usage, and require help with getting the best out of the BL facilities. Also, in contrast to the access to peers taken for granted by academics, many BIPC customers work in relative isolation, and can suffer from lack of social resources. So as to maximize the 'user experience' of this group it can be argued that the BL uses a network-oriented, many-to-many marketing type approach to increase the level of user resources so that they can better co-create value in conjunction with the BL.

Thus, the cultural operant resources of BIPC customers, such as specialized knowledge and skills (Arnould et al. 2006), are facilitated by both BL and partner (e.g. London Development Agency) resources, including:

- workshops (e.g. 'Introduction to Intellectual Property', 'How to Search' workshops on patents, trademarks, registered designs and copyright, 'How to Find' workshops on using business information to assess markets, produce plans and pinpoint customers)
- advice sessions with the 'Inventor in Residence' and other experts, offering free bespoke 'consultancy'
- a free e-course on intellectual property
- website information.

Social resources (highlighting relationships and communities) are facilitated by, for example:

- 'Inspiring Entrepreneurs' networking events and talks by famous entrepreneurs (which are also available on YouTube)
- a Facebook group
- blogs
- a monthly e-newsletter
- coaching, mentoring and 'Ideas into Action' workshops (BL 2007, 2008).

Many of the above activities could also facilitate the development of physical operant resources such as energy, emotion and strength (Arnould et al. 2006) among BIPC customers, for example by the use of successful exemplars, which could provide motivation and encouragement to individuals to persevere with what may be at times difficult and complex situations in which they find themselves as they seek to exploit their intellectual property and/or establish businesses. Indeed, the BL encourages its users to communicate their positive experiences of the BL:

> Are You a Business & IP Centre success story? Has the Business and IP Centre helped you get your idea off the ground or made a real difference to your existing business? If so, we would like to hear from you.
>
> We are looking for successful entrepreneurs and inventors to be part of our case study programme. If you qualify to be part of the programme, your story could be featured on our website, in our press coverage and in promotional material in the Centre. To apply to be a Business & IP Centre success story, visit www.bl.uk/bipc/success.html. (Promotional postcard distributed to users of the Business and Intellectual Property Centre)

This use of user case studies has been a central tenet of the BL's communications activities for some time, with much promotional literature and the institution's Annual Report and Accounts in recent years incorporating user case studies, emphasizing how user resources have been enhanced by BL facilities and services – in other words, how value has been co-created through interaction.

Values-based communities

A key criterion for the definition of non-territorial-based communities is common values/interests etc., and in the context of consumers, we can identify patterns of consumption that may be defined in this way. A term that has been used to describe such specialized communities of consumers is 'neo-tribes' – 'where members share values, lifestyles or self-images rather than demographic traits' (Weatherell et al. 2003: 234). An obvious example of this can occur with regard to the food we eat, and the term 'conscious consumer' has been used to describe those that demonstrate higher levels of concern about industrialized forms of food provisioning and greater knowledge of the socio-economic benefits of buying food that has been grown or reared locally. In recent years this 'neo-tribe' of 'conscious consumers' has become more important, and one, more overtly, experiential aspect of this has been the development and growth of farmers' markets.

Farmers' markets have been defined in various ways. However, there is a consensus as to their common characteristics:

- involving direct selling to the consumer by the person who grew, reared or pro-duced the foods
- in a common facility where the above activity is practised by numerous farmers
- who sell *local* produce, usually defined as constituting foodstuffs originating from a defined area, usually within a 30 50-mile radius of the market location (McEachern et al. 2010).

The number of farmers' markets has grown substantially in the last decade. La Trobe (2001) states that there were two farmers' markets in 1997, this figure increasing to 120 by 1999. Bentley et al. (2003) state that 250 were in existence by 2000 and FARMA (2006) estimate that there are currently over 500 such markets in the UK. Despite the potential benefits that farmers' markets can provide for the local community and economy within which they are located, the farmers themselves, and the consumers who patronize them (outlined in more detail by McEachern et al. 2010), shopping within them remains a minority activity and experience, even among those 'conscious consumers' most likely to espouse those values relating to issues relating to sustainable and ethical consumption inherent in farmers' markets. Such perceptions were investigated in a research project with which one of the authors was involved (for more details see McEachern et al. 2010).

This research identified a key task for those responsible for the management of farmers' markets as being to move consumers' perceptions of shopping at such events from being an occasional 'leisure' pursuit to a regular, ongoing shopping pattern. One means by which this could perhaps be achieved may be through better communications of the benefits of farmers' markets, but equally through the management of the farmers' market 'experience'. Indeed, farmers' markets have been thought of by McGrath et al. (1993) in terms of the servicescape, which has been defined as the built environment surrounding the service (Bitner 1992), incorporating ambience, function and design (Bitner 2000). Other research (Baker et al. 1992, 1994) has added a social dimension, in which people can shape and influence the physical space of the built environment and its impact. Indeed, the servuction system mentioned in the previous section of this chapter could be of use in terms of thinking about how an experience context could be created in which those conscious consumers (and others) could demonstrate their chosen consumption patterns.

Thus, as was mentioned above, it can be seen that the territorial and non-territorial approaches to community are not mutually exclusive. Indeed, given the fact that, by definition, they are grounded in a locale (as highlighted above) and are manifestations of 'short' food supply chains (Marsden et al. 2000), then McEachern et al. (2010) argue that farmers' markets have an obvious opportunity to capitalize upon conscious consumers' concerns relating to sustainability, and also perceptions relating to the importance of locality and community for some customers (Szmigin et al. 2003). Therefore, any marketing communications activity that farmers' markets may develop to emphasize their inherent attraction could highlight their benefits in terms of their contribution to the local economy, and in terms of fostering a sense of community within a particular locale. Indeed, given the ubiquity of multiple retailers and subsequent concerns relating to the 'cloning' of Britain's high streets (see New Economics Foundation 2004), then the potential of farmers' markets as a means to differentiate retail provision within an urban location (linking to the previous section) should not be ignored.

This focus on 'place' and community (i.e. stressing the first- and second-order connections identified in Figure 9.1) may be the most appropriate avenue for farmers' markets to try to differentiate their offering, particularly as performance on issues relating to 'ethical' consumption are increasingly highlighted by their supermarket rivals in an attempt to appeal to 'conscious' and, indeed, more general consumers, to create consumer goodwill and obtain competitive advantage. Often supermarkets focus on issues such as organic produce and Fair Trade, which may not necessarily benefit *local* producers – by emphasizing their inherent *locality* and their experiential aspects more overtly, farmers' markets may be able to secure an effective market positioning in to the future.

Issue-based communities

Another criterion which we could use to classify non-territorial communities may relate to specific issues that bind people together into communities (if only temporarily). Thus, in the context of place marketing (described earlier in this chapter) Warnaby et al. (2002, 2004) identified initiative-specific interaction, with different combinations of actors responsible for the marketing of a locality coming together for a finite period to develop specific marketing activities. This introduces an overtly temporal dimension to the concept of communities within experiential networks, where individuals and groups may collaborate to achieve a particular objective, which, once achieved may be followed by the dissolution of the community network.

A good example of this kind of community was investigated by one of the authors in relation to the campaign to save a local independent cinema in a particular district in Liverpool (for further details, see Baron and Harris 2008).

Woolton Picture House opened in 1927, and surviving downturns in cinema-going in the 1970s and 1980s, that caused the closure of many similar cinemas, the Woolton cinema began to flourish again in the 1990s. It was made famous as being the cinema frequented by John Lennon and his contemporaries in the 1960s. The lines 'I saw a film today, oh boy/The English army had just won the war' from Lennon and McCartney's 1967 'A Day in the Life' was written after Lennon had seen a film at the Woolton cinema. However, the owner's death in June 2006 led to the cinema being put up for sale, and in September 2006 the final curtain fell on the cinema.

This led to a consumer campaign led by some residents in Woolton Village to save 'their cinema', which began with a conversation between those people who ultimately became the campaign leaders in a pub in Woolton Village. The campaign started with an emotional plea to save the cinema to the audience during the interval of the final performance, of *Pirates of the Caribbean*, on 3 September 2006. Following leaflet distribution, notices in the village and a mention on Radio Merseyside, a first public meeting was held in September 2006 in the upper room of a local pub. More than three times as many people (over 150) turned up than expected to support the campaign to save the cinema. There followed a number of initiatives and activities: public meetings, leafleting, local newspapers (*Liverpool Echo* and *Liverpool Post*) and radio (Radio Merseyside), the website, continuous local awareness creation through 'leg work' (at the Woolton Farmers' Market, for example), and fundraising efforts, such as 'gigs' (featuring well-known Liverpool musicians) and 'table sales', which were also the locations for campaign-related merchandise sales (such as 'Save Woolton Cinema' T-shirts, badges and key rings).

It became clear, at a very early stage, that the campaign would not raise the money needed (£500,000) to purchase the cinema, and place the cinema in the hands of the local community, which had been an early aspiration. Also, it was decided that it was not really feasible to prepare a funding application to forward to bodies such as the Arts Council to subsidize the cinema. The eventual purchase of the cinema, on 20 February 2007, by a consortium of south Liverpool businessmen, dedicated to getting the cinema business back up-and-running, represented the culmination of myriad consumer and co-consumer efforts to prevent the site and building from being purchased for non-cinema-based-property development. Baron and Harris (2008), in their reporting of the detail of the campaign, emphasize the use of consumer capabilities and resource integration by a network of individuals, collectively motivated by the desire of the organizers of the campaign to continue what they considered to be the authentic cinematic experience, and which was 'bought into' by many within the local community.

Conclusion

This chapter has looked at the concept of 'community' in relation to the consumer experience, recognizing that because of the social resources (Arnould et al. 2006) available to consumers, they can – and do – act collectively within what we have termed 'experiential networks'. We have looked at different ways in which to think about communities in this context, using the distinction between territorial and non-territorial approaches to conceptualizing community (Azarya, 1996) and have identified a number of different examples of how communities might be classified from a consumer experience perspective, using case studies drawn from research projects with which the authors have been involved. A key question that we need to consider is *how* such communities are created and maintained (especially those classified in terms of non-territorial bases, where members of the communities may be widely dispersed). One dimension of this, which has been alluded to in this and earlier chapters, is the role of information technology, and the next chapter considers this in more detail.

Learning propositions

- Consumers are often 'social' creatures and exist (and act, individually or collectively) within various patterns of relationships, which can be termed 'experiential networks'.
- These experiential networks can be classified according to territorial and non-territorial criteria.
- Non-territorial experience networks can be further subdivided into communities of practice, values-based communities and issue-based communities.

Activities and discussion questions

- In relation to your own consumption behaviour, can you identify any 'experience networks' of which you are a member?
- How is your consumption behaviour affected by these 'experience networks'?

References

Arnould, E.J., Price L.L. and Malshe, A. (2006) 'Toward a Cultural Resource-Based Theory of the Customer', in R.F. Lusch and S.L. Vargo (eds), *The Service-Dominant Logic of Marketing: Dialog, Debate and Directions*, Armonk, NY: M.E. Sharpe; 320–333.

Ashworth, G. (1993) 'Marketing of Places: What are we Doing?', in G. Ave and F. Corsico (eds), *Urban Marketing in Europe*, Turin: Torino Incontra; 643–649.

Ashworth, G.J. and Voogd, H. (1990a) *Selling the City*, London: Belhaven.

Ashworth, G.J. and Voogd, H. (1990b) 'Can Places be Sold for Tourism?', in G. Ashworth and B. Goodall (eds), *Marketing Tourism Places*, London: Routledge; 1–16.

Azarya, V. (1996) 'Community', in A. Kuper and J. Kuper (eds), *The Social Science Encyclopedia* (2nd edition), London and New York: Routledge; 114–115.

Badot, O. and Filser, M. (2007) 'Re-enchantment of Retailing – Toward Utopian Islands', in A. Caru and B. Cova (eds) *Consuming Experience*, London and New York: Routledge; 166–181.

Baker, J., Levy, M. and Grewal, D. (1992) 'An Experimental Approach to Making Retail Store Environment Decisions', *Journal of Retailing*, 68(4): 445–460.

Baker, J., Grewal, D. and Parasuraman, A. (1994) 'The Influence of Store Environment on Quality Inferences and Store Image', *Journal of the Academy of Marketing Science*, 22(4): 328–333.

Baron, S. and Harris, K. (2008) 'Consumers as Resource Integrators', *Journal of Marketing Management*, 24(1–2): 113–130.

Baron, S. and Warnaby, G. (2008) 'Individual Customers Use and Integration of Resources: Empirical Findings and Organizational Implications in the Context of Value Co-creation', paper presented at The Otago Forum 2: The Service-Dominant Logic of Marketing: From Propositions to Practice, Otago.

Bentley, G., Hallsworth, A.G. and Bryan, A. (2003) 'The Countryside in the City – Situating a Farmers' Market in Birmingham', *Local Economy*, 18(2): 109–120.

Bitner, M.J. (1992) 'Servicescapes: The Impact of Physical Surroundings on Customers and Employees', *Journal of Marketing*, 56(April): 57–71.

Bitner, M.J. (2000) 'The Servicescape', in T.A. Swartz and D. Iaccobucci (eds), *Handbook of Services Marketing and Management*, Thousand Oaks, CA: Sage; 37–50.

British Council of Shopping Centres (BCSC) (2007) *Future of Retail Property: Future Shopping Places*, London: British Council of Shopping Centres.

British Library (2007) British Library Business & IP Centre: A Capital Resource for Enterprise and Innovation, London: British Library.

British Library (2008) *Annual Report and Accounts 2007/08*, Norwich: TSO (The Stationery Office).

Corsico, F. (1993) 'Urban Marketing, a Tool for Cities and Business Enterprises, a Condition for Property Development, a Challenge for Urban Planning', in G. Ave and F. Corsico (eds), *Urban Marketing in Europe*, Turin: Torino Incontra; 75–88.

FARMA (2006) 'What is a Farmers' Market?' available at www.farmersmarkets. net.home.htm (accessed 28 September 2006).

Forsberg, H., Medway, D. and Warnaby, G. (1999) 'Town Centre Management by Co-operation: Evidence from Sweden', *Cities*, 16(5): 315–322.

Gummesson, E. (2006) 'Many-to-many Marketing as Grand Theory: A Nordic School Contribution', in R.F. Lusch and S.L. Vargo (eds), *The Service-Dominant Logic of Marketing: Dialog, Debate, and Directions*, Armonk NY and London: M.E. Sharpe; 339–353.

Iacobucci, D. (ed.) (1996) *Networks in Marketing*, Thousand Oaks, CA: Sage Publications.

Kotler, P., Asplund, C., Rein, I. and Haider, D. (1999) *Marketing Places Europe: Attracting Investments, Industries, and Visitors to European Cities, Communities, Regions and Nations*, Harlow: Financial Times/Prentice Hall.

Langeard, E., Bateson, J., Lovelock, C. and Eiglier, P. (1981) *Marketing of Services: New Insights from Consumers and Managers*, Report no. 81–104. Cambridge, MA: Marketing Sciences Institute.

La Trobe, H. (2001) 'Farmers' Markets: Consuming Local Rural Produce', *International Journal of Consumer Studies*, 25(3): 181–192.

Marsden, T., Banks, J. and Bristow, G. (2000) 'Food Supply Chain Approaches: Exploring their Role in Rural Development', *Sociologica Ruralis*, 40(4): 424–439.

McEachern, M., Warnaby, G., Carrigan, M. and Szmigin, I. (2010) 'Thinking Locally, Acting Locally?: Conscious Consumers and Farmers' Markets', *Journal of Marketing Management* (in press).

McGrath, M.A., Sherry, J.F. and Heisley, D.D. (1993) 'An Ethnographic Study of an Urban Periodic Marketplace: Lessons from the Midvale Farmers' Market', *Journal of Retailing*, 69(3): 280–319.

New Economics Foundation (2004) *Clone Town Britain: The Loss of Identity on the Nation's High Streets*, London: New Economics Foundation.

Short, J.R. and Kim, Y.H. (1999) *Globalisation and the City*, Harlow: Longman.

Sleipen, W. (1988) *Marketing van de Historische Omgeving*. Breda: Netherlands Research Institute for Tourism. Cited in G.J. Ashworth and H.Voogd (1990a) *Selling the City*, London: Belhaven.

Szmigin, I., Maddock, S. and Carrigan, M. (2003) 'Conceptualising Community Consumption: Farmers' Markets and the Older Customer', *British Food Journal*, 105(8): 542–550.

Stubbs, B., Warnaby, G. and Medway, D. (2002) 'Marketing at the Public/Private Sector Interface: Town Centre Management Schemes in the South of England', *Cities*, 19(5): 317–326.

Turok, I. (2009) 'The Distinctive City: Pitfalls in the Pursuit of Differential Advantage', *Environment and Planning A*, 41(1): 13–30.

Van den Berg, L. and Braun, E. (1999) 'Urban Competitiveness, Marketing and the Need for Organising Capacity', *Urban Studies*, 36(5–6): 987–999.

Vargo, S.L. and Lusch, R.F. (2008) 'Service-Dominant Logic: Continuing the Evolution', *Journal of the Academy of Marketing Science*, 36(1): 1–10.

Ward, S.V. (1998) *Selling Places: The Marketing and Promotion of Towns and Cities 1850–2000*, London: E. & F.N. Spon.

Warnaby, G. (2009) 'Managing the Urban Consumption Experience?', *Local Economy*, 24(2): 105–110.

Warnaby, G. and Davies, B.J. (1997) 'Commentary: Cities as Service Factories? Using the Servuction System for Marketing Cities as Shopping Destinations', *International Journal of Retail & Distribution Management*, 25(6): 204–210.

Warnaby, G., Alexander, A. and Medway, D. (1998) 'Town Centre Management in the UK: A Review, Synthesis and Research Agenda', *International Review of Retail, Distribution and Consumer Research*, 8(1): 15–31.

Warnaby, G., Bennison, D., Davies, B.J. and Hughes, H. (2002) 'Marketing UK Towns and Cities as Shopping Destinations', *Journal of Marketing Management*, 18(9–10): 877–904.

Warnaby, G., Bennison, D., Davies, B.J. and Hughes, H. (2004) 'People and Partnerships: Marketing Urban Retailing', *International Journal of Retail & Distribution Management*, 32(11): 545–556.

Warnaby, G., Bennison, D. and Davies, B.J. (2005a) 'Retailing and the Marketing of Urban Places: A UK Perspective', *International Review of Retail, Distribution and Consumer Research*, 15(2): 191–215.

Warnaby, G., Bennison, D. and Davies, B.J. (2005b) 'Marketing Town Centres: Retailing and Town Centre Management', *Local Economy*, 20(2): 183–204.

Weatherell, C., Tregear, A. and Allinson, J. (2003) 'In Search of the Concerned Customer: UK Public Perceptions of Food, Farming and Buying Local', *Journal of Rural Studies*, 19: 233–244.

10 Social Networks: C2C Exchanges and Relationships

Learning objectives

- To demonstrate the importance of social network sites in twenty-first century communication networks.
- To explore and identify the reasons for the popularity of social network websites.
- To catalogue the main uses of social network sites by individuals.
- To gauge the opportunities and pitfalls associated with organizations' engagements with social network sites.

Introduction

In Chapters 7 and 8, through the application of consumer experience modelling (CEM), we have advocated an increased focus on C2C interactions as part of relationship networks. As Gummesson observes, 'C2C interaction and the customers' role in both the value proposition and value actualisation is a growing area for research and practical applications' (2007: 11). Physical, face-to-face C2C interactions have been researched (see, for example, Nicholls (2005)), but have not had as much attention from services and relationship marketing management, as have interactions between customers and service employees, or between customers and the physical service settings (servicescapes). To quote Gummesson again, 'Unfortunately, the providers may not see the contribution of [C2C] involvement and fail to support it' (2007: 16). However, the widespread adoption of mobile technology and the internet by consumers has meant that ICT-mediated C2C interactions complement, and add to the face-to-face C2C interactions, and, as with the British Library example in Chapter 6, can have important network effects and implications for organizations.

In particular, the *social network website* is a twenty-first century phenomenon which has changed the interactions, relationships and networks landscapes, through the increased opportunities for C2C interactions. For example, according to eMarketer (www.emarketer.com), 15.4 million (39 per cent) of UK internet users interacted by using a social network once a month in 2009, and it is estimated that the figure will rise to 21.9 million (50 per cent) by 2013. On a global scale, the CNET News social networks rankings in February 2009 showed that the three most popular sites had monthly visits as follows: Facebook, almost 1.2 billion; MySpace, over 800 million; Twitter, over 50 million. YouTube statistics show that 78.3 million videos were uploaded in March 2008. The use of social networks is widely believed to be driven by younger people. It has been said that Generation Y (people born between the early 1980s and late 1990s) 'has always had the computer in their lives. They know nothing of life before Google and conduct their social lives differently to any other generation thanks to MySpace and Facebook' (Anonymous 2009).

Of course, the sheer numbers involved with social networks, and its growth, has not gone unnoticed by organizations that see commercial possibilities and opportunities (Jones 2007; Foster 2008). For example, Brottlund (2009) identifies many companies, including Absolut Vodka, Adidas, American Express, Boeing, Coca-Cola, Dell, Motorola, Pizza Hut, Southwest Airlines and Starbucks, that use social networking as a means of boosting sales. It has also spawned a crop of business 'how-to' books: e.g. *Facebook Marketing* (Holzner 2009) ('Leveraging social media to grow your business'); *YouTube for Business* (Miller 2009) ('All types of businesses are getting into the YouTube scene: local businesses, major national marketers, ad agencies, real estate agencies, consultants …'); *Twitter Power* (Comm 2009) ('The goal of using Twitter is to build relationships – especially relationships that can benefit your company').

In this chapter, therefore, we explore the reasons for the growth of social networks, how they are used and managed by consumers, and the potential for organizations to address this phenomenon in their relationship marketing activities and strategies. First, however, we define and look briefly at the history and development of social network websites.

Definition and history of social network sites

A useful definition of social network sites is offered by boyd and Ellison (2007: 2).

They are web-based services that allow individuals to:

1   construct a public or semi-public profile within a bounded system
2   articulate a list of other users with whom they share a connection
3   view and traverse their list of connections and those made by others within the system.

They also point out strongly that social network sites are not normally used by individuals for the purpose of meeting strangers, but are used mainly to communicate with people who are already part of an extended social network.

The first social network site was created in 1997, but the most popular three sites at the time of writing were created later; MySpace in 2003, Facebook (for everyone to use) in 2006 and Twitter in 2006 (boyd and Ellison 2007). As is seen above, these three sites have, between them, over 2 billion visits per month. The features of the sites vary. In this chapter we focus mainly on Facebook, the most popular social network website at the time of writing.

Facebook began as an electronic version of a college-student yearbook at Harvard University. College-student yearbooks were usually created so that freshmen (first-year students) could know something about the fellow students in their year: their backgrounds, hobbies, skills, likes, dislikes, etc., accompanied by a photograph. Many colleges and universities handed out hard-copy yearbooks after the first week of attendance, once the students had provided the appropriate information. An electronic version of the yearbook, however, came with additional facilities for the students to chat, and swap emails, and so a social network was created through the website. Initially, it was available only to Harvard University students. Then it was expanded to other colleges, high schools (in 2005), and ultimately to anyone aged 13 or over, in 2006. Even before it became available to everyone, commentators were appreciating its importance. Raskin, for example, observed that 'Stories abound about how everyone from marketers, to job recruiters, to college admissions counsellors, to teachers and even law enforcement are using Facebook to see what students are doing' (2006: 57). With wider participation since 2006, organizations are looking at building applications into Facebook that can be spread by viral networking (Dobele et al. 2007; Ferguson 2008; Foster 2008).

Consumer experiences with Facebook

In keeping with this book's focus on consumer experiences, we now present two accounts, written by Facebook users. Through the accounts, we can see how the features of Facebook may be used.

The first account is written by Phil, who is 31 years of age, and works as an information provider for financial advisers. He has a Bachelor's Degree in Politics and a postgraduate qualification in journalism. He lives in the northwest of England. The second account is written by Pooja, aged 25, who is from India, but is currently working as a freelance marketing researcher in England. She successfully completed her MBA in the UK 18 months ago.

Phil's Account

I first became aware of Facebook about two years ago when I started to receive email 'invitations' to join it, mostly from former colleagues and university friends. I had never been one for embracing new internet fads but in this case I decided to give it a go, mainly because it was recommended to me by people who would normally be equally sceptical of such websites.

Once I'd bitten the bullet my initial reaction was a mixture of being slightly disconcerted and feeling flattered; within literally a few hours of signing up I received several 'friend' requests from people I had lost touch with several years before. A large number of these were people who I was friendly with but who I had not necessarily socialized with in the past, and therefore had never swapped mobile numbers and email addresses. I suppose the word I'm looking for is 'acquaintance', rather than 'friend' but I found Facebook to be an invaluable means of breaking down social barriers to establish contact with a wider social circle (on the basis that you need a plausible reason to ask for someone's mobile phone number, whereas you can send a casual message on Facebook because 'Facebook is not a big deal and everyone uses it').

In terms of the several applications that can be used on Facebook, I pretty much disregard all of them and just use it primarily for communication purposes and occasionally to share my thoughts with the world via what I (optimistically) think to be amusing status updates. Every time I log-in, someone I barely know from school or a previous job has sent me (well, me and everyone else in their friend list) a 'challenge' about my movie knowledge, or knowledge of 80s TV shows. All are ignored, as are various childish and pointless vampire/werewolf attacks.

I think it's fair to say that I have a love–hate relationship with Facebook these days. Part of me hates the exhibitionism of it all, and the fact that some people feel equally as comfortable sharing with the world the contents of the sandwich they have just eaten as they do their latest relationship break-up. I am also wary of pictures of me in a 'tired and emotional state' appearing on there and being seen by people who, pre-Facebook, would never have been privy to such snapshots into my life.

A friend got it right by not signing up, and instead relying on his girlfriend to keep him informed of our social circle via her own account; so he basically got all the benefits, without having to put up with all the irritation. But, as surely as night follows day, he gave in and, as of this weekend, became friend number 223 ...

Pooja's Account

The most important feature of Facebook (FB) is that it offers me privacy. I can have complete control of my account in terms of adding friends, and sharing photos with the people on my friends list. Also if I want to send any information which I don't want others to read, instead of writing on the wall, I can click and send messages.

It also gives me a platform to interact with my old school/college/university friends. It is where I can be in touch with them all the time. For example, when we write our latest updates (on the 'What is on your mind' feature), friends respond, which makes it very interactive, and gives me a clue about their latest events in life. It is fun and entertaining to have an account because there may be some event/party/get-together in town coming up, and an invitation is sent out to friends through FB.

Sometimes I may not really check any sort of news, or current updates, but my friends might update news related status messages, and hence I may find out about the news much quicker then I would have, and can follow up later.

I also use FB for building up new contacts which might be helpful for professional and personal reasons. I think it is good that you can have your own page where you would want to create your own community or promote any company, TV show, idea, etc., and ask people to join as fans. FB is amazing to use because I do not need to remember individual email addresses. It is really addictive. Once you have an account you wouldn't dare to delete!

I access FB at least 2–3 times in a day. Usually, when logged on, I am on FB for a minimum of 10–15 minutes each time. The facilities I use are photo album upload, and tabs to leave messages on any sorts of updates, birthday applications, personality quiz applications, or news updates. I choose friends when the invitation is sent out by a person to accept me as a friend. Also there is a tab on the homepage which states people you may know, and common friends are listed, so I can send an invite. Finally, on top there is a search tab and you can enter name of the person you are looking for and add as a friend (friend finder tool).

I have the following companies as friends: GIEU (University of Liverpool); The University of Liverpool – Alumni Relations; Jai Hind College; Hindu Student Forum – Liverpool. I am a 'fan' of Rani Mukherjee (Actress), the Simpsons, Bombay, Ek cutting chai (Indian Tea), Susan Boyle (*Britain's Got Talent*), and The Ali Khan Brothers (Musicians).

Some really interesting recent news was on 'Earth Hour' – spreading the message to save energy. People updated their status on FB to inform others that they would participate in such an event. Hence, people who were originally unaware of such an event did read about it in detail, and it was interesting to find out that the participation level of the people who turned off their lights after 8.30–9.30 was really massive.

I also use other social sites: Orkut and LinkedIn.

Nature of the C2C exchanges

Survey research, undertaken by Ellison et al. (2007) and Joinson (2008) has focused on Facebook user practices, benefits and motivations.

Ellison et al. (2007), in a survey of 286 Michigan State University undergraduates (of which 94 per cent were Facebook users), found that the users would spend between a mean of 10–30 minutes per day on Facebook, with the most frequently cited number of 'friends' as being between 150–200. There was a significantly higher Facebook usage involving friends that they already knew offline than those involving meeting new people. Ellison et al. affirm that 'Our participants overwhelmingly used Facebook to keep in touch with old friends and to maintain or intensify relationships characterised by some form of offline connection ...' (2007: 18).

Joinson (2008), in two surveys of general Facebook users (not just students), confirmed these findings, drawing a distinction between the more frequent 'social searching' usage of Facebook (finding out information about existing offline contacts) and less frequent 'social browsing' usage of Facebook (developing new connections with the possibility of subsequent offline interaction). He also identified two forms of activities related to 'keeping in touch'. The first is surveillance; keeping a check on what old contacts are currently doing, how they are behaving and what they look like. The second is social capital building gratification associated with being able to '... build, invest in and maintain ties with distant friends and contacts'.

The personal accounts by Phil and Pooja tend to support the findings of these surveys, and acknowledge the addictive nature of Facebook. Two immediate problems arise when organizations or companies contemplate entering the Facebook interactions. They may not be considered as offline 'friends' and their contributions, if considered irritating by the majority of Facebook users, may result in a great amount of negative word-of-mouth. Let us look now at the possibilities for organizations to provide messages that encourage positive C2C interactions between Facebook users.

C2C interactions and relationships

The following quotation from Professor Glenn Reynolds of the University of Tennessee, in Cook and Hopkins, demonstrates the importance of C2C interactions for relationship building in the twenty-first century.

> The Internet is a powerful tool. But most attention seems to focus on its use as a means of vertical communications: from one to many.
> ... But as important as this is – and it's very important indeed – it's probably dwarfed by the much more numerous horizontal communications that the Internet, and related technologies like cell phones, text message and the like permit. They allow a kind of horizontal knowledge that is often less obvious, but in many ways at least as powerful, as the vertical kind.
> Horizontal knowledge is communication amongst individuals, who may or may not know each other, but who are loosely coordinated by their involvement with something, or someone, of mutual interest. And it's extremely powerful, because it makes people much smarter. (2008: iii)

The proof of the pudding ...

In the course of gathering information for this book, Steve Baron asked a work colleague, who is a Facebook user, to post the following message to a restricted list of 'friends', including ex- and present students at the University of Liverpool.

> My colleague, Steve Baron, is writing a chapter on social network sites in a book on Relationship Marketing. If you know of any *organizations or companies* (including the one you work for) that have a Facebook or MySpace page, can you let me know, and I'll forward to Steve. Please pass on this message to anyone else you know who may be able to help.

Of course, this is not the same as communicating with people via a Facebook page, but it acts as a pointer to the reach of a social network. The response was interesting. On the positive side, within five hours, there had been two very interesting leads, and one enquiry for clarification. The leads related to a small firm in Northern Ireland, 'Suki Tea', which had used Facebook to win a contract in China, and to an agency that uses Facebook to find people for last-minute jobs and to publish photos of big events. Also, an email to Steve's colleague, as a follow-up to the Facebook message, provided a web address, www.insidefacebook.com, that lists companies that have a Facebook page.

On following up on Suki Tea, it transpired that the contract that was won was in Japan. According to Siliconrepublic.com, Ireland's technology news service, 6 May 2009, 'Belfast start-up Suki Tea Company has won a major contract to supply gourmet teas to a leading tea house in Tokyo, after a recommendation was posted via Facebook ... it has created a unique and highly successful website, which it is using very cleverly and effectively to build an appealing personality for the business in this era of social networking online'. Suki Tea Facebook was launched on 9 October, 2008.

It is fair to say that we, as authors, may have become 'smarter' as a result of this exposure to Facebook possibilities. However, on the negative side, the message impact was both short-lived – no responses beyond the first five hours – and seemingly uninspiring, in that it generated only three responses from over 70 recipients.

What can and should organizations do?

According to Li, 'Most marketers salivate at the tremendous reach of social networking sites like MySpace and Facebook' (2007: 2). While this might not be a pretty image, it reflects the view that there are rich pickings to be had for those organizations that embrace appropriately the C2C phenomenon that is supported by social network sites. The key word is 'appropriately' because costly mistakes can be made through organizations unthinkingly invading what consumers regard as their own space. The name 'MySpace' is not only a brand name, but also a clear signal. So how can, and should, private and public organizations reap benefits from the social network happenings?

We look at some published accounts of organizational involvement with social network sites, and examine what appear to be the lessons to be learnt.

Unilever and the co-creation experience

Needham (2008) provides an example of how Unilever engaged with the social network site Headbox, used mainly by 16–25-year-olds, to co-create value with young people and also generate positive word-of-mouth.

Applying the mantra of marketing *with* young people, rather than marketing *to* them (a feature of the S-D logic of marketing), Unilever identified 'youth advocates' through Headbox. They are the ones who regularly write blogs and have brands as friends on their profile pages. They are acknowledged as creative with a high social standing amongst friends. The idea is to co-create value with these consumers, through involving them with the design and launching of new Unilever products. A trial of these ideas involved taking 18 Headbox youth advocates to Alicante in Spain for three days to talk through their own product ideas and designs, as well as suggestions as how they might be marketed to their peers. This was followed up with presentations in London to senior Unilever executives.

According to Needham: 'After the Alicante project our 18 Headboxers enthused for days on their Facebook pages about how brilliant their Unilever experience had been. The combined number of friends who would have read or engaged with these exchanges was over 10,000.'

Libraries and their users

We have seen, through the British Library context in Chapter 6, that library users have social networks. Recognition of this has stimulated library managers to consider engaging with social network sites. Alcock (2009) has chronicled the findings of a pilot study of the experience of the University of Wolverhampton in the UK of using Facebook to reach the library users. Recognizing that many of their students use Facebook to communicate with their fellow students and to organize group working within their various courses, and that academic staff were beginning to use Facebook as a forum for social interaction with students, the library staff at the University of Wolverhampton piloted a project aimed at creating a Facebook page for its Learning Centres.

They had two main concerns with engaging with Facebook. First, they did not want to be seen to be invading the students' private and personal space. By setting up a Facebook page, rather than a profile, they ensured that they would communicate only with students who designated themselves as 'fans' of the page, and that students could control who sees their profiles.

Second, they were worried that Facebook would be used primarily to feed back moans and groans about the library service, and that there may be some inappropriate comments by students for all to see. In the event, this concern proved not to be a problem. The pilot was generally successful with Learning Centre updates being gratefully received by over 200 fans, and feedback largely positive.

On a national scale, the British Library has been piloting the use of social network sites to create greater awareness of its Business and Intellectual Property Centre (BIPC) which offers services to inventors, entrepreneurs and small business owners (Infield 2009). The BIPC team chose Facebook as its preferred site, knowing that it is populated by large numbers of graduates and professionals. The British Library Entrepreneur and SME network page on Facebook quickly attracted fans/members, and the BIPC team decided that, once the membership reached 1,000 (which they achieved within six months), they would invite the members to a 'real' face-to-face networking event at the British Library. They were very pleased that over 70 people turned up. The event was videoed, and, together with successful entrepreneur stories, was placed on YouTube on a BIPC-dedicated YouTube channel. The channel captured just below 8,500 views in three months. The BIPC is now experimenting with Twitter, the fastest growing social network site at the time of writing.

Ernst and young employee hiring

Ernst and Young (EY) has a page on Facebook dealing exclusively with careers. EY hires over 5,000 US college students each year for internships and entry-level career opportunities. On the page, EY has acquired over 28,000 fans, at the time of writing, who contribute information and frequent the discussion board. The move to create and maintain the page incurs costs: fee to Facebook, staff costs to maintain the page and respond quickly to students who contact them via the page, and potential intangible costs of negative views attracting a wide audience.

Nevertheless, it has been viewed as a success, creating contacts between students, graduates, EY staff and campus recruiters across North America. It has also attracted other business people who are seeking advice on how to set up Facebook pages of a similar kind.

Non-profit organizations and Facebook

Waters et al. (2009) carried out a study of the use of Facebook by not-for-profit (NFP) organizations in sectors such as arts, education, health and religion, in order to examine how the NFP organizations 'can engage their stakeholders and foster relationship growth' (Waters et al. 2009: 102). They looked at a sample of over 200 such organizations and categorized their Facebook usage according to three criteria:

- organizational disclosure: level of description, history, listed administrators, etc. included on the page
- information dissemination: news links, posted photographs, discussion wall, press releases, etc.
- involvement: facilities for interaction, e.g. email addresses/phone numbers, calendar of events, volunteer opportunities.

The study concluded that most pages scored reasonably highly on organizational disclosure, but failed to take advantage of involvement in terms of the interactive nature of social networking. In the language of the S-D logic of marketing, facilities for co-creation of value with members was missing from the pages. The authors of the study pointed out opportunities, currently not being offered, for videos and photographs from volunteers to be encouraged especially if the NFP organization lacks resources and equipment. Additionally, volunteers may be able to ensure that daily maintenance is given to the page, as it appears, from the sample survey, that most NFPs 'lack the resources and time to provide constant attention to a Facebook page', and 'creating a profile and abandoning it ... could turn off potential supporters if they witness inactivity on the site' (Waters et al. 2009: 105).

Tapping in on customer creativity

In May 2009, WD-40 started its own social network – The Money-Saving Tool community. Most of us may be able to recall squirting the car lubricant WD-40 onto wet car-battery leads or onto squeaky wheels, and being encouraged to try WD-40 to cure many car ailments as a first-try.

The social network site has the tagline 'Join The Money Saving Tool community and share your money-saving stories, photos and videos'. The first 40 submissions received a WD-40 value pack as a prize. According to the website BrandFreak.com, 'At this budding Peyton Place of cyberspace, members are encouraged to share money-saving tips and tricks – through stories, photos, videos, what have you – to show the creative ways they protect their investments and avoid paying for expensive repairs or replacement goods'.

By mid-May 2009 there were over 2,000 different uses of WD-40 offered by customers, many of which cannot be repeated here.

Bringing it all together

Interactions and relationships between and amongst individuals, or individual consumers, have been relatively under-explored in traditional relationship marketing discourse, despite the greater recognition of the importance of C2C interactions as emphasized in this book.

Social network websites are a twenty-first century phenomenon. They are extremely popular as shown by the usage statistics on Facebook, MySpace, Twitter and YouTube quoted earlier. Their popularity and potential has attracted many organizations and companies to create Facebook pages or profiles. According to InsideFacebook.com, by May 2009, there were 21,655 companies on Facebook. The previous section gave a snapshot of Facebook activities of a very small minority of these organizations. Additional insights can be gleaned from Exhibit 10.1 which shows the benefits that Brazen PR, a public relations company in Manchester, see from using Facebook and Twitter (see http://www.brazen-world.com/).

Exhibit 10.1   Brazen PR's use of social network sites, according to the owner, Nina Webb

Why create a Facebook page?

As one of the country's top PR consultancies, it is paramount that we demonstrate our communication abilities: it's the bread and butter of what we do. With today's modern marketer tuned into the advantages and importance of social networking, what example are we setting to perspective clients if we, as a business, have no online presence? At Brazen we use a number of social networks but chose Facebook because of its mass audience and interaction capabilities. We see our profile as a passport into our world, where people can experience our environment and interact directly with our Brazen citizens (employees). Brazen is more than just a PR consultancy, it is a living organization, and we really wanted to bring our unique culture alive.

What is your experience? Good or bad?

The Brazen Facebook profile has been of benefit to the overall Brazen brand. We don't have thousands upon thousands of friends, but that is because we have a niche appeal: only those who want to know us more personally will befriend us and it's more about quality than quantity. In essence, our Facebook profile serves its purpose well. It's a domain where we can quickly and easily upload a snapshot of our world or share a news broadcast, and Facebook allows us to do just that.

How important is it to you?

As the communication experts that we are, it is vital that we illustrate our professional skills and qualities. The Marketing and PR industry is no longer just about print, broadcast and word of mouth, but also digital which is revolutionizing the way we work. As a relatively new medium, we are all pioneers shaping the way that business is conducted within the future and to be blunt, if

(Cont'd)

---

you're not already beating the online drum, you're going to get left behind. This is what clients expect as a standard service and if we're not seen to be involved within social networks, it really doesn't instill confidence of our own abilities. For that kudos alone, our Facebook profile is not important, but imperative.

Who are your friends?

Our friends vary, but each has a vested interest within Brazen and what we do. Along with all our citizens, we have a mixture of people from ex-citizens who want to keep tabs on what's happening in Brazen world, journalists and editors who are on the hunt for a story, and even suppliers such as photographers who are scouting for business. We encourage clients to join, as we see them as much a part of Brazen World as our citizens.

How do you maintain/update the page?

Status updates are linked directly via our other social medium, Twitter. Essentially this kills two birds with one stone, and we aim to update our status at least three times a day. To keep it fresh, we also encourage all of our citizens to suggest status updates. This could be amazing coverage, interesting articles relating to our industry, or even generic banter. The profile really does update naturally and that's because it's fun – our world is fun and we want everyone else to join in.

How does it complement other forms of networking?

The secret is don't just choose one social network, but don't choose them all either. Research what is available and select which formats most complement your business or aim. For example, we were originally planning to create a Brazen MySpace page but chose not to due to it being primarily used by creative individuals such as musicians and artists. Social networking takes a lot of time and effort, so only use what is essential and, if you are going to do it, make sure you stick at it! In terms of what complements Facebook the best, we also utilise Twitter and find it's the perfect match. Summarizing, both are very similar in terms of method and establishing networks but, at the same time, operate from opposite ends of the table which actually plays to our advantage. The best way to describe this; Facebook is for people you used to know, while Twitter is for those you want to know. In reference to business, it keeps your friends close, and your future clients closer.

Our message throughout the book has been to examine interactions from a consumer experience perspective to gain insights into the interactions, relationships and networks that contribute to well-being and quality-of-life. Research into online social networking affords great opportunities to learn more of these aspects. The published research into Facebook usage, supported by some short, introspective personal accounts, suggests strongly that individuals use Facebook to communicate with people with whom they have, or have had an offline relationship. Online communication with strangers, whether they are individuals or organizations, is engaged in far less frequently. Topics of the conversations appear to be gossip-related and recent news-related, possibly coupled with topical-knowledge quizzes, photographs, details of upcoming events, or video links. More 'heavyweight' topics, such as Steve's attempt to gain links to social networking usage by companies, are likely to gain very few responses, and may be of interest only over a very short time-span. A picture emerges of a 'typical individual' spending up to 30 minutes per day on Facebook, communicating with any of about 200 'friends'. It is predicted that half of UK internet users will log on to online social network sites by 2013. Taking a wider view of social networks, it is highly probable that, by 2013, almost all UK citizens will know personally someone (friend, family member) who participates an online social network site, even if they, themselves, do not.

Despite the closeness of the individual relationships on Facebook, some organizations and companies do seem to have developed effective pages, and created devoted fans. In these cases, working with an aim of value co-creation with customers is proving to be a successful strategy. How? Two tentative suggestions are offered.

First, it appears that successful company Facebook pages facilitate activities in which consumers are already engaged, rather than making overt sales propositions. For example, the Ernst and Young careers/internship page makes it easier for prospective employees/interns to contact the company, other people in the same position and college recruiters, and the University of Wolverhampton Resource Centre website makes information gathering and communication for group working more efficient. 'Suki Tea' communicate with, and provide information for, consumers seeking fair-trade products. However, such uses of Facebook pages require constant maintenance by the sponsoring organization, because once the facilitation, through updates and responses, falters, the customers can easily lose interest as seems to be the case with some of the not-for-profit organizations.

Second, where the organizational page actively encourages users to be active and/or creative, there is likely to be a greater response, as with the Unilever example. The WD-40 social network site is also a good example. Community members have sent in stories of novel uses of WD-40, often accompanied by short videos, which, in turn, has encouraged more members to be more inventive, with better videos, etc. Such are the features of the more effective viral marketing and consumer campaigns (such as saving energy). What is not known is the lifetime of such initiatives, the maintenance costs and the possibility of the tarnishing of a brand image if the members go 'over the top' with their responses. Indeed, it has been noted that some large companies, including Vodafone, First Direct and AA, have removed pages from online social network sites because of their brand being juxtaposed with material from extreme political organizations (Anonymous 2008).

Finally, we should note that there may be some serious ethical issues associated with social networks, especially related to the potentially addictive behaviours that are resulting. According to Kunz and Liu (2009), the social network sites could lead to harmful outcomes for addictive customers: those who invest a great deal of time on social networks, possess motives to reinforce their behaviour and experience withdrawal symptoms should they ever be prevented access. Their preliminary findings suggest that the main influences on addiction are arousal (a consumption emotion), entertainment (a consumption motivation) and extraversion (a consumer personality trait). Kunz and Liu plea for more research aimed at preventing 'harmful experiences from excessive usage of [social network] sites', and suggest that 'it would be interesting to compare different online business models regarding their addictive potential for the consumer' (2009: 6).

There is, in our view, an opportunity for some very interesting further research into the whole domain of social network sites – research that explores the life-world of consumers. This may involve the development of marketing research ideas and methods that follow from the premises of the S-D logic of marketing. In Chapter 11, we explore the possibilities.

Learning propositions

- Social network sites are mainly used to maintain relationships with existing (offline) friends.
- Social network sites demonstrate extensive networks that individuals possess.
- Organizations have mixed success when engaging with social network sites: they may reap benefits by either facilitating activities with which consumers are already engaged, and/or by encouraging active participation on behalf of network users.
- C2C interactions, through social network sites will (a) increase and (b) increase in importance for organizations.

Activities

- Politicians' social network usage:

  It was generally agreed that Barack Obama's use of social network sites, such as YouTube, had been successful as part of his presidential campaign (see case study, Chapter 1). Conversely, Gordon Brown's attempt at using YouTube was not well received (see, for example, *The Times* report of 6 May 2009, 'Gordon Brown's YouTube fightback', and subsequent news reports on the same topic). How would you explain the apparent differences in the outcomes of YouTube engagement between Barack Obama and Gordon Brown?

- Your own social network:

  Calculate the size of your own personal network as follows: Start with your number of friends on Facebook or MySpace (say, 200). Assume that half of the friends of each of their friends are your friends also (leaving, say, 100 new friends each). Then your 'friends of friends' network consists of $200 \times 100 = 20,000$ people. Repeat this for six degrees of separation. How many people are in this network?

- Possibilities for your own organization:

  Investigate how your organization is, or could be part of a social network site.

References

Alcock, J. (2009) *Using Facebook Pages to Reach Users: the Experience of University of Wolverhampton*, http://www.wlv.ac.uk/lib/facebook (accessed 19 May 2009).

Anonymous (2008) 'MySpace or Yours?', *Strategic Direction*, 24(8): 15–18.

Anonymous (2009) 'Jonny-No-Stars is no More?', Book Review in *Development and Learning in Organizations*, 23(1): 27–29.

boyd, d.m. and Ellison, N.B. (2007) 'Social Network Sites: Definition, History and Scholarship', *Journal of Computer-Mediated Communication*, 13(1), article 11.

Brottlund, B. (2009) 'Companies Using Social Networking to Boost Sales', *Resourcenation.com*, 19 February.

Comm, J. (2009) *Twitter Power*, Hoboken, NJ: John Wiley & Sons Inc.

Cook, T. and Hopkins, L. (2008) *Social Media White Paper* (3rd edn). http://trevorcook.typepad.com/weblog (accessed 24 November 2009).

Dobele, A., Lindgreen, A., Beverland, M., Vanhamme, J. and van Wijk, R. (2007) 'Why Pass on Viral Messages? Because They Connect Emotionally', *Business Horizons*, 50: 291–304.

Ellison, N.B., Steinfield, C. and Lampe, C. (2007) 'The Benefits of Facebook Friends: Social Capital and College Students' Use of Online Social Network Sites', *Journal of Computer-Mediated Communication*, 12(4): 1–24

Ferguson, R. (2008) 'Word of Mouth and Viral Marketing: Taking the Temperature of the Hottest Trends in Marketing', *Journal of Consumer Marketing*, 25(3): 179–182.

Foster, K. (2008) 'JBS Interviews Three Business Leaders', *Journal of Business Strategy*, 29(4): 51–56.

Gummesson, E. (2007) 'Exit Services Marketing – Enter Service Marketing', *Journal of Customer Behaviour*, 6(2): 113–141.

Holzner, S. (2009) *Facebook Marketing*, Indianapolis, IN: Que Publishing.

Infield, N. (2009) 'Engaging with Social Media in the Business & Intellectual Property Centre (BIPC) at the British Library', *Business Information Review*, 26(1): 57–58.

Joinson, A. (2008) '"Looking at", "Looking up" or "Keeping up with" People? Motives and Uses of Facebook', *CHI*, Florence, Italy, 5–10 April.

Jones, G. (2007) 'Facebook's Big Sell', *Marketing*, October 17: 15.

Kunz, W.H. and Liu, R. (2009) 'Why Do Consumers Get Addicted to Online Communities? Toward an Understanding of the Underlying Influencing Factors', in J.-P. Helper and J.-L. Nicolas (eds), *Marketing and the Core Disciplines*. 38th EMAC Conference Proceedings: Nantes. p. 156.

Li, C. (2007) *Marketing on Social Network Sites*, Forrester Research, 5 July.

Miller, M. (2009) *YouTube for Business*, Indianapolis, IN: Pearson Education.

Needham, A. (2008) 'Word of Mouth, Youth and their Brands', *Young Consumers*, 9(1): 60–62.

Nicholls, R. (2005) *Interaction between Service Customers*, Poznan, Poland: Poznan University of Economics.

Raskin, R. (2006) 'Facebook Faces its Future', *Young Consumers*, Quarter 1: 56–58.

Waters, R.D., Burnett, E., Lamm, A. and Lucas, J. (2009) 'Engaging Stakeholders through Social Networking: How Nonprofit Organizations are using Facebook', *Public Relations Review*, 35(2): 102–106.

Part III
Conclusion

11 Issues for the Future

The conclusions are structured in three sections. In Section 1, we provide a brief overview of the material presented in Parts I and II. Section 2 is devoted to a discussion of the potential to innovate with marketing research in line with the foundational premises of the service-dominant logic of marketing and approaches that take a consumer experience perspective on relationships. In Section 3, pedagogical features that arise from the approach adopted in Part II, particularly in respect of the CEM process, are considered.

1: Overview of the book

Relationship marketing has had a 30-year history prior to the publication of this book. As a sub-discipline of marketing, it has matured and developed a number of sub-themes, as portrayed in Chapters 2 and 3. Greater understanding of the sub-themes is being continually developed to the benefit of academics and practitioners.

In this book, however, in Part II, we have advocated a change of perspective on interactions and relationships in order to increase the likelihood of the relevance of relationship marketing to a changing world in which the role of the consumer has changed (largely as a result of widespread accessibility to information and communication technology), and in which the 'consumer experience' is becoming increasingly central to marketing strategies and decisions. Some of the constructs emanating from, but not exclusive to, the extremely important debate on the service-dominant logic of marketing – co-creation of value, use and integration of resources by both organizations and consumers, the notion that value is idiosyncratic, experiential, contextual and meaning-laden – have provided a rationale for the approach taken in the book. We recognize that, compared to many other books on relationship marketing, we have not covered B2B relationships in any depth. However, a companion book in this series, Brennan et al. (2008), covers this area far more adequately than we could hope to, and we are left with space to develop ideas on a consumer experience perspective on relationship marketing.

It has to be acknowledged that the ideas presented in Part II are by no means exhaustive in taking a consumer experience perspective on relationship marketing. However, they have been tested out with third-year undergraduate classes in the UK and have generated extremely positive feedback. Indeed, the book has been structured in such a way as to fit a 10–12-week semester-based course on relationship marketing; one in which students can adopt a researcher role and contribute to the emerging knowledge. By adopting the approaches in Part II, students become involved in the life-world complexities and practices of segments of consumers. This can constitute an unforgettable learning experience.

The consumer experience perspective brings with it an increased emphasis on C2C interactions. We are not alone in emphasizing these interactions. As Chapter 10 illustrates, social networks and social communities are increasingly important, but relatively under-researched, despite the current influx of academic conference papers on the subject, and the large numbers of companies rising to the challenges of becoming 'a friend'. It also makes more specific the goal of consumer well-being: perhaps we should regularly consider 'consumer implications' before attempting to address 'managerial implications' of marketing innovations and initiatives.

Many of the citations in Parts I and II refer to articles, papers and practices in the years 2006–09, and so the ideas are relatively new, and, of course, this means there is still plenty more to do to verify, adapt and develop them. Nevertheless, we strongly believe that they can form a platform for exciting new developments in relationship marketing. While, we have involved companies with our ideas (for example, the British Library), and the notion of focusing on the overall consumer experience has been applauded by company representatives (as one CEO put it 'we prefer "jungle" research, to "zoo" research'), we are striving to work with more organizations to explore how useful the ideas are to them.

2: Researching relationship marketing

In Chapter 10, it was suggested that research into relationship marketing, especially research which takes a consumer experience perspective, may require innovative approaches. In this chapter, we offer some approaches that are taken from non-marketing disciplines, and others that specifically take account of the resources that consumers use and integrate. However, it is recognized that the foundations of the material presented in Chapters 2 and 3 were laid with respect to research carried out through conventional model-building and hypothesis testing. Therefore, we start this section with examples

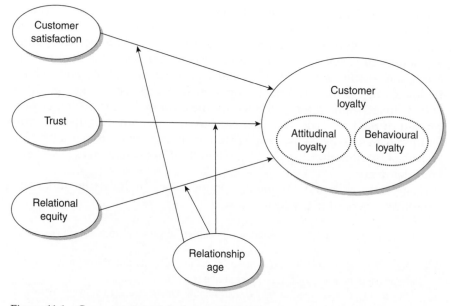

Figure 11.1   Conceptual model of customer loyalty
Source: Adapted from Raimondo et al. (2008)

of important, conventional research approaches to topics of relationship marketing, before considering examples of some alternative approaches.

Conventional approaches to research into relationship marketing

Research into aspects of relationship marketing is currently dominated by quantitative methods. A (visual) conceptual model is usually proposed that specifies the likely determinants of a dependent variable of interest (for example, customer loyalty or relationship strength), and data are collected to test hypotheses regarding the identified determinants and the dependent variable. Models may include mediating variables (demonstrating indirect relationships between the determinants and the dependent variable) or moderators (such as age and/or gender) that are likely to lead to differences in outcomes.

Two examples from 2008/09 research are summarized below to illustrate the more conventional approaches to research on aspects of relationship marketing.

1 A conceptual model of customer loyalty

Raimondo et al. (2008: 144) proposed the conceptual model of customer loyalty shown in Figure 11.1. Customer satisfaction and trust are seen as drivers of customer loyalty, which in turn is made up of attitudinal and behavioural loyalty. None of that part of the model is new. There are many studies that have explored statistical relationships between these variables. The focus of the study, and the contribution to the literature, is a measure of the effects of relational equity on attitudinal and behavioural loyalty, and the moderating role of relationship age on these effects. Relational equity is defined by the authors as 'the customer perception of the proportionality between her or his own benefit–cost ratio and the firm's benefit–cost ratio within a continuous customer–provider relationship'. Relationship age is the length of time customers have been with the firm.

Using data collected on mobile phone users in Italy, the following hypotheses were formally tested.

H1: Relational equity has a positive influence on (a) attitudinal loyalty and (b) behavioural loyalty.
H2: The effects of relational equity on (a) attitudinal loyalty and (b) behavioural loyalty increases along with relationship age.
H3: The effects of satisfaction on (a) attitudinal loyalty and (b) behavioural loyalty decreases along with relationship age.
H4: The effects of trust on (a) attitudinal loyalty and (b) behavioural loyalty increases along with relationship age.

As the authors state:

> Results ... show that, in highly competitive and transparent contexts, relational equity is a relevant determinant of customer loyalty and that its effect increases along with the age of the relationship. As we expected, the effect of satisfaction on behavioural loyalty decreases over time. However, we did not find support for the same moderating effect in the attitudinal loyalty model. Contrary to our expectations, trust shows a time-independent effect on customer loyalty. These results proved to be robust to diverse statistical diagnostics. (Raimondo et al. 2008:155)

The implications for managers of the research findings were mainly described in terms of advice on the design of customer loyalty programmes – usage of relationship to differentiate CRM practices and loyalty programmes, avoiding 'incremental benefit to new customers that does not correspond to a proportional advantage for long-term customers' (Raimondo et al. 2008: 157).

2 A conceptual model of the antecedents to customer-reported relationship strength

Dagger et al. (2009: 376) proposed the conceptual model of customer-reported relationship strength (CRRS) shown in Figure 11.2. Again, the

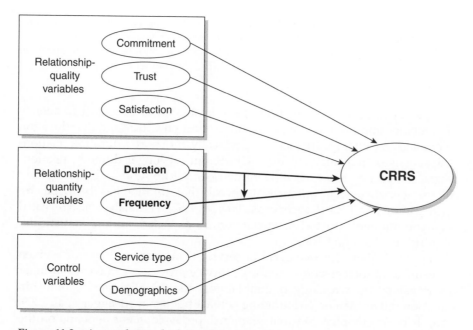

Figure 11.2   Antecedents of relationship strength
Source: Adapted from Dagger et al. (2009)

familiar constructs of commitment, trust and satisfaction (relationship-quality variables) are postulated as antecedents of CRRS, and CRRS is believed to depend on service type and customer demographics, but the main focus and contribution of the research is on the effects of relationship quantity variables (duration and frequency) on CRRS (as shown in bold in Figure 11.2).

The dependent variable, CRRS, is the customer-perceived extent, degree, or magnitude of the association between a customer and service provider. Frequency of contact is the number of interactions per period (one year in this case) between the exchange partners. The duration of the relationship is the length of time a relationship between the exchange partners has existed (similar to relationship age in the previous example). Using data collected from samples of Australian customers of nine service types – travel agents, hairdressers, family doctors, photo-printing service, general banking, pest control, cinemas, airlines and fast-food outlets – the following hypotheses were formally tested:

H1: The greater the frequency of contact in a relationship, the higher will be the customer-reported level of relationship strength.
H2: The longer the duration of a relationship, the higher will be the customer-reported level of relationship strength.

H3: Relationship duration moderates the effect of contact frequency such that contact frequency will enhance CRRS more when relationship duration is long.

H4: Among relationships with the same number of total contacts, longer relationship duration will be associated with greater CRRS, but higher contact frequency will not.

As the authors state, '… our findings indicate that both contact frequency and relationship duration have a positive effect on CRRS, and that duration moderates the effect of frequency. Specifically, for shorter duration relationships, contact frequency enhances CRRS; but for longer duration relationships, contact frequency has little influence on CRRS', and '… by controlling for number of contacts, our analysis reveals that duration has its own incremental effect on CRRS' (Dagger et al. 2009: 381–382). The analysis also revealed that commitment, trust and satisfaction, as expected, all had statistically significant effects on CRRS.

The implications for managers of service firms suggest that 'for a given investment in total customer contacts, service providers can create stronger relationships by working on maintaining and highlighting relationship duration rather than on encouraging contact frequency' (Dagger et al. 2009: 383). It is also emphasized that relationship development depends on the service type: CRRS was stronger in the more customized services (travel agents, hairdressers, family doctors).

The pros and cons of the conventional approaches

The two examples above provide excellent exemplars of the predominant approach to research into aspects of relationship marketing. The statistical analyses have not been emphasized here, but they have both been undertaken with great rigour and care, following the recommended processes for assessing reliability and validity of the measures employed. They and other similar studies have added significantly to our understanding of customer loyalty and relationship strength.

Our overall view, however, is that such approaches are necessary but not sufficient to fully understand interactions and relationships in the twenty-first century. Our reasons for reaching this conclusion are summarized below:

- Conventional approaches tend to treat the role of the respondents (customers) as largely passive. Respondents are only required to fill in answers to predetermined questions. The S-D logic of marketing celebrates customers as active participants who co-create value through using and integrating their operant resources. Should not research into relationship marketing acknowledge these customer characteristics?
- Conventional approaches seem to have a rather narrow firm-focus view of relationships. C2C interactions and networks, for example, are hardly ever formally

included in the models. Where they are, they are seen from a firm perspective, not a consumer experience perspective.

- However well specified the model, and however strong the theory to support it, the regression analyses that are employed often result in R^2 values less that 0.5, and rarely more than 0.6, however many independent variables are included. That means that, 40 per cent or more of the variations in the dependent variables are unexplained statistically, even assuming respondents are comfortable with, and careful with using Likert scales of measurement. Conventional approaches alone are unlikely to unearth the added explanation that could be crucial to strategy-making.
- There is a tendency to concentrate on one-to-one relationships in conventional quantitative research, which can ignore the complexity of networks of interactions and relationships. As Gummesson puts it, 'A more innovative use of research approaches is necessary' Quantitative marketing research in its application often represents a fundamentalist and narrow view of science and the search for reality' (1997: 271).

So what are the alternatives?

Here we consider two potential avenues for innovative marketing research into relationship marketing: exploring approaches adopted in other disciplines and exploring the directions implied by the S-D logic of marketing.

Approaches adopted in other disciplines

In this section, we have identified two approaches that are relatively under-used in research into relationship marketing, certainly in terms of what is published, but which are the backbones of research in other disciplines.

1 The ethnographic approach

Ethnographies are common in sociological and anthropological research and are adopted in consumer culture theory (Arnould and Thompson 2005), but are very rarely used to further understanding of relationship marketing. Yet, as seen in the following example (in educational research), there is potential to use an ethnographic approach to explore how personal networks contribute to consumer problem-solving.

Horvat et al. (2003) undertook ethnographic research with third- and fourth-grade American children and their families. The purpose was to examine social class differences (i.e. between 'poor', 'working class' and 'middle class') in the relationships between families and school. Data consisted of interviews with, and observations of children and their families in three different schools. The observations consisted of '... both in-class and out-of-classroom activities. The classroom observations included routine classroom activities and lessons. Researchers also observed parent–teacher conferences, PTA meetings and special events such as graduation, school fairs, book fairs, Back-to-School Night, and classroom celebrations of Halloween and Valentine's day' (Horvat et al. 2003: 324–325). The purpose was to provide a detailed understanding of the experiences of school-children and their parents, especially with respect to how certain problems were resolved.

We summarize here their findings related to two problem areas – responding to inappropriate teacher behaviour, and customizing children's school careers – especially regarding the networks employed by the different social classes.

Responding to inappropriate teacher behaviour: This relates to the few occasions that teachers lost their temper with pupils or even yelled or pushed them. How did parents react? The findings, supported by numerous *verbatim* accounts collected through the ethnography, suggest strongly that 'Middle-class parents responded in a very different fashion ... than did working-class and poor parents. Middle-class parents mobilized resources to respond collectively. By contrast, in working-class and poor families, these incidents were ... addressed at the individual level' (Horvat et al. 2003: 332).

Customizing children's school careers: This relates to the manner in which parents deal with special educational needs of their offspring at both ends of the scale; child with learning difficulties or 'gifted' child. Here it was found that middle-class parents, in contrast to poor or working-class parents, were more proactive, and were able to mobilize network members to garner additional information relating to the educational need of their children.

From consideration of the aspects above, and other evidence derived from the ethnography, Horvet et al. (2003) drew the conclusion that (in this context), the characteristics of networks vary across the different social classes. In particular, they found much evidence that middle-class parents had many network ties connecting them to other middle-class parents, whereas the networks invoked by working-class and poor families were predominantly based on kinship/family.

The above example is highly contextual, but there are opportunities for the relationship marketing researcher to adopt an ethnographical approach to determine the properties and nature of networks employed by different segments – customers, employees, businesses.

2 Social network analysis

Social networks were the subject of Chapter 10. Their *structures* have been analysed, by researchers in computer-mediated communication, using social network analysis (SNA). SNA is often used to examine the positions of individuals within online social networks, and the overall structure of communication patterns within online communities (Pfeil and Zaphiris 2009). Such

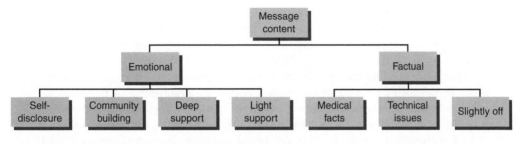

Figure 11.3   Classification of social message content

knowledge can contribute greatly to understanding of the interactions summarized in Figure 9.1.

What is involved with SNA? The paper by Pfeil and Zaphiris (2009) provides a good example of the application of SNA; in this case in a study of the use of SeniorNet, an empathetic online community for older people. A preliminary qualitative study of the use of SeniorNet over a 1.5 year period resulted in a classification of the content of the posted messages (see Figure 11.3).

One of the aims of the paper was to examine whether there is an association between the communication content and the social network patterns exhibited by the structure of the communications. At the second level of Figure 11.3, they were able to examine whether the social network structures differed according to whether the communication content was emotional or factual. (Similar comparisons were made at the third level of Figure 11.3. Interested readers are advised to consult the original paper.)

To determine whether social network structures differed for emotional or factual content, a SNA software package (Cryam Netminder II) was employed to calculate measures such as density, inclusiveness and closeness of the network, and to draw sociograms to visualize the network and its dynamics. The authors summarized their findings as follows:

> emotional communication content is linked to a dense social network, in which more members are included in the message exchange, often as both sender and receiver of messages. Additionally, emotional communication is associated with closeness between members of the community. In contrast to that, structures that were based on factual communication were found to be loose and only included a few of the members. (Pfeil and Zaphiris 2009: 10)

In other words, emotional communication scored higher than factual communication on the dimensions of density, inclusiveness and closeness of the network. This led the authors to conclude that '... emotional communication is an essential part of the discussion board and should not be underestimated. It is the emotional part of the conversation that is associated with a strong connection between people' (Pfeil and Zaphiris 2009: 15), and that

'This knowledge can help practitioners and scholars to design successful empathetic online communities and better understand how relationships between members within empathetic online communities develop out of conversations they engage in' (Pfeil and Zaphiris 2009: 16).

Notwithstanding the specific example above, there are great opportunities for (relationship) marketers to gain a better understanding of the associations between communication content of conversations and interactions, and the network structures that result, through employing methodologies and methods of analyses that are being used in the computer-mediated communication domain.

Directions implied by the S-D logic of marketing

Foundational Premise 10 of the S-D logic of marketing – value is always uniquely and phenomenologically determined by the beneficiary (Vargo and Lusch 2008) – implies that a greater emphasis should be given to interpretivist approaches to marketing research. There is scope for the development of research approaches that accommodate the increasing willingness for consumers to express themselves and be active participants. That is, innovation is required, both with collecting and interpreting qualitative data that represents the voice of the consumer. It should also be recognized that consumer voice data is available in abundance on the internet (Web 2.0) through blogs, consumer discussion groups and social interaction sites. Availability of qualitative data is perhaps less of a problem than its interpretation.

We chronicle here five approaches (I to V) that have been used to obtain and interpret data on consumer experiences, since the advent of the S-D logic.[1] I and II specifically address the task of understanding the use and integration of consumer operant resources. III, IV and V provide examples of how to harness the potential of consumer resources in the co-creation of the value of marketing research. To our knowledge, each approach had original features at the time of implementation.

Seeking an understanding of how customers/consumers employ their operant resources in creating experiences

The experiential contexts of I and II were library usage and cinema going, respectively. More details are now given:

I: Library usage (see Chapter 6) In this approach, working with the organization in question, the British Library, user voice was generated on a user forum as a result of posing one question: 'If you want to support us, please let us know why the British Library is important to you'. The question was posed because of potential government cuts in funding for the British Library. It generated almost a thousand responses. The first tranche (565 messages) was analysed according to a guiding framework offered by Arnould et al. (2006) on the use and integration of consumer resources. In particular the division of consumer operant resources into cultural, social and physical resources provided a starting point for further useful and contextual divisions. The analysis had resonance with senior executives of the British Library who were able to see their users through a different lens (see Baron and Warnaby 2008).

II: Cinema going (see Chapter 9)   Here, while still adopting the Arnould et al. (2006) categories of consumer operant resources, the focus was on the dynamics of consumer resources integration. This was achieved through analysing the development (and ultimate success) of a consumer campaign to save a local cinema by tracing the use and integration of operant resources of the five trustees of the 'save the cinema' campaign over a three-month period. Data were captured through personal interviews of the trustees and the web-based and other news literature that underpinned the campaign. The findings emphasized how speedily consumers can enhance their individual and collective operant resources when stimulated by a cause about which they felt very strongly (see Baron and Harris 2008).

In both I and II, consumers had a strong urge to voice their opinions, and so demonstrated the operant resources they have at their disposal. Example I shows that a single question can generate a high volume of consumer responses with associated managerial implications, while II emphasizes the importance of gaining further understanding of the dynamics associated with consumer resource integration and use.

Acknowledging the potential of consumer resources in the co-creation of the value of marketing research

There is another side to the notion that consumers use and integrate their operant resources. Given the resources that consumers possess, there is considerable scope for stimulating them to use these same resources for the purposes of research. Consumers are often labelled respondents in the marketing research process. The word 'respondent' connotes a reactive role for the consumer, whereas approaches III–V below (in the contexts of text messaging, shopping and restaurant dining, respectively) demonstrate that consumers can contribute much more to the process than merely replying to researcher questions.

III: Text messaging   A total of 113 undergraduate students were asked to keep diaries, for four weeks, of their text messaging activities, and to critically reflect on their experiences. The data consisted, therefore, of multiple consumer diaries that not only demonstrated behaviour, through the diary entries, but also contained contextual meaning – and value-laden reflections made by the diarists. The combined data were interpreted by the authors, using existing technology acceptance model constructs (Venkatesh et. al. 2003), to demonstrate the embeddedness of the technology (text messaging) in the everyday lives of the users. The approach clearly identified the consumers' role in co-creation of value, something that was absent in the technology acceptance models derived from survey research (see Baron et al. 2006).

IV: Shopping A variation on the approach above involved 232 students being asked to write introspective accounts of their experiences on visiting a department store. This resulted in a data set consisting of *multiple* personal introspections that was interpreted by three independent researchers, unguided by existing constructs; a customer-involving procedure that is a world away from the customer satisfaction surveys that still dominate the literature. The accounts demonstrated overwhelmingly, from a consumer experience perspective, that the store under consideration had inadequate value propositions, and they anticipated the subsequent closure of the store (see Patterson et al. 2008).

V: Restaurant dining In the theatre domain, performances are seen and discussed by critics. The critics consider the gestalt performance, and are sensitized as to what elements contribute to the overall intended effect of the performance and, conversely, to what elements are inconsistent. Many services, such as those offered by restaurants, are likened to performances, and so, in an attempt to provide fresh insights on the restaurant-dining experience, 'customer critic' research was undertaken. Here, prior to dining in a restaurant in the north of England, a small sample of potential restaurant diners was trained and sensitized as to how to critique a performance. They then undertook the dining experience. Finally, they engaged in a post-performance critical assessment of the experience. The customers, therefore, had been given a complete role in co-creating the research findings. The findings presented to the restaurant management highlighted numerous inconsistencies in the overall performance, and provided strategic insights into the nature of the overall intended effect of the dining experience (see Harris et al. 2007).

In III–V, the consumer role is more of a research partner than of a conventional 'respondent'. Consumers can be encouraged (often with advice or specialist training) to reflect, be introspective, or be constructively critical; skills normally taken to be the province of the researcher(s). In each of III–V, consumers were given greater freedom to contribute thoughts openly and spontaneously, and this has contributed to the richness and practical relevance of the findings. In such ways, S-D logic's FP6 can be explicitly acknowledged in the context of marketing research.

Example III clearly demonstrates that consumers go way beyond mere technology acceptance, and embrace (mobile) technology as part of their way of life. The following quote, from the study of text messaging behaviour, could easily relate to use of social network sites such as Facebook or Twitter, and expresses eloquently the feelings involved in networking with peers.

> I was quite shocked at how many texts were incoming and outgoing in just one week. You don't think about it until you are recording each one and all the different types of text you receive. Each one making some sort of impact on my life (however little it may be) makes me feel strangely complete.

In IV and V, the interactions are between consumers and a single organization. However, they both unearth the complexities involved with such interactions. It is not simply one single moment of truth that matters to the consumers, more the holistic experience. As shoppers in study IV put it:

> The atmosphere was dull, the products were dull and even the few members of staff looked like they wanted to take their own lives in some sort of extreme suicide pact to highlight the overexposure of handicrafts to the human soul. Enough was enough. It was time to move on.

> It's not necessarily true that Lewis's did something wrong, maybe it's just that they didn't do anything at all. As all the other stores evolved around them, they just carried on as they were. This is, I feel, where their problem lies. The Lewis's store in Liverpool is a perfect example of this. In one simple word the store is dated! I certainly wouldn't go back there, and soon I think nobody else will either!

Similarly, in study V:

> A number of the critics felt that the staff did little to reinforce the 'quality' food image. In particular, most critics were disappointed that the staff seemed to be disinterested in the recipes and, in some cases, lacked detailed appreciation of the content of some of the more unusual combinations. Because the food was so good, one of the critics commented, *'you would have expected the staff to be both proud and knowledgeable and want to show off about it'*. There was a discussion about the intention of the restaurant to reflect the 'regional/north Lancashire' position. Critics agreed that the menu and recipes reflected this, but there was nothing else in the performance to reinforce it. One critic commented on the fact that the accents of the waitresses were certainly not Lancastrian! Another felt that the whole environment with its harsh, clinical feel was incongruous with the image of Lancastrian food, i.e. *'hearty, wholesome dishes eaten in a cosy warm environment'*. Although the food was excellent, many felt that they would not return.

In each case, the holistic consumer/customer experience is seen to affect their loyalty to the organization. We feel that imaginative, interpretivist research methods, such as the ones above, are needed to capture more clearly the reasons for customer loyalty/disloyalty.

Researching consumer resources

Foundational Premise 9 of the S-D logic, which postulates that *all* economic actors are resource integrators, includes customers/consumers as resource integrators. This has proven especially enlightening when considering the potential of appropriate marketing research methods. There is a real need to discover just how consumers employ and integrate their resources during the course of their experiences and in the process of value co-creation as in, for example, I and II. This requires research processes that uncover everyday consumer practices and interactions, and the various networks of which they are a part, and acknowledges that consumers, like organizations, can play roles as providers as well as beneficiaries. Simply asking questions of consumers, as is done in many surveys, is unlikely to reflect the richness and dynamics of consumer experiences, and to uncover the subtleties and dynamics of consumer resource use and integration.

Preparing consumers to be partners

Treating consumers as partners, rather than simply respondents, does, however, introduce an additional, potentially controversial element to the marketing research process. With the possible exception of blogging or campaigns (I and II), consumers do not naturally reflect on their actions and feelings or order their thoughts on the experiences in which they engage. None of us, unless prompted, stop to ponder on our everyday, seemingly routine interactions and feelings. Therefore, consumers need 'training' on how to be reflective, how to articulate their introspections, and how to analyse their feelings. In addition, consumers as partners need to be made aware that their 'voice' is valued. The training was integral to the methods employed in III–V. However, there is a subtle balance to be achieved between drawing out consumer voice and 'stage-managing' their contribution. Where consumer voice data is already available on the internet, our limited experience suggests that data related to consumer campaigns (as in I) may be more focused and articulate.

The approaches I–V provide a range of contexts in which the S-D logic might inform marketers regarding issues relating to consumers' *life-worlds* (Arnould, 2007). The data generated in the approaches were very large, and phrased in the consumer's own voice, which requires interpretation by researchers. The processes by which the data are obtained – and particularly analysed – can be very time-consuming and resource-intensive. However, such practicalities need to be balanced against the obvious advantages of generating new insights into consumers' life-worlds that may not have been available elsewhere. Grasping the challenges of adapting marketing research methodologies to the contingencies of the S-D logic should provide a fruitful research agenda into the future, for academics and practitioners alike.

Networking opportunities brought about by information and communication technology have created exciting opportunities for academics and practitioners involved with relationship marketing. We argue that the more conventional, largely quantitative marketing research methods that have served us well in the past need to be supplemented by innovative methods that acknowledge the networks and interactions that play such an important part in the lives of customer and consumer experiences. Some ideas have been presented which have great potential to uncover new insights. They are by no means exhaustive, and we fully expect that the next few years will see a burgeoning of new, and adapted, research methods that can be applied to relationship marketing, and that are in keeping with the S-D logic of marketing and the inter-disciplinary requirements of service science (Spohrer 2009).

3: Pedagogical features – learning by doing

It is reasonable to ask whether the CEM process (Chapters 7 and 8) can be incorporated into student learning, and what might be the potential benefits and drawbacks of so doing. In a paper presented to the UK Academy of Marketing Conference in 2006, and subsequently published in *The Marketing Review* (Baron and Harris 2006), we outlined, as a case study, our first attempt to incorporate CEM into the curriculum of a Relationship Marketing course in the context of the service-dominant logic of marketing. In this book, after two more runs-through of CEM with final-year undergraduate students, we offer some brief thoughts based on both the teacher and student evaluations. Interested readers should refer to the paper above for a more comprehensive account.

- *Learning*: 'This feels like we are doing some research. Am I right?' So asked one of the students involved. It reflected the sometimes bemused reactions of many of the students undertaking the activity. Having to use skills, such as qualitative data interpretation, synthesis and creativity seemed strange, at first, but was valued by the completion of the project.
- *Being the consumer advocate*: Most of the students' other learning/teaching in marketing had taken a focal (large) firm perspective. This often presents difficulties when students have no real feel for the marketplace or the particular competencies of the firm. It is even more difficult for students who are studying outside their own countries. Being required to study an experience domain from a consumer experience perspective, and act as a consumer advocate by considering consumer implications explicitly, is, once the surprise has worn off, a more comfortable and familiar position for the student to be in. Even if neither they nor their friends have ever discussed the gap-year experience, the primary data-collection exercises (interviews, focus groups, consumer diaries, blogs) soon makes them accustomed

to the consumer experience domain. It is not long before they can speak with some degree of authority and comfort about key issues faced by consumers in the domain.

- *Time/timing*: The CEM process, if done properly, is time-consuming. Furthermore, the acknowledged benefits of using CEM are often not apparent until towards the end of the process. If the software package (NVivo in this case) could be taught prior to the CEM project, then that would reduce some of the time spent with data coding and retrieval. Nevertheless, for students who have little familiarity with qualitative data analysis, the requirement for systematic and thorough data collection and analysis may stretch their patience in the initial stages.
- *Working in groups*: It is strongly advised that students undertake such projects in groups (of 4-5 people). Apart from the obvious benefits of being able to share out the data-collection requirements, the process described in this chapter appears to work well through the 'brainstorming' of ideas between members of the group, based on the many tables of consumer value enhancers and inhibitors that have been developed. The stage of translating consumer implications into potential strategic responses from contributors to the experience domain, whilst probably the most intellectually challenging component of the process, is often regarded by the students as the most rewarding component. From the tutor's perspective, the ideas presented by the students never fail to be imaginative, and many are grounded not only in the findings from CEM, but also in further, voluntary research undertaken by the students to support the feasibility of their ideas.

Finally, although the focus is on active learning, it is advisable to offer a further opportunity, once the project has been completed, to discuss CEM in the wider context of dominant logics of marketing.

Final thought

In Chapter 1, we acknowledged the substantial role of Philip Kotler in marketing in the 1960s. Kotler is still writing, and it is interesting that, in a co-authored 2009 publication (written during a worldwide recession), he states that, 'Marketers must further master resiliency if they are to engage the marketplace forcefully, break through turbulence and chaos, and *connect with customers and consumers*' (Kotler and Caslione 2009: 187; our emphasis). Just how marketers connect with customers and consumers is a key question. We hope that this book provides some original ideas.

References

Arnould, E.J. (2007) 'Service-Dominant Logic and Consumer Culture Theory: Natural Allies in an Emerging Paradigm', *Consumer Culture Theory Research in Consumer Behavior*, 11: 57–76.

Arnould, E.J. and Thompson, C.J. (2005) 'Consumer Culture Theory (CCT): Twenty Years of Research', *Journal of Consumer Research*, 31(March): 868–882.

Arnould, E.J., Price, L.L. and Malshe, A. (2006) 'Toward a Cultural Resource-Based Theory of The Customer', in R.F. Lusch and S.L.Vargo (eds), *The Service-Dominant Logic of Marketing: Dialog, Debate and Directions*, Armonk, NY: M.E. Sharpe; 320–333.

Baron, S. and Harris, K. (2006) 'A New Dominant Logic in Marketing: Pedagogical Logic Implications', *The Marketing Review*, 6(4): 289–300.

Baron, S. and Harris, K. (2008) 'Consumers as Resource Integrators', *Journal of Marketing Management*, 24(1–2): 113–130.

Baron, S., Patterson, A. and Harris, K. (2006) 'Beyond Technology Acceptance; Understanding Consumer Practice', *International Journal of Service Industry Management*, 17(2): 111–135.

Baron, S. and Warnaby, G. (2008) 'Individual Customers' Use and Integration of Resources: Empirical Findings and Organizational Implications in the Context of Value Co-Creation', *Otago Forum 2: Academic Papers*, 61–79.

Brennan, R., Canning, L. and McDowell, R. (2008) *Business-to-Business Marketing*, London: Sage Publications.

Dagger, T.S., Danaher, P.J. and Gibbs, B.J. (2009) 'How Often Versus How Long', *Journal of Service Research*, 11(4): 371–388.

Gummesson, E. (1997) 'Relationship Marketing as a Paradigm Shift: Some Conclusions from the 30R Approach', *Management Decision*, 35(4): 267–272.

Harris, K., Harris, R., Elliott, D. and Baron, S. (2007) 'A Theatrical Perspective on Service Performance Evaluation: The Contribution of Critical Discourse and Aesthetics', *10th Quality in Services Symposium*, Orlando, Florida, 14–17 June.

Horvat, E.M., Weininger, E.B. and Lareau, A. (2003) 'From Social Ties to Social Capital: Class Differences in the Relations Between Schools and Parent Networks', *American Educational Research Journal*, 40(2): 319–351.

Kotler, P. and Caslione, J.A. (2009) 'How Marketers Can Respond to Recession and Turbulence', *Journal of Customer Behaviour*, 8 (Summer): 187–191.

Patterson, A., Hodgson, J. and Shi, J. (2008) 'Chronicles of Customer Experience: The Downfall of Lewis's Foretold', *Journal of Marketing Management*, 24(1–2): 29–45.

Pfeil, U. and Zaphiris, P. (2009) 'Investigating Social Network Patterns Within an Empathic Online Community for Older People', *Computers in Human Behavior*, Doi: 10.1016/j.chb.2009.05.001.

Raimondo, M.A., Miceli, G. and Costabile, M. (2008) 'How Relationship Age Moderates Loyalty Formation', *Journal of Service Research*, (1192): 142–160.

Spohrer, J. (2009) 'Welcome to our Declaration of Interdependence', *Service Science*, 1(1): i–ii.

Vargo, S.L. and Lusch, R.F. (2008) 'Service-Dominant Logic: Continuing the Evolution', *Journal of the Academy of Marketing Science*, 36: 1–10.

Venkatesh, V., Morris, M.G., Davis, G.B. and Davis, F.D. (2003) 'User Acceptance of Information Technology: Towards a Unified View', *MIS Quarterly*, 27(3): 425–478.

Note

---

1 This section is based on a paper by Baron, Patterson, Warnaby and Harris, entitled 'Service-Dominant Logic: Marketing Research Implications and Opportunities', presented at the Academy of Marketing Conference, Leeds Metropolitan University, July 2009.

Index

The Qualitative Research Kit

Edited by Uwe Flick

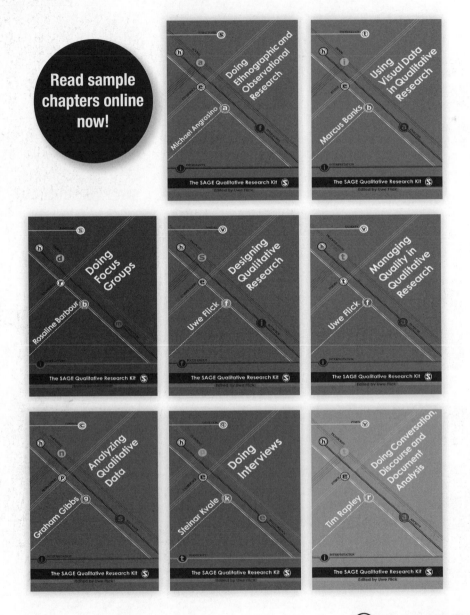

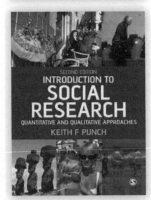
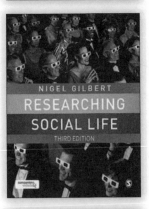